Toni Morrison's Secret Drive

Toni Morrison's Secret Drive

A Reader-Response Study of the Fiction and Its Rhetoric

DAVID S. GOLDSTEIN *and*
SHAWNRECE D. CAMPBELL

Foreword by Helane Adams Androne

McFarland & Company, Inc., Publishers
Jefferson, North Carolina

This book has undergone peer review.

ISBN (print) 978-1-4766-7937-2
ISBN (ebook) 978-1-4766-4109-6

LIBRARY OF CONGRESS AND BRITISH LIBRARY
CATALOGUING DATA ARE AVAILABLE

Library of Congress Control Number 2020047202

© 2021 David S. Goldstein *and* Shawnrece D. Campbell. All rights reserved

No part of this book may be reproduced or transmitted in any form or by any means, electronic or mechanical, including photocopying or recording, or by any information storage and retrieval system, without permission in writing from the publisher.

Front cover image Toni Morrison, circa 1978 (Photofest)

Printed in the United States of America

*McFarland & Company, Inc., Publishers
Box 611, Jefferson, North Carolina 28640
www.mcfarlandpub.com*

If I had to use one word to describe Toni Morrison's work, it would be "love." It is fitting, then, that I lovingly dedicate this book to my marvelous adult children, Justus and Chunnan.
—David S. Goldstein

I would like to dedicate this book to my mother Jacqueline, the spirit of Toni Morrison, and the loves of my life: Shinnique, Tyler, Jacqueline, Sahara, Elijah, Eniah, Mariana, Christian, Rebecca, and Tony.
—Shawnrece D. Campbell

Acknowledgments

I cannot thank my co-author, Dr. Shawnrece D. Campbell, enough for her work on this project. I doubt I ever would have been able to finish it on my own. What a pleasure it has been to learn from her scholarship; her perspectives complemented but also challenged my own.

We benefited greatly from reports from two exceptionally thoughtful readers of our early manuscript, one of whom, Dr. Marilyn S. Mobley, subsequently granted permission to be identified, and from the guidance that Senior Editor Gary Mitchem and his team at McFarland provided.

My academic home, the School of Interdisciplinary Arts and Sciences at the University of Washington Bothell, provided support for four invaluable writing retreats at the extraordinary Whiteley Center at UW Friday Harbor Laboratories on San Juan Island, Washington, which made the difference between a work-in-progress and a completed manuscript. The colleagues who accompanied me on those trips, especially Drs. Benjamin Gardner, Kristin Gustafson, and Gwen Ottinger, provided helpful suggestions, delightful companionship, and terrific chili. I am grateful to Dr. Bruce Burgett, dean of our school, for sending us. I also benefited greatly in the early stages of this project by Drs. Jamie L. Shirley and the late Dickson D. Bruce, Jr. Two extraordinary undergraduate students, Brooke Byun (University of Washington) and Eugene Lee (Amherst College), provided outstanding research assistance, for which I am grateful. Thanks, as well, to Drew Gamboa, who created the index.

I acknowledge, with respect, that the places where I live and work are the unceded, occupied, ancestral lands of the Coast Salish peoples. My university campus sits on customary grounds of the Sammamish/Willow People and my home sits on those of the Duwamish People. I am grateful to be a guest in these lands.

Portions of Chapter 1 were revised and expanded from "Race/[Gender]: Toni Morrison's 'Recitatif'" (*Journal of the Short Story in English* 27 [Autumn 1996]: 83–95) and "Race and Response: Toni Morrison's 'Recitatif'" (*Short Story* 5 [Spring 1997]: 77–86), with kind permission from Presses Universitaires de Rennes and the University of Texas at Brownsville.

Ever supportive of my scholarly work, Melissa Plotsky brings joy to my daily life inside and outside the academy.

My debt to the late Toni Morrison, whom I never had the honor of meeting, is immeasurable and inexpressible. Much of what I value in my education and my understanding of my place in the world comes from her astonishing wisdom and sublime art. Wherever this book falls short, as it inevitably does, in no way reflects upon her, or, for that matter, upon anyone who knowingly or unwittingly contributed to it.

—David S. Goldstein

* * *

I am incredibly grateful to David S. Goldstein for inviting me to help him complete this project. It has been a joy to work with him in bringing this manuscript to completion and to learn from his perspective. I also thank our reviewers for their insight and Senior Editor Gary Mitchem and the team at McFarland.

I would also like to thank Stetson University for providing me sabbatical support as researched conducted during that period was incorporated into this project and the Stetson University College of Arts and Sciences for supporting my attendance at various national and international conferences so that I could present various elements of this project to an audience of peers and use their feedback in refining it.

Of course, I am forever grateful to my children Shinnique, Tyler, and Jacqueline; grandchildren Sahara, Elijah, Eniah, Mariana, and Christian; partner Tony Johnson; and daughter-in-law Rebecca for their support, love, and encouragement. Each one provides sunlight to my day.

To Toni Morrison, the preacher in the clearing whom I unfortunately never had the chance to meet, thank you for getting me. That is the thought that stayed with me after reading *The Bluest Eye* for the first time. The MacTeer sisters longing to understand why their journey living in this world was the way it was echoed my own desire to understand the world around me, and Morrison's ingenious way of asking her readers to analyze why they believe what they believe resonated with the feistiness of my soul's refusal to allow others to define me or how I lived life on this earth and what I could achieve. Her body of work coached and mentored me. Her words, written and oral, were friends to me. Profound sadness encompassed me when I learned that she had transitioned out of this life, but I took solace in the fact that she had left a legacy of living water that I and millions of others could go back to and drink from again and again.

—Shawnrece D. Campbell

Table of Contents

Acknowledgments	vii
Foreword by Helane Adams Androne	1
Preface	7
Introduction	11
1. "Recitatif"	23
2. The Bluest Eye	46
3. Song of Solomon	71
4. Beloved	87
5. Paradise	114
6. Home	126
7. Sula, Tar Baby *and* A Mercy	140
Conclusion	157
Chapter Notes	169
Works Cited	177
Index	187

Foreword
by Helane Adams Androne

The night before I was scheduled to present a conference paper on Toni Morrison's only short story, "Recitatif," I had a dream. As I stood before the audience, a full room of Morrison scholars, I revealed my dream as the introduction to my conference paper. In the dream, I stood behind a lectern and, as I read my paper, Toni Morrison walked into the room ... and I promptly shifted to the right and threw up my lunch. Now, I am not this type of "star-struck" scholar, so in some ways this dream was perplexing. Was my visceral reaction a response to the possibility of Morrison entering the room or was it something more? In my dream, Morrison entered into that space between me and her story, and it apparently triggered me to give up everything.

To be fair, Morrison's stories have always positioned her unpredictably. Given her ongoing use of archetype, signifying on historical trauma, her way of pointing directly to the racist and classist oppressions systemically devised to undermine the healing of whole communities, it is ironic that she has been framed as a serious intellectual and speaker of "the race," while subsequently becoming the focus of popular culture book clubs. Even so, Morrison's stories signify for many the difficult work of exposure, confrontation, and healing. Novels like *Beloved* and *The Bluest Eye* have been characterized, and have indeed come to characterize, what has become the genre of "trauma fiction." True, in structure and content, Morrison's stories unravel the damage, the shame, the trauma of entire communities from within the psyches of a handful of characters. Her characters fight themselves and each other to recover, forget, and weave back together the experiences of troubling, tightening pasts.

Alan Gibbs notes that Morrison's *Beloved* demonstrates an "aesthetic [that] extends beyond the rather limited set of accepted trauma representational practices. Morrison's novel has more to offer than these narrow paradigms, for example in its dramatization of trauma's major problematic as presence and insistence rather than absence" (Gibbs 72). Decoding the narrative and structural work of her representations of trauma is certainly part of the work Morrison provides. bell hooks reminds us, however, that along with authors such as Toni Cade Bambara, Alice Walker, and Gloria Naylor, Morrison is part of a specific project of acknowledgment, confrontation, and healing:

> Much of the celebrated fiction by black women writers is concerned with identifying our pain and imaginatively constructing maps for healing ... [they] address the deep, often unnamed psychic wounding that takes place in the daily lives of black folks in this society.... Indeed, many non-black people also find healing maps in this work they can use in daily life [hooks 11].

From the playing of the dozens that shifts one text toward unexpected violence, to the deliberate construction of clearings, open spaces and buried clues in another, each one of Morrison's stories points the reader to the tools for revelation. In one moment readers are perplexed by what cannot be re/membered, in another they are exhausted by the weight of revelation carried by her characters. We gasp, we speak back to the text, angry and shocked at the sharp, frightening oppressions playing out, on, and through, black lives on the page. Our shock melts into realizations that Morrison's stories have pointed to painful truths, there finally spoken, somehow having fought back the threat of historical silence.

Secret Drive takes familiar tropes and devices in Morrison's fiction and decodes how she uses them to provoke intellectual activism—personal and communal—through reader response. This is not to suggest that all readers respond in the same way, however; in fact, an important intervention Goldstein and Campbell make here is in the open consideration of disparate readings of the same texts—most easily noted in readings of Morrison's only short story, "Recitatif," which notoriously boggles readers into acknowledging their own deeply held stereotypes. In her essay, "Unspeakable Things Unspoken," Morrison acknowledges her desire for "an intimacy between the reader and the page," which she strategizes accomplishing in *Sula* by purposely "introducing an outside-the-circle reader into the circle" (Morrison "Unspeakable Things..." 1989). And so, while reader response theory is privileged here, Goldstein and Campbell juxtapose that consideration with how these texts also demonstrate intersectionality and an integration that suggests Morrison's strategic efforts to represent transformation and healing.

In the same moment she speaks to inner circles, Morrison also speaks to the way her work is always "about, for and out of black culture." *Toni Morrison's Secret Drive* tugs on this principle and provides a compelling opportunity to better understand what Campbell's African-centered ethnomedical critique offers in the examination of Morrison's work on communal healing and transformation. Morrison has admitted her agenda to take readers on a deep dive into the psyche and behaviors of oppression, into what one believes about justice, history, and humanity. Indeed, fighting against silence is a matter of "psychic well being" that bell hooks identifies as necessary to "black liberation" (hooks 15). Morrison's stories, which consistently narrativize psychic individual and communal trauma, also represent an activist impulse that counters "traditional therapy, mainstream psychoanalytical practices, [which] often do not consider 'race' an important issue" (hooks 15). Digging deeper into real and theoretical readers, attending to how they are drawn in through carefully constructed intimacies within the "interior lives" of Morrison's characters thus, without neglecting the intersectional project of communal healing from injustice, is a welcome addition to existing scholarship on Morrison. *Toni Morrison's Secret Drive* shows how Morrison gets readers to not only recognize such damaging systems, but also how reader engagement with Morrison's techniques result in "recruiting readers in her political and social project" toward healing (Conclusion). You will find that this book finally makes the connection between how Morrison makes you feel as you read her work and what having read her work with such introspection inspires you to do. In doing so, our authors acknowledge that reading Morrison is, and has always been, intellectual *and* emotional work.

Scholars regularly recognize that reading Morrison's stories is a complex enterprise. It requires active deconstruction of the sacred cows of Western capitalist life. Most critical analysis of her work is a confrontation with its narrative formalities that demonstrate these moves; however, as hooks suggests, the experience of her work demands a response to these moves outside the texts and inside ourselves. But Goldstein and Campbell construct a critical bridge between the principles of reader-response and critical analysis that asks us to step into the narrative more fully to notice *how* Morrison accomplishes what happens to *us* when we confront fractured memories that decry absence, and why it is that we find ourselves taking part in their reconstruction.

And so, *Secret Drive* takes on that benign understanding that Morrison always has been after reader participation. Much scholarship shows how Morrison unscrolls the map back to painful pasts. What Morrison actually asks of readers, however, is not so safe. It is entirely possible to find oneself cornered in one's own biases as much as in those of another. Such pain and historical reflection is what makes Morrison's work as significant now as ever, as police brutality in the United States sparks a global response and unprecedented resurgence in activism and clamoring for anti-racist resources. Global scrutiny and multicultural protest against the systems and symbols of slavery, arguably triggered by the close, sequential deaths of Ahmaud Arbery, Breonna Taylor, and George Floyd—added to a list attended to more carefully because of the emergence of #BlackLivesMatter as a response to the growing list of black victims of contemporary white aggression. Morrison's work braces literary resources that help us understand the complex traumas experienced as a result of America's racist slave system; her texts point toward speaking truths to ourselves and to each other, anticipating how we suffer, face, and transcend the enormity of our system's reach. Therefore, this book, taken alongside those primary stories, matters because it engages the curiosities found in Morrison's narrative maps as it also helps us wonder about our relationship to the truths she reveals and the work she demands. *Toni Morrison's Secret Drive* examines and recounts what we know of Morrison's characters and plots, but it demonstrates through authors who themselves are co-creating meaning, even as they demonstrate a vast potentiality of responses, that we can peer through these strategies to see the journey ahead. What indeed is the reach of our assumptions about race? How discomforted are we as readers if the map is distorted, resistant to our norms? How exactly does Morrison draw the reader into the inner circle of story-making, requiring not only that one responds to the text, but also that one participates in reflective, active transformation?

The answers, our authors suggest, are found within the gaps, between the shadowed author presence and the signifiers. In those moments I picture Morrison as a griot sitting within the page, turning slowly toward her reader, pausing with upturned chin, waiting for the reader to understand and signal to continue. She takes note of our efforts, reveals more, then urges us further into stories of imperfect humans marked and twisted by the systems we recognize outside the page. Her stories capture the voices, humor, politics and uncertainties of which we are most afraid, most relieved, by which we are most humbled. Her work means to tear, push, cause us to dis/re-member trauma and distance. It is this that Goldstein and Campbell point to in Morrison's stories—the suggestions within these narratives that you know better now, but the nagging sense that perhaps you do not.

There is no shortage of scholarship on most aspects of Morrison's noted and deliberate rebellion against traditional narrative formulas or predictabilities. I have myself spent much of my academic life exposing literary structures of memory, the rites of passage that emerge in the journey to remember, those that confront and transform. Despite extensive scholarship on Morrison, there remains a long road beyond the head-scratching neglect or rationalistic dismissal of the reader in the same way that scholarship tends to shift its feet when faced with representations of the supernatural. Morrison's work, however, acknowledges the "profound unshaken belief in the spiritual power of black people to transform our world and live with integrity and oneness despite oppressive social realities" (hooks 8). It has been painfully clear that until recently, academic study could only acknowledge the distance between author and reader. It is a different effort to go beyond rhetorical description to shed light on Morrison's skillful use of "introspection" and "retrospection" to provoke reader activisms. This lens makes this book stand out from other scholarship.

And so, as I return to my memory of being at the lectern at the conference, and re/member my visceral response within the dream, I imagine for a moment that it was not simply the enormity of reputation that fed my subconscious the night before. I had labored with Morrison while reading her work, and I had further labored by engaging in the activist impulse of writing back to it my way of knowing things, exposed the meanings I made within the absences she wrote, placing in public view my entry into the inner circle to which we were invited. Morrison did, in fact, enter that room (to a collective gasp); and, as I responded to her work, she settled into her seat unremarkably, and listened. It was a generous act of curiosity—or, perhaps, a curious act of generosity. In either case, reading *Toni Morrison's Secret Drive* reminded me of that experience—the closing of the distance between Morrison, her texts, and the work of we, her readers. I am left engaged, appreciative, and responding.

Works Cited

Gibbs, Alan. *Contemporary American Trauma Narratives*. Edinburgh University Press. 2014.
hooks, bell. *Sisters of the Yam: Black Women and Self Recovery*. South End Press. 1993.
Morrison, Toni. *Beloved*. Penguin, 1987.
———. *The Bluest Eye*. Washington Square-Pocket, 1970.
———. "Recitatif." *Confirmation: An Anthology of African American Women*. Ed. [Imamu] Amiri Baraka (LeRoi Jones) and Amina Baraka. Morrow, 1983. 243–61.
———. "Rootedness: The Ancestor as Foundation." *Black Women Writers (1950-1980): A Critical Evaluation*. Ed. Mari Evans. Anchor, 1984. 339–45.
———. *Sula*. Plume-NAL, 1973.
———. "Unspeakable Things Unspoken: The Afro-American Presence in American Literature." *Michigan Quarterly Review* 28 (1989): 1–34.

Helane Adams Androne is a professor of English and the chair of the Department of Interdisciplinary and Communication Studies at Miami University. Her influential article on Morrison's short story "Recitatif" is credited as one of the first pieces of literary criticism to focus on the significance of Maggie's character in the story. She publishes widely in African American and Latinx literature.

Preface

The two authors of this book come to Toni Morrison in different ways and from different backgrounds. We argue throughout the book that Morrison's singular genius lies in drawing readers deeply into her tales, thereby inspiring them to co-create meaning, filling in gaps with their own thoughts, experiences, expectations, and implicit biases. For the purposes of transparency and illustration, then, we believe it is worthwhile to elucidate where each of us comes from, literally and figuratively, as readers and as Morrison critics. Our personal and professional histories undoubtedly influence our respective readings of Morrison.

Goldstein, a half-generation older than Campbell, never intended to become a Morrison scholar. As an undergraduate English major in what was then a terribly traditional department, he began to wonder where the women writers and writers of color—and, for the matter, non–British writers—were. Subsequently, in a master's program in American civilization, a seminar with Janice Radway introduced him to the idea that readers of literature—not just the authors and the works themselves—are worthy of study; that is, introduced him to reader-response criticism. These two conceptual threads—what was then the American literary canon's paucity of women writers and writers of color, and the idea that readers matter—led to a doctoral program in comparative culture (ethnic studies), in which he set out to use Morrison's short story, "Recitatif," as a basis for studying how readers' backgrounds might influence their interpretations of a literary work. His advisor wisely suggested that the study be expanded to see if the results could shed light on ways some of Morrison's novels guide readers' responses.

The more Goldstein learned about Morrison's preternatural ability to move readers, the more he realized that he could spend a career, and a lifetime, studying her work. He had not anticipated that Morrison would provide a rigorous education for him—a white, middle-class man raised in the 1970s in a mostly white Southern California suburb—not just about literature, but about history, memory, trauma, politics, love, and more. Although he says he studied Morrison in graduate school, it is more accurate to say that Morrison *was* his graduate school.

Similarly, Morrison is why Campbell switched from focusing on Arthurian romances in graduate school to texts written by authors of color and subsequently took a teaching fellow position in the Department of Pan African Studies at her doctoral institution, Kent State University. During the first semester of her doctoral program, she was introduced to a group of women writers of color, including Morrison, Gayl Jones, and Toni Cade Bambara, with whom she was unfamiliar, having been exposed only to Richard Wright's work. Had Morrison not been such a dedicated editor who was determined to introduce this body of work, as well as her own writing, to the rest of the world, Campbell may never have made that sharp left turn toward works by other authors of color and would have missed the liberation ideology that Morrison taught her to treasure.

Campbell savored the moments she sipped on Morrison's words over the years and enjoyed sharing moments of delightful epiphany with her students. Her pleasure in watching her students' eyes light up spurred Campbell's desire to continually study Morrison, to use Morrison's work to teach non–African Americans about black U.S. culture, and to affirm and interrogate African American ways of knowing and being in the world. Campbell is most thankful to Morrison for allowing herself to be a conduit of light full of tough love and wisdom to humanity, and especially to fellow African American women.

These two Morrison scholars began collaborating on this manuscript in 2012. As readers from different backgrounds, we found that each of us was drawn to some of Morrison's novels more than others, which affirmed for us the validity of a reader-response approach to Morrison's work. Because we were studying an author who was then still living—she published *Home* and *God Help the Child* after we began working together—we continuously updated our study and kept current with the evolving scholarly literature. We never strayed, however, from our belief that Morrison is the most important American writer of the mid-twentieth and early twenty-first centuries and merits ongoing critical attention.

Especially since her receipt of the Nobel Prize in 1993, attention to Morrison's work in scholarship and in pedagogy is burgeoning. Despite increasing numbers of titles focusing on Morrison, many of which comment upon her extraordinary ability to engage interactively with readers, no work of which we are aware analyzes in detail precisely *how* her texts accomplish this quintessentially Morrisonian task. This book aims to fill that gap in Morrison scholarship.

We argue that Morrison's texts, through ingenious rhetorical strategies, induce responses among readers that recruit them into Morrison's anti-racist mission. Only by figuratively inserting themselves into the stories and then carrying the stories' themes out of the text and manifest them in their own world will readers make a political and social difference. Starting with an explanation of our reader-response approach, we describe an original, empirical study of actual readers' responses to Morrison's first published short story, "Recitatif,"[1] and then analyze specifically how each of her eleven novels—concentrating especially on eight—use gaps and enigmas to inspire readers' self-reflection.

Morrison's strategy of enlisting readers' participation, her socially and politically active orientation, and the "oral" quality of her fiction are well-established in scholarship on her work. We hope (1) to build upon and extend this conversation with an extended analysis of her particular tactic of textual gaps and enigmas that help her writing achieve reader participation; (2) to provide a more precise analysis of her writing as political activism, specifically its tactic of inspiring self-reflection and social action among its readers—a tactic that initiates a process of deconstructing race; and (3) to offer a synthesis of significant scholarship—roughly 250 sources—on Morrison's remarkable oeuvre.[2]

We wish to note that even when we disagree with other scholars' interpretations and conclusions, we do so with respect and gratitude, and with the hope that all of us who study this remarkable writer do so in the communal spirit that Morrison had hoped to foster. We also know that we have not incorporated, and cannot synthesize, all significant Morrison scholarship, nor do we claim that we cite all of the most important articles and books on Morrison—rather, only the ones that help us evince, hone, or interrogate our argument. Moreover, we look forward to engaging future studies of Morrison, especially those that take a reader-response approach. We collectively still have much to learn.

Introduction

Describing the scene in a Harlem nightclub in the 1920s, the narrator of Toni Morrison's novel, *Jazz*, says of the dancing patrons: "They believe they know before the music does what their hands, their feet are to do, but that illusion is the music's secret drive: the control it tricks them into believing is theirs; the anticipation it anticipates" (65). The music's guidance of the dancers' responses is a fitting metaphor for Morrison's fiction. Her writing anticipates the readers' anticipation, and guides their responses while allowing them to think that they are in control. Her texts, through ingenious rhetorical strategies, induce responses among readers that recruit them into Morrison's social justice mission. This book seeks to explicate the "secret drive" of Morrison's fiction.

Morrison (1931–2019) needs her readers. She alone cannot accomplish her work's mission: to "deconstruct" race as a pernicious, socially constructed concept and to eradicate racism in contemporary American society. Only by guiding readers toward an introspective evaluation of their own prejudices, toward recognizing the oppressive power of white, cultural hegemony in the United States, and toward understanding the continuing, overwhelming legacy of North American slavery can she effect change. She can do this only one reader at a time: "The peace I am thinking of is the dance of an open mind when it engages another equally open one—an activity that occurs most naturally, most often in the reading/writing world we live in" (*Dancing* 7). Deepening one's understanding of oneself and the world is the goal not only of her literature, but of life: "In order to get to a happy place—what I call happy, even though people are dropping dead all over my books—is the acquisition of knowledge. If you know something at the end that you didn't know before, it's almost wisdom. And if I can hit that chord, then everything else was worth it. Knowing something you didn't know before. Becoming something" (Kaiser and Manyika).

Although most fiction writers acknowledge their relationship with readers,[1] none engages readers more consciously and brilliantly than Morrison. Indeed, nearly all Morrison scholars remark upon the Nobel laureate's stunning ability to involve her readers in her fiction. Morrison herself states in an interview with Claudia Tate: "My writing expects, demands to have participatory reading" (125). Reader-response critics have been arguing for decades that meaning is co-created between texts and readers, but Morrison is particularly conscious of and oriented toward her readers. She neither simply delivers stories to them nor explicitly instructs them, but rather guides them to self-enlightenment. The rhetorical devices she employs in her texts are therefore specifically intended to elicit her readers' participation. Only by figuratively inserting themselves into the story and then carrying the story's themes out of the text and into their own world will readers make a political and social difference.

In her speech to the Swedish Academy upon receiving the Nobel Prize, Morrison tells a quintessentially Morrisonian tale. She speaks of a story in which a group of young people visits an old, blind, wise woman to make fun of her. One of them mockingly asks her whether the bird in the youngster's hand is alive or dead. The old woman remains silent, so the youngster asks again. "Finally she speaks, and her voice is soft but stern," Morrison says. "'I don't know,' she says. 'I don't know whether the bird you are holding is dead or alive, but what I do know is that it is in your hands. It is in your hands'" (11). Morrison then glosses the story: "I choose to read the bird as language and the woman as a practiced writer.... Being a writer, [the old woman] thinks of language partly as a system, partly as a living thing over which one has control, but mostly as agency—as an act with consequences" (12–13). Language, she says, can stagnate and die, "content to admire its own paralysis" (13). With her own work in mind, Morrison continues: "Language can never 'pin down' slavery, genocide, war. Nor should it yearn for the arrogance to be able to do so. Its force, its felicity, is in its reach toward the ineffable" (21). Morrison returns to the tale at her speech's conclusion, reiterating that once the old woman, in her silence, admonishes the youngsters as they contemplate the meaning of the words she had spoken, opening in them endless, profound questions about life and death—after she has prepared them by inspiring thought and feeling—until the old woman eventually says, "Finally, ... I trust you now. I trust you with the bird that is not in your hands because you have truly caught it. Look. How lovely it is, this thing we have done—together" (30). How appropriate that Morrison explicates, far more artfully than we, the collaboration she offers—indeed, insists upon—to her readers. Once she has trained readers, she trusts us to work with her to create profound art. What a gift.

Political and social change is, indeed, Morrison's acknowledged goal. She demands not only that readers participate in making meaning with the texts, but that they act upon what they learn about themselves and their world. In this regard, Morrison exemplifies the tenets of the African

American artistic movement known as Black Aesthetics. Proponents of Black Aesthetics, the critical movement begun in the 1960s and 1970s that promotes the rejection of white cultural values in favor of a distinctive "mystique of blackness" (Leitch 335), have called for the re-discovery of uniquely black cultural modes and forms of expression as a means for throwing off what are seen as racist, colonizing, mainstream forms. Larry Neal, one of the movement's premier intellectuals, holds as quintessentially black forms of expression both black music, especially jazz and blues, and oral, communal expression such as those found in folktales ("And Shine" 655), both of which figure prominently in Morrison's writing. Black literature, he insists in "The Black Arts Movement," has to embrace these forms rather than the formalistic modes of expression found in what he sees as the oppressive, European literary tradition (39). Thus, art and politics are inseparable; Black Aesthetics is a movement of liberation, a position echoed by Hoyt W. Fuller.[2]

Another prominent proponent of Black Aesthetics, LeRoi Jones (now known as Imamu Amiri Baraka), lays out the black artist's responsibility this way:

> The Black Artist's role in America is to aid in the destruction of America as he knows it. His role is to report and reflect so precisely the nature of society, and of himself in that society, that other men will be moved by the exactness of his rendering... [Jones 251].

No one can doubt that Morrison fits the description of the responsible black artist according to Jones's definition (except, of course, for his use of the male pronoun). Morrison is known for her vivid depictions of racism and poverty and their deleterious effects not only on the oppressed, but on the oppressor, as well. We show in Chapter 4 that the prejudice of Bodwin, a white abolitionist in Morrison's masterpiece, *Beloved*, ultimately drains from him the invigorating drive he felt during the movement's heyday. The depiction of his disappointment and bitterness in the novel exemplifies one relatively mild manifestation of racism's injury upon the oppressors. A more powerful example in *Beloved* is Stamp Paid's realization that whites project upon blacks their own savagery; whites' fear of black people leads to their own debasement.

Storytelling is Morrison's means for effecting social change. Although all fiction writers are storytellers, Morrison is particularly acclaimed for the "oral" quality of her writing. "I like the act of reading my works because I measure their value in terms of how they sound. That's not the only thing, but it's an important thing to me," she has said (Kaiser and Manyinka). Well-known for integrating conversational diction and syntax into her dialogue, Morrison is a recognized master of vernacular black dialect. She follows in a tradition of which Zora Neale Hurston is the acknowledged pioneer, although each uses significantly different ways of representing that dialect in writing. Hurston, trained as an anthropologist, reproduces the actual sounds of the speech by transliterating the dialect (e.g., "mouf" for "mouth"); Morrison prefers to capture cadence and rhythm rather than specific word pronunciations.

Morrison (obviously) considers herself a storyteller—she sees herself as a descendent of the African village storyteller, or *griot*—and her stories themselves feature numerous storytellers, evidencing how crucial she considers storytelling to be. Storytelling particularly empowers black women; by telling their own stories, they validate their own experiences. In fact, the *medium* of storytelling is as important to black women writers as is the content of the stories. So intertwined, they are essentially indistinguishable. For Morrison, storytelling about storytellers contributes to her strategy of enlisting reader participation and thereby furthers her project of deconstructing racism. The connection between the oral quality of her work and its mission to elicit reader (auditor) participation in the text—and ultimately in social change—is best made by Morrison herself, when she likens herself to the African American preacher who "requires his congregation to speak, to join him in the sermon, to behave in a certain way, to stand up and to weep and to cry and to accede or to change and to modify" ("Rootedness" 341). Stories carry myths and myths carry communal and cultural memory. To Morrison, and to her fellow masters in the African American women's writing tradition, this role of stories means nothing less than cultural survival.

As opposed to the Western literary tradition that privileges an ostensibly objective reality, African American writing privileges collective memory of reality. That is, in literate societies, history is recorded and is believed to be objective reality. In pre-literate societies, collective memory serves as history. Western societies impose a division between myth and reality; traditional societies do not. African peoples' sense of themselves depended upon collective memory, transmitted orally from one generation to the next, predominantly by women, who thus created an oral archive. The community orientation that is simultaneously characteristic of and reinforced by storytelling is crucial to Morrison: "Storytelling was 'a shared activity between the men and women' in her family, and she attempts to write within that oral tradition," Stelamaris Coser writes (88).[3] Memory is a dominant theme in Morrison's work and is inextricably linked with her use of storytelling.

When a piece of African American literature simulates traditional, oral storytelling style and thereby itself becomes a conveyor of collective memory and myth, it becomes what Henry Louis Gates, Jr., calls a "speakerly text" (*Signifying Monkey* 198). In such a text, the story, although written, relies upon what Hurston calls "word pictures" or "thought pictures" that constitute "hieroglyphics": "The white man thinks in a written language [while] the Negro thinks in hieroglyphics," Hurston says (qtd. in Gates, *Signifying Monkey*, 199). Writing about Hurston's classic novel, *Their*

Eyes Were Watching God, Gates notes that her characters' diction and "free indirect discourse" reflect features "that Hurston argued were fundamental to black oral narration" (199). Such features are liberally represented in Morrison's work, as we discuss in the forthcoming chapters.

Another aspect of African American literature highlighted by Gates is revision, in which an artist draws upon a previous work and remakes it into an original work. Depending on the motivation of the revision, the new work can be a parody or a pastiche of the original. Gates, citing definitions from the *Oxford Classical Dictionary*, thus distinguishes the two forms: "pastiche, which caricatures the manner of an original without adherence to its actual words, and parody proper, in which an original, usually well known, is distorted, with the minimum of verbal or literal change, to convey a new sense, often incongruous with the form" (*Signifying Monkey* 107). Gates argues that all literary traditions are series of intertextual revisions. The African American literary tradition includes unmerciful parodies, in which writers engage in "motivated" revision in order to shake up power relations, and pastiches, in which writers adopt and refashion the work of predecessors in a way that honors the originals. Morrison's work contains both forms of revision. For example, as we argue in Chapter 2, she parodies a banal Dick-and-Jane reading primer in *The Bluest Eye*, and revises, as pastiche, Richard Wright's great novel, *Native Son*.

By creating speakerly texts and rendering black "hieroglyphics" in her own way, Morrison revises Hurston. (Although Morrison claims she had read only a short story by Hurston before she herself began to write [Naylor and Morrison 589–90], she notes that the connections between the two writers made by numerous critics testify to the contention that "the world as perceived by black women at certain times does exist" [590].) In her metaphorical, figurative language, especially in her rendering of black vernacular dialogue, Morrison extends Hurston's seminal fiction and non-fiction. In her choice of subjects, too, Morrison builds upon Hurston: Disgusted by the stereotypical ways other writers have depicted black people, both Hurston and Morrison seek to depict authentically the people and experiences of black America. Hurston writes of Southern black folk, specifically those of her home state of Florida. Morrison also writes about black folk, but mostly those in the North; both *The Bluest Eye* and *Beloved* are set in her native Ohio. Both authors use multivocality in their narratives, reflecting "the dual consciousness code defined by Du Bois," according to Michael Awkward (12), who specifically sees Hurston's *Their Eyes Were Watching God* as "the primary precursor" of *The Bluest Eye* (12).

Morrison's original contributions to the tradition—the storytelling tradition of African American writers and especially African American women writers—are the masterful use of what we call *textual* and *meta-textual enigmas* to motivate readers' involvement and an intentionally political goal of challenging racism and sexism. This political agenda further distinguishes Morrison's work from Hurston's. Hurston is excoriated (unfairly, in our view) by the leaders of the Black Aesthetics movement because they see no political purpose in her art. Morrison does not subordinate the aesthetic considerations of her literature to a political cause, but establishes political goals *through* her novels' aesthetics.

All of Morrison's texts focus on the bane of racism and the naturalized (i.e., perceived as primordial and therefore unquestioned), oppressive nature of racial categorization and upon gender stereotyping, and, more broadly, the complicated ways in which identity markers interact—what Kimberlé Crenshaw termed "intersectionality." Morrison explicitly and continuously addresses these concerns when discussing her position as a writer and as an individual. For example, she has stated, "Racism will destroy love," and has identified gender conflict as "a cultural illness" (qtd. in Coser 104). So, when her texts lead readers to question why they interpret clues and fill gaps using preconceived ideas of race, they also begin to deconstruct those racial attitudes and prejudices. Morrison's texts act upon readers who in turn become actors in the broader narrative of "real life." As her readership grows in terms of both numbers and self-awareness, Morrison increases her impact upon deeply ingrained racial attitudes in contemporary Western society.

Morrison uses several tactics in the reader-centered strategy of her work. Each of her works of fiction clears an ideological space for itself; that is, each discomforts readers, getting them to question their most basic and unexamined assumptions about race, races, history, and literary form.[4] Figuratively wiping blank the minds of readers, the stories can then build within readers' minds a new vision, a new apprehension of reality as Morrison sees it. This tactic relies upon another tactic: the blending of African, American, and African American artistic forms of expression. Morrison's combination of African elements (e.g., a mimicking of the African *griot*—or storytelling—tradition) and Euro-American elements (e.g., the genre of the novel) is appropriate because she seeks to overturn pat categories of themes and forms, just as she tries to undermine Western readers' predilection for generalizing about human beings based on assumed racial traits.[5]

In more than forty years of interviews and through much of her non-fiction, cultural criticism, Morrison insists that she would never privilege a white perspective, would never write from a view that for writers and for readers, white is the default setting. No matter how many times a hapless, white interviewer asks her the insulting question about her attention to race—as if a white writer conjuring white characters were an unraced activity—Morrison consistently responds that black characters are no more and no less universal than white characters. As she famously, and with astonishing patience, recalls to Charlie Rose in a 1993 interview that one reviewer of her second novel, *Sula*, wondered when Morrison would confront what the reviewer saw as African Americans' "real" conflict, which is with white people, "as though our lives have no meaning and no depth without the white gaze. And I spent my entire writing life trying to make sure that the white gaze was not the dominant one in any one of my books" (Morrison and Rose).

Morrison's friend, the activist and intellectual Angela Davis (whose memoir Morrison had edited when she was at Knopf), supports Morrison's point, saying, "Toni Morrison's project resides precisely in the effort to discredit the notion that this white male gaze must be omnipresent" (Greenfield-Sanders). Although Morrison refuses to pander to or write to the white gaze,[6] she welcomes white readers, for whom, we suggest, Morrison has some lessons to impart. We hope, in this study, to suggest ways in which Morrison inspires responses among readers of disparate backgrounds; that is, at the risk of reductionism, we hope to examine how the same body of texts can prompt sometimes similar and sometimes disparate responses, depending largely on readers' individual backgrounds.

It is useful to outline some of our own assumptions underlying this work. First, like Morrison, we see "race" as a social construction, not a genetically or biologically meaningful concept. From Ashley Montagu to Henry Louis Gates, Jr., scholars have irrefutably established that race is meaningless in a genetic or biological sense, yet continues to hold meaning—albeit in shifting ways—in a social and cultural sense.[7] The key to understanding "race" in the United States is to recognize that Americans attach a great deal of meaning to these phenotypic differences. Furthermore, many of these supposed cultural differences emerge from historical circumstances, most notably slavery. Because Americans seem unable to resist assuming genuine difference among individuals based solely on physical markers, the fiction of race is an extremely powerful social force. We can understand better the race-based social hierarchy if we understand what people believe about race, even if what they believe is mistaken. In the following chapters, we argue that Morrison operates from this perspective and, moreover, that she seeks to expose simultaneously the falseness of racial stereotypes and the power of their persistence in American ideology.

Following from the definition of race as a social construction, we use the term "racism" in the following chapters in accordance with Gates's simple and useful definition of it: "I would say that 'racism' exists when one generalizes about the attributes of an individual (and treats him or her accordingly)" ("Talkin'" 403). Whenever possible, we use the more precise terms "prejudice" and "discrimination," by which we mean, respectively, negative attitudes toward an individual member of a group or an entire group based on supposed characteristics of the group, and actual acts—intentional or unintentional—against such an individual or group.

Morrison's exposure of "race" as a fiction—one with a powerful ability to oppress those considered inferior based upon traits ascribed to them by the dominant culture—is what we mean when we say that she attempts to "deconstruct" race. We are loosely borrowing the term from deconstruction theory as propounded by Jacques Derrida, who argues that Western culture values the written word over the spoken word, which tends to codify axiological oppositions such as "voice/writing, sound/silence, being/nonbeing, consciousness/the unconscious, ... signified/signifier" (Leitch 271), in which the first term is privileged at the expense of the second. By breaking down, or "deconstructing," the polarities represented in written language, Derrida also attacks the power dynamics reflected in and perpetuated by these binaries. Derrida notes, for example, that separateness and difference become codified in an idiom, pointing out that "there's no racism without a language" (Derrida 331). Language is used to make differences, and to make differences seem natural and primordial. Racism is thus a "system of marks" which "outlines space in order to assign forced residence or to close off borders. It does not discern, it discriminates" (Derrida 331), he writes. For example, the dichotomy *white/black* is rooted in language, and is thereby given social reality.

Given that Derrida's theory of deconstruction tries to overturn or reverse the privileging of the first term in these binary pairs of terms, one can see why some feminist scholars embrace deconstruction, for one such pair is male/female, in which, in the writing-centric tradition, the male, as reflected in its primary position in the pair, is considered the stronger. In challenging the binary pair, feminists also challenge male privilege. Analogously, Morrison's challenge, through her fiction, of the white/black pairing constitutes a challenge to white privilege. In fact, Morrison challenges such overgeneralizing categorizations in the first place. In this way, her fiction "deconstructs" both the racial categorizations in use in the United States and the actual white privilege that they codify and perpetuate.

Morrison's recognition of the power of discourse, and the active attempt to undermine the status quo, echo the thinking of Michel Foucault. Foucault insists that the elite of a given period assume the privilege of defining social norms, and that their definitions justify and perpetuate the elite's power. Morrison's work points up not only the insidiousness of categorizing human beings, but also the inequities of power and privilege that result from the practice.

Morrison clearly is aware of the "unnoticed power" of labeling. For example, in "Friday on the Potomac," she speaks of the "white discourse" in which "a reference to a black person's body is de rigueur" (xiv). By defining black people, black behavior, and "black" itself, whites were able to make into a spectacle the Clarence Thomas confirmation hearings. Putting into play their stereotypes of blacks' sexual permissiveness and irrationality, whites perpetuated their control over a matter as politically and socially important as the confirmation of a justice of the United States Supreme Court. "Predictably, the nominee was required to shuck" (xx), she states. Her concern with the power of discourse is not reserved strictly for high-profile matters, however. As we discuss in Chapter 2, the conclusion of *The Bluest Eye* (esp. 159) exposes the way discourse—in this case, the definitions of "beautiful" versus "ugly," "valuable" versus "garbage"—utterly destroy a young black girl. Morrison's work, fiction and non-fiction, seeks to demystify and disarm "white" hegemonic discourse.

Morrison accomplishes her deconstruction of race and racism by designing her texts to produce certain responses in her readers such that they will carry out her mission. This study focuses on how and why Morrison's fiction guides readers' responses. A brief discussion of reader-response theories helps illuminate this topic.

Many varieties of reader-response criticism exist, but the uniting element among them is assertion belief that readers—the third element in M.H. Abrams's triangle of author, work, and reader (Beach 1)—merit the attention of literary critics, and, in fact, should be their central concern. Beyond this commonality, however, the scholars loosely labeled "reader-response critics" disagree on many points, such as the relative importance of texts and readers (Do texts exercise nearly total control of readers' responses? Do texts have virtually no authority, leaving meaning-making almost exclusively to readers?) and even what is meant by "readers."

In developing our understanding of how Morrison's reader-directed rhetorical devices operate, we draw principally upon the work of Wolfgang Iser. According to Iser, readers continually modify their expectations of what is to follow in the text they are reading. Literary texts rarely fulfill such expectations—rarely present all of the plot- and character-related detail and display all of the anticipated features of the genre—so readers continually readjust their expectations against what they remember of previous sentences. Iser states: "Thus, the reader, in establishing these interrelations between past, present and future, actually causes the text to reveal its potential multiplicity of connections" (*Implied Reader* 278). The text triggers readers' interpretive faculties, which create in their minds the world presented by the text. Iser calls the product of this creative activity—which "endows" the text with its "reality"—the "virtual dimension" of the text, which is "not the text itself, nor is it the imagination of the reader: it is the coming together of the text and imagination" (*Implied Reader* 279).

It is crucial to note that Iser is not concerned with "real readers," but with the hypothetical construct toward which a text's rhetorical devices are aimed. That is, he is interested in what in *texts* guides readers' responses, not in what actually happens in the minds of "real readers." The hypothetical reader is thus "implied" by the text's rhetorical strategies. "Real readers" might or might not behave the way the so-called "implied reader" does. The implied reader has "roots firmly planted in the structure of the text" (*Act* 34), Iser writes. As Gabriele Schwab puts it, Iser's concept of the "implied reader" refers not "to the individual, the empirical, or to the ideal reader of a literary text, but to its strategies and structures of communication or its 'guiding devices' that exert at least a certain control over the reader's response" (130–31). It is always possible, she points out, that "the text cannot adapt to any individual reader who, in turn, can never fully verify his or her response in a face-to-face situation" (131).

One stratagem used by texts to guide the responses of their implied readers is what Iser calls *gaps*. What a text does not explicitly say—what is left unsaid—must be supplied by the readers. These gaps force readers to connect segments of the text that are explicitly present. As the viewpoint shifts throughout the text as the text is read—for example, when the action in a novel shifts from one character to another—the theme at each moment shifts, as well. Readers naturally associate the shifting themes with themes from outside the text. By cueing readers to connect the text's internal elements with those outside the text, the gaps condition readers' view of the shifting themes and thus guide the development of readers' responses to the text (*Act*, esp. 108–34).

Iser's model emphasizes textual guidance of readers' responses. "The reader is free to fill in the blanks but is at the same time constrained by the patterns supplied in the text; the text proposes, or instructs, and the reader disposes, or constructs" (142), as Elizabeth Freund puts it. Meaning comes at the merger of text and reader, separate from those two elements. Iser states: "As text and reader thus merge into a single situation, the division between subject and object no longer applies, and it therefore follows that meaning is no longer an object to be defined, but is an effect to be experienced" (*Act* 9–10). This model facilitates our analysis of Morrison's fiction because we are most interested in how the gaps in her fiction work on the "implied reader," i.e., how the text guides the "implied reader" to respond as desired. What we call *textual* and *meta-textual enigmas* in Morrison's fiction are manifestations of the textual gaps posited by Iser.

Because readers draw from their own experiences to help fill textual gaps, it stands to reason that responses to a given text will vary in different time periods. Iser's colleague, Hans Robert Jauss, complements Iser's model with his conception of a reading public's *horizon of expectations*. The literary conventions of a particular period inform readers' expectations of a text and color their reading of it.[8]

Introduction 21

Steven Mailloux's model of reading, based on rhetorical theory, also takes into account the conventions of a historical moment. His specific discussion of Nathaniel Hawthorne's short story, "Rappaccini's Daughter," is the most useful part of his analysis (*Interpretive Conventions* 73–92). Mailloux notes that readers come to realize that the story's narrator is unreliable, leading them to reconsider their earlier judgments and rely instead upon their own engagement with the textual evidence before them, assessing characters and situations according to their own sense of morality developed through their own life experiences. This same tactic—use of an unreliable narrator—arises throughout Morrison's work. For example, *Jazz* features a narrator who is so unreliable that readers must consider for themselves the veracity of the narrator's perspective; that is, readers must think for themselves. Jane Lilienfeld notes that "the mysterious narrator of *Jazz* is repeatedly proven to be wrong. Because of the narrator's unreliability, the parts of the novel depicting the past are as destabilized as the representations of the Harlem Renaissance. The motivations for characters' choices are obliquely suggested, often obscure to the characters, and a puzzlement for the first time reader" (44). Lilienfeld concludes:

> By situating the narratee as a co-creator of the text, the implied authors [of Morrison's *Jazz* and Virginia Woolf's *To the Lighthouse*] incorporate the reader in a community that does not erase difference, but demonstrates through narrative strategies of reading postures the possibility of shared knowledge. Requiring the reader to share in the work of constructing the narrative merges artistry with political meaning. Alluding to social, political, and cultural history and insisting that the reader understand these allusions in order to understand event, experience, re/memory, and outcome, Woolf and Morrison create narratives that are simultaneously artful and political [57].

Tracey Sherard argues, in fact, that Morrison uses the novel's narrator allegorically as akin to both a jazz record and the phonograph on which it plays. "At the end of the novel," Sherard writes, "the narrator, metaphorically 'playing' a record on a phonograph, must acknowledge that it was wrong in its anticipated narrative of 'bluesy' outcomes for its characters" (par. 3). The characters respond, consciously or unconsciously, to the narrative's music, sometimes in consonance and sometimes in resistance, but never indifferently. By symbolically suggesting that the history of jazz needs to be reconsidered from a more female point of view, Morrison leads readers to reconsider the geographical and historical context of jazz's development in the United States, especially its heyday in Harlem in the 1920s, Sherard argues. Thus, as in Morrison's preceding and succeeding novels, *Jazz* pushes readers off-balance through textual enigmas in order to reorient them toward a more nuanced, just, and humane perspective on history and society. Morrison's later novel, *Love*, also features an unreliable narrator—in fact, as readers discover late in the story, who tells the tale from beyond the grave. Moreover, Morrison's texts push readers toward self-criticism as a technique for teaching them.

Based on these conceptions of different kinds of readers and how texts influence their responses, we begin this study by examining, in Chapter 1, how a group of "real readers"—participants in an empirical study that one of us (David S. Goldstein) conducted—responded to Morrison's paradigmatic short story, "Recitatif." We use the responses of these "real readers" to point up aspects of the text that guide the responses and suggest how readers' life experiences might influence their readings of a text. We center our discussion upon the text's guidance of readers toward an introspective assessment of their own assumptions about race. We turn in Chapter 2 to Morrison's first novel, *The Bluest Eye*. In that chapter, we demonstrate how the text critiques white, hegemonic standards of beauty, and how such standards harm not only black Americans, but white as well. In Chapter 3, we discuss how Morrison builds empathy for Milkman and Pilate in *Song of Solomon* in order to lure readers to a communal rather than individual orientation. Chapter 4 analyzes Morrison's attempted recovery of slave history, which is partly lost and partly ignored in the contemporary American psyche. The text—her novel, *Beloved*—leads readers to infer that only by owning up to that painful history can they and the nation heal, recover, and forge new and equitable race relations. We describe in Chapter 5 how, in many ways, Morrison has come full circle with the publication of *Paradise* in 1998. In Chapter 6, we appropriately discuss how Morrison uses her creative and compassionate talent to take us, figuratively, home in her novel *Home* (2013). Chapter 7 explores intersectionality in Morrison's work, examining in detail *Sula* (1973), *Tar Baby* (1981), and *A Mercy* (2008). Although we do not dedicate entire chapters to Morrison's remaining novels—*Jazz* (1992), *Love* (2003), and *God Help the Child* (2015)—we do include discussions of each of them as they illuminate the principal novels we examine.

1

"Recitatif"

Despite being the only short story ever written by Nobel laureate Toni Morrison and a topic of her own speaking and writing, "Recitatif" has received very little, but slowly growing, scholarly attention. This curious fact might reflect either a critical bias against the short story genre—which, following Alastair Fowler, Michael Bérubé has suggested (322)—or the relative obscurity of the anthology in which it first appeared in 1983 (the out-of-print *Confirmation: An Anthology of African American Women*, edited by Amiri Baraka and Amina Baraka).[1] In any case, as Morrison herself has said, "Recitatif" puts into play the very themes and rhetorical devices for which her novels have been recognized (*Playing* xi).

In fact, "Recitatif" can be viewed as a nineteen-page distillation of Morrison's grand project of deconstructing race which characterizes her remarkable oeuvre. Like all of her fiction, the story's strategies are designed to induce readers' involvement in its thematic goal. To accomplish this task, "Recitatif" foregrounds race, placing less explicit emphasis on gender. The text also "stages" within the text the "real world" debate about school desegregation and mandatory busing and models a particularly African American storytelling style. The author's use of cleverly ambiguous racial codes in her descriptions of the main characters is the story's most outstanding feature, and is a prime example of Morrison's use of textual and meta-textual enigmas.

"Recitatif" keeps its readers off-balance from its outset. Its plot turns, language tricks, and story line gaps disturb readers, prodding them out of lazy reading and complacency and into fuller, deeper engagement with the text. These unusual textual elements push readers to solve the mysteries, fill in the gaps, and thereby complete the story. By participating in making meaning out of the text, readers experience the story on a more visceral level than they otherwise would. Furthermore, they respond on a meta-analytical level, encouraged to consider why the text's elements influenced their responses in particular ways. By using such rhetorical devices to pull readers into meaning-making and self-reflection, Morrison also pulls readers into questioning their own assumptions, particularly about race.

As Elizabeth Abel discovered when she shared this story with her black colleague, Lula Fragd, Morrison slyly plants clues regarding the two protagonists' respective races without revealing which girl is black and which is white. Abel, who is white, found that the same clues that led her to believe that Twyla is white convinced Fragd that Twyla is black. Abel supposes that their divergent interpretations of the same set of clues result from their very different experiences. Despite being highly and similarly trained literary critics, Abel's life experiences as a white woman and Fragd's as a black woman lead them to opposite interpretations of the textual clues. Karla F.C. Holloway (who is black) and Stephanie A. Demetrakopoulos (who is white) similarly present divergent, personal readings of Morrison's works in their collaborative book, *New Dimensions of Spirituality*. In their introduction they state: "Although a sensitivity to the issues of women's reality initially unifies our analysis, the schism of individual racial and cultural perspectives eventually clearly distinguishes it" (4–5). They thus acknowledge that race is a potent force in shaping individual response.[2]

Hoping to build upon the questions raised by Abel's anecdotal report and the individual, divergent readings of Morrison's work presented by Holloway and Demetrakopoulos, one of this volume's co-authors, David Goldstein, sought to identify the textual clues planted throughout "Recitatif" that influence readers' responses, particularly their conjectures about the characters' racial identities. The sixty-seven "real readers" of this empirical study, who read the story and completed a questionnaire, cited a variety of clues in formulating their guesses. Often, some readers cited the same clues as a basis for opposite guesses. The responses provided by this set of "real readers" indicate, as we discuss throughout this chapter, that Morrison's tactics for unsettling and disturbing readers are remarkably successful.[3]

The readers' uneasiness begins with the story's first paragraph, when a narrator, speaking in first person, begins to tell how she and a girl named Roberta were taken to a shelter called St. Bonny's. Readers cannot identify the narrator, but from the narrator's casual language (e.g., referring to a restroom as a "john" [249]) and mistakes in grammar (e.g., "…when Roberta and me came…" [243]; using sentence fragments and improper punctuation), which occur throughout the narrative, readers begin to make assumptions about her class status. Most significantly, the text's first page introduces readers to the principal mystery of the text: the racial identities of the two girls. The second paragraph, which indirectly provides the narrator's identity, Twyla, indicates that Roberta is "from a whole other race" (243). Members of Roberta's race, which is not specified here or anywhere else in the text, "never washed their hair and they smelled funny" (243), according to Twyla's mother. In this instance, readers can be certain that by "they" Twyla is referring to members of Roberta's race. Later, when she disparagingly speaks about the residents of the wealthy part of town, she remarks, "Everything is so easy for them" (252). In a stroke, readers' confidence that "they" and "them" mean the other race is shattered; perhaps Twyla means the other class. At this early point in the story, however, readers are only beginning to work on the puzzle of the characters' racial identities, not yet realizing that the text will never yield that information.

By the story's second page, readers begin to sort through textual clues regarding the characters' racial identities. The clues identified by the "real readers" in the empirical study tended to fall into two categories: physical (e.g., the physiques of the characters and their mothers and features such as hair texture) and cultural (e.g., language usage, characters' names, knowledge of culturally important persons and historical events, and exhibitions of bigotry).

One culturally related clue that many "real readers" noted was the characters' food preferences. Twyla tells readers that Roberta hated the institution's food, which included Spam, Salisbury steak, and Jello. Readers might consider such food to be that of white people or black people, depending on their own experiences. Although readers might consider such bland fare to be typical of institutions like St. Bonaventure (which, Twyla eventually reveals, is the shelter's proper name), the fact that Roberta refuses to eat it evidences, to some readers, either Roberta's whiteness or her blackness; the "real readers" in the empirical study tended to conclude the latter.

Later in the story, when the girls' mothers come to visit (Twyla explains that she and Roberta "weren't real orphans with beautiful dead parents in the sky. We were dumped" by incompetent mothers [244]), Roberta's mother brings chicken legs, ham sandwiches, oranges, chocolate-covered graham crackers, and milk. Whatever conclusions readers reached based on the girls' opinions of St. Bonaventure's food now must be reconsidered. If the chicken legs are fried, perhaps this lunch indicates that Roberta is African American, readers relying on stereotypical notions might assume. On the other hand, the description of Roberta drinking milk from a Thermos conjures in the minds of some readers images of a white girl. Morrison apparently expects this association.[4] Finally, if readers' assumptions about who eats what kind of food are not already shaky, Twyla then remarks, "The wrong food is always with the wrong people" (248), further destabilizing readers' conclusions. The fact that the "real readers" who noted these food-related clues reached divergent conclusions about the characters' racial identities evidences these clues' ambiguity.

The characters' names themselves also resist readers' pat conclusions. Roberta, a feminine form of Robert, is a centuries-old European name, leading some readers to associate it with the white race. On the other hand, some readers might be familiar with African Americans named Roberta, such as singer Roberta Flack.⁵ Furthermore, about halfway into the story, readers learn that Roberta's surname is Fisk, which might remind some readers of Fisk University, a historically black college in Nashville.

Twyla, a more uncommon name, might lead some readers to believe she is black if they associate African Americans with less traditional given names. Twyla Tharp, the dancer and choreographer, however, is white. Although Twyla deprives readers of the potential clue of her birth name, she reveals her post-marriage surname, Benson (251), which might call to some readers' minds the popular jazz guitarist and singer George Benson, who is African American. Readers then learn that Roberta has married a man named Kenneth Norton, which also is the name of a black heavyweight boxer. Depending upon readers' knowledge and assumptions, they disregard some of these clues and incorporate others in their conjectures about the characters' racial identities. In Goldstein's empirical study, several respondents referred to the characters' names, but reached divergent racial inferences based upon the names. Readers familiar with more than one of these name-related clues face the more difficult task of assigning relative weight to them, probably never feeling certain of their conclusions.

As the "real readers" of the empirical study showed, readers' assumptions of phenotypic, corporeal markers also influence their conclusions about the characters' races. To the extent that their assumptions about those markers conflict with other textual clues, readers continuously second-guess themselves each time they encounter a new clue. The first body-related clue comes early in the story, when the girls curl each other's hair before their mothers arrive. Readers might wonder why, if one of them is black (as is clear from Twyla's earlier comment that "we looked like salt and pepper" [244]), she needs her hair curled.

The uncertainty is only beginning at this point. Meeting again in the coffee shop some years later, Roberta sports "big and wild" hair (249), suggesting an afro. The next description of Roberta's hair comes when Twyla sees her in the grocery store. Twyla reports that "her huge hair was sleek now, smooth around a small, nicely shaped head" (252). Did Roberta straighten her (naturally curly) hair or stop curling her (naturally straight) hair? Did the black girl—either Twyla or Roberta—require curling to control unruly, but already curly, hair? Morrison notably avoids the adjective "kinky," which readers more likely would associate with African American hair texture.

In a later encounter at a demonstration against busing for school desegregation, startled by their mutual animosity, Roberta says to Twyla, "I used to curl your hair," to which Twyla responds, "I hated your hands in my hair" (257). Was Twyla's hair straight, then? And if so, does that mean she is white? Readers struggle to form mental pictures of the characters out of these troubling clues.

Twyla's descriptions of the girls' mothers provide more but equally ambiguous clues for readers. Twyla is horrified when her mother arrives for a visit wearing "those green slacks I hated and hated even more now because didn't she know we were going to chapel? And that fur jacket with the pocket linings so ripped she had to pull to get her hands out of them" (246). Do ratty and garish clothes suggest to white readers that Twyla's mother is black, and therefore Twyla is black? Do black readers think such descriptions indicate "white trash" (a contemptuous, primarily Southern term for a poor white person)? Are there cross-over assumptions, such as black readers associating shabby clothes with blacks and white readers imagining Twyla's mother as "white trash"?

If readers do make one of these associations, they must ask themselves *why*. Is it because they associate ratty clothing with one race or the other? Do they associate ragged clothing with poverty, and then jump to the association of poverty with one race or the other? Indeed, the empirical study's "real readers" demonstrated that the same clues led to different conclusions regarding the meaning of the evidence.

Twyla then remarks that her mother's green slacks "made her behind stick out" (247). Do the slacks make it appear that her buttocks stick out although they really do not, or do they emphasize buttocks that really do stick out? And if the latter, do protruding buttocks suggest an African American physique? Several readers—nearly all of whom concluded that Twyla is black—referred to this aspect of Twyla's mother's body, but did not specify precisely why they associated the trait with African Americans. What we do know is that in white, Western society, protruding buttocks connote racial "otherness."[6]

Added to this unflattering description of Twyla's mother is her depiction of Roberta's mother, which, if readers are prone to associate body shape with one race or another according to prevailing stereotypes, complicates their conclusions. If readers think that protruding buttocks indicate Twyla's mother's blackness, they somehow must reconcile this description of Roberta's mother: "She was big. Bigger than any man and on her chest was the biggest cross I'd ever seen" (247). Readers inclined to rely on physical markers on which to base racial identification, and who subscribe to the stereotype of the obese black woman such as the mammy caricature (*Ethnic Notions*), are unsettled by these descriptions. (Indeed, a few of the readers who noted Roberta's mother's stature conjectured that she is black.) Moreover, readers must question why they view the descriptions as contradictory, as if obesity and protruding buttocks—traits ascribed to Roberta's mother and Twyla's mother, respectively—belong together.

The cultural clue of the cross, too, provides a clue that is difficult to interpret: does this assertion of her piety indicate a more flamboyant faith, such as Southern Baptist, typically associated with African American Christians? Combined with the physical clues centered on physique, the cultural clue of religious piety bewildered the empirical study's "real readers."

Twyla describes the mothers' behaviors—another set of cultural clues—in ways that challenge readers seeking to use behaviors rather than physiques as a basis for their conjectures. First, Roberta's mother refuses to shake the hand of Twyla's mother. Is it because she is a white bigot, a resentful black woman, or a black bigot? Or is her rebuff unrelated to race? Perhaps it is based on perceived class difference. Or maybe Roberta's mother is simply anti-social. The subsequent response of Twyla's mother exacerbates readers' confusion. At the entrance to the chapel, where the rebuff occurs, she loudly says, "That bitch!" (247), an interjection so crass and inappropriate that Twyla thinks her mother "really needed to be killed" (248). Is such behavior associated with one race? Or is it class? Or simply upbringing?

The confusion between class and race also arises when readers encounter the scene in which Twyla and Roberta face off on opposite sides of the issue of mandatory busing for school desegregation. Roberta stands opposed to busing; Twyla then counter-protests in favor of it. Does Roberta oppose busing because she opposes desegregation? If so, is her opinion related to her race? If so, is her race white or black? Many blacks have opposed busing, desegregation, or both; readers with a reasonably sophisticated understanding of the civil rights era know they cannot assume that her opposition to busing means she is a white racist. In fact, the "real readers" in the empirical study who took note of Roberta's anti-busing protests were less likely to assume she is black than the readers who did not mention her political stance.

Readers also must consider whether Roberta, who by this time has acquired the trappings—and presumably the attitudes—of affluence, opposes busing on the grounds that her children will be sent to inferior schools. Her convictions about busing might be entirely unrelated to race. When it becomes clear that Twyla's stance stems more from her resentment of Roberta than from her own political opinions, readers cannot derive more insight from the situation.

Despite its slipperiness, the apparent class difference between Twyla and Roberta significantly influenced some of the respondents in the empirical study. Although no white respondents mentioned a character's class as evidence of her race, a quarter of the respondents of color cited class as a basis for their guesses of Roberta's race, half saying she is white and half saying she is black. If these "real readers" are an indication, non-white readers are particularly attentive to the text's class-oriented clues, but read the clues divergently.

Although class figures prominently in the story, gender is, of course, present but relegated to the background relative to racism. Sexism concerns Morrison as much as does racism; she believes that "the conflict of genders is a cultural illness" (qtd. in Strouse 56). All of her novels deal on some level with sex and gender. Yet in "Recitatif" Morrison refrains from dealing explicitly with gender. Although gender always operates in a narrative involving humans, the text draws readers' attention more directly to race. From lay readers' perspective, gender demands much less attention. The pains to which Morrison goes to avoid making gender an issue obvious to readers of this story are worth examining because they emphasize, by contrast, how sharply she brings issues of race to the fore.

Both protagonists in "Recitatif" are female. They meet in a home for girls, of which the entire staff is female. The story depicts no male/female conflict, unlike every one of her novels. The only males who appear in the story at all—some police officers at the scene of the demonstration and the two young men accompanying Roberta when they enter Twyla's coffee shop—are inconsequential. Twyla's and Roberta's husbands and sons are mentioned in passing; they do not participate in the action of the story. Concentrating primarily on women sidesteps the social problem of sex-based "othering" which elsewhere figures prominently in Morrison's writing and thus focuses readers almost exclusively on the racial issues raised in and by the story. That is, the tenuous sisterhood of these characters—in some ways reminiscent of that between Eva and Sula in *Sula*—remains a crucial feature of the tale, but readers, especially lay readers, are less apt to concentrate on gender when the narrative's central conflict is between two females than if it were between men and women, such as in *Paradise*.

Not only are male/female relationships in "Recitatif," such as between the two women and their husbands, pushed somewhat into the background; even there, they pose no challenge to the hegemonic status quo. Unlike Morrison's novels, in which strong women contest male domination, "Recitatif" depicts conservative gender roles in the women's marriages. Twyla states, "Strife came to us that fall.... I couldn't figure it out from one day to the next. I knew I was supposed to feel something strong, but I didn't know what, and James wasn't any help" (255–56), indicating that she expects her husband to explain confusing current events and, moreover, to tell her how to feel about them. Even the more worldly Roberta suggests she has a traditional marriage in which her husband earns money and she spends it. When Twyla asks Roberta what he does for a living, Roberta replies, "Computers and stuff. What do I know?" (254). It is enough for her that her husband provides for her; how he earns the money does not concern her. These traditional gender roles for husbands and wives are atypical for Morrison's fiction. Unlike her novels, "Recitatif" is too short to tackle Morrison's dual targets of racism and sexism. By declining to foreground in her readers' attention issues of gender, this story mounts a stronger attack on matters of race.[7]

With virtually no covert reference to men, Morrison neutralizes the problem of pronouns that ostensibly are gender-neutral but actually are not (which, of course, is not to say that gender is absent if men are absent). She also disarms the potential problem of different recollections about the story among men and women. Male and female readers are not given the opportunity to respond differently. With this story, Morrison wishes to confound preconceptions of race; splitting readers by gender would not further this purpose. This tactic worked with the "real readers" in the first author's (Goldstein's) empirical study; men and women responded equivalently. In contrast to Morrison's carefully ambiguous manipulation of race, which it is her purpose to demystify—or, more accurately, to lead her readers to demystify—"Recitatif" privileges race rather than gender, although, as Susana M. Morris notes, the distressed friendship between Twyla and Roberta is imbued with gender, and, in fact, disentangling race and gender "does not allow for the ways in which considering race and gender together can illuminate critical discourse" ("Sisters" 164).[8] Although we agree with Morris, we wish here to focus more on what the story says about race insofar as that theme dominates all of her literary and non-fiction works.

Toward her goal of deconstructing race in "Recitatif," Morrison uses some textual enigmas specifically to elicit readers' sympathy as well as discomfort. For example, when Roberta and two friends happen to visit the coffee shop in which Twyla works, she tells the three that she lives in Newburgh (a Hudson River Valley town about fifty miles north of New York City and only twenty miles from one of Morrison's two homes [Furman 3]). Roberta responds, "Newburgh? No kidding?" Twyla reports, "She laughed then a private laugh that included the guys but only the guys, and they laughed with her" (250), leaving Twyla, and the reader, to wonder what is funny about Newburgh. Because readers are dependent on Twyla's reporting, they also are excluded from the private joke, and also share Twyla's frustration and, by extension, her embarrassment.

Other culturally related clues relate to Twyla's apparent naiveté and ignorance. One example is the coffee shop scene, when Twyla reveals her ignorance of Jimi Hendrix. All but one of the empirical study's "real readers" who used this clue guessed that Roberta was black. Interestingly, no respondents who grew up in an African American community referred to this clue. This result bears out Abel's anecdotal report that she, a white reader, assumed that Roberta was black because she knew of Hendrix and Twyla did not, while her African American colleague pointed out that black readers would know that most of Hendrix's fans were white (474).

Twyla also expresses remarkable ignorance about race relations in the United States. When Roberta explains her earlier coldness to Twyla, she says, "Oh, Twyla, you know how it was in those days: black—white. You know how everything was." Twyla tells the reader:

> But I didn't know. I thought it was just the opposite. Busloads of blacks and whites came into Howard Johnson's together. They roamed together then: students, musicians, lovers, protesters. You got to see everything at Howard Johnson's and blacks were very friendly with whites in those days [255].

Although the reader cannot pin down precisely when the coffee shop scene takes place, it most likely occurs after Twyla was about sixteen (old enough to work full time), which was in 1953, but before the characters reunite again, presumably around 1965. During this Jim Crow period, it is possible that a young, white person might be unaware of the tensions underlying apparently good relations between the races. Readers might consider this explanation of Twyla's remark as an indication that Twyla is white. Twyla's later comments, though, lead readers to think that her naive belief that race relations were good might stem from a general lack of awareness about social matters, not only about race relations. About busing, she says, "I thought it was a good thing until I heard it was a bad thing. I mean I didn't know" (256). If she simply is unused to thinking about social issues, her unenlightened sense of race relations might not signify whiteness, after all. Again, readers' conclusions are stymied.

Readers must work hard to unravel the story's timeframe, a tactic that challenges Western concepts of linear time. (We discuss in Chapter 4 how this tactic resurfaces in *Beloved*.) Twyla includes no dates by which readers can establish with certainty when events occur. Readers know that the girls are eight years old when together at St. Bonaventure, and Twyla's incidental mention upon their second accidental reunion at a grocery store that "twenty years disappeared" (253) indicates that they are twenty-eight at that point. When Twyla later reports that racial strife struck their town that fall, most readers will assume that the period is the mid–1960s, when racial violence plagued many American cities. Working backward, readers can deduce that Roberta and Twyla resided at St. Bonaventure around 1945. The narrator's present must be after the 1960s but is not specified. She must be at least forty but might be as old as sixty-six (considering that "Recitatif" was published in 1983). The uncertainty about the narrator's present undermines confidence in readers' conclusions about Twyla's age and the story's timeframe in general, even when logically deduced.

Like so many elements in the story, time is complicated because it is left unexplained; the timeframe remains open. Appropriately, silence (e.g., Maggie's muteness) and absence recur as themes in "Recitatif," and augment Morrison's rhetorical strategy of inducing the reader to complete the text. The story ends not with a statement but a question about Maggie's fate. The puzzles of what really happened to Maggie, whether she was black or not, and whether Roberta and Twyla participated in the orchard incident increasingly trouble the story's readers as they progress.

Early in Twyla's narrative, she says she often dreams of the orchard but does not know why. "Nothing really happened there" (244), she says. This comment is most problematic. The entire narrative comprises Twyla's recollections of past events. If, as readers naturally assume when reading a first-person account, the narrator is speaking to them in the present, then why would Twyla say that nothing really happened in the orchard? Telling a retrospective story, she ought to know that the incident with Maggie, which obsesses her throughout the story, is not only significant but crucial.

The enigma of Maggie is emphasized by Twyla's description: "The kitchen woman with legs like parentheses" (245). Parentheses indicate something of secondary importance, which, added to Maggie's muteness, connote a passive, marginalized victim, a cipher; the bow legs conjure the image of a zero itself. Reduced to nothing, Maggie is robbed of agency, which leaves for her only the role of pawn in the battle of memories waged by Twyla and Roberta over three decades. Twyla first tells readers that Maggie fell down in the orchard and the older girls at the shelter assaulted her. When she meets Roberta in the grocery store, Roberta contradicts Twyla's recollection of the incident with Maggie, telling her that Maggie did not trip; the girls pushed Maggie down. Twyla refuses to believe this account, but Roberta's insistence plants doubt in her mind (255). With the introduction of Twyla's uncertainty about her own memory, readers, dependent entirely on Twyla as a source of information, also begin to feel unsure.

Just as Morrison employs codes regarding race which readers must supply themselves on the basis of their own preconceptions, Howard Sklar convincingly argues that Morrison employs the same tactic for disability—Morrison withholds explicit identification of Maggie's disabilities to instigate readers' application of their own biases and preconceptions. Morrison fully intends for readers to be unsure of the nature of Maggie's disabilities, Sklar notes. Moreover, as Twyla's and Roberta's empathy for Maggie develops (albeit quite late), they model empathy rather than judgment or derision for readers.[9]

The uncertainty intensifies as the narrative progresses. At their next unpleasant reunion, at which each woman stands literally and figuratively on opposite sides of a busing and desegregation demonstration, Roberta says to Twyla, "You're the same little state kid who kicked a poor old black lady when she was down on the ground. You kicked a black lady and you have the nerve to call me a bigot" (257). This new version of the story introduces the notion that Twyla and perhaps Roberta participated in tormenting Maggie, and that Maggie, whom at first Twyla described as "sandy-colored" (245), was black. Twyla's unspoken response is, "What was she saying? Black? Maggie wasn't black" (258). Later, Twyla acknowledges that, although she is sure that she did not kick Maggie, Maggie might have been black: "When I thought about it I actually couldn't be certain" (259). To readers, this incident is becoming a *Rashomon* of sorts, leaving them, like viewers of Akira Kurosawa's film, to wonder which version of the story to believe.

Finally, Twyla seems fairly certain: "I didn't kick her; I didn't join in with the gar girls and kick that lady, but I sure did want to" (259), a version that Roberta finally corroborates during their last reunion at Christmas when she tearfully confesses that they had not kicked Maggie. But the uncertainty continues when Roberta says, "I really did think she was black. I didn't make that up. I really thought so. But now I can't be sure" (261). If neither she nor Twyla feel certain about Maggie's race, neither can readers. Then, the story concludes with Roberta's unanswered question, "What the hell happened to Maggie?" (261). Twyla's earlier statement that she and Roberta knew how to believe what had to be believed (253) becomes quite ironic, for readers have found that the characters, and therefore the readers, do not know what to believe.

For most of the story's time period, Twyla and Roberta argue about Maggie's race, implicitly agreeing that Maggie's race is important. So concerned are they with Maggie's race that their disagreement overwhelms what begins at St. Bonaventure as a strong friendship based on the powerful, common experience of inadequate parenting. By depicting the characters' rapprochement as a result of the characters' abandonment of their need to label Maggie by race, the story presents readers with a model for reducing racial tensions in society. However, Helane Adams Androne reads the space between racial binary codes as Roberta and Twyla's connection to healing through a problematic archetypal mother figure in which analysis of the "absent/present [mothering] paradigm shows how mothers' identities actually collide and intersect with archetypal identities, and how women use culture and memory to cope with trauma" (133–34). Androne represents a shift in more recent criticism on "Recitatif" that focuses on the significance of Maggie's disability, racelessness, and mothering as signs and symbols moving away from binary racial coding. Shanna Benjamin points out that the "boundaries circumscribing Maggie's representation of the parenthetical past" are "an allegory for black/white relations, ... representing the residual, racialized perspectives precipitating from America's slave past. Silent and bow-legged, ever-present yet readily marginalized, Maggie symbolizes the silent truth imbedded within the parenthetical narratives of America's racialized history" (89).

Maggie is indeed extremely significant to the text, yet, as Benjamin acknowledges, is also marginalized. The boundaries created by the historical legacy of racism in the U.S., signified by the parentheses of Maggie's legs, prevent her from being central to the text as it is the history of racial codifications that creates her disability and marginalization. While there is a space for potential healing within the parentheses where historical racial codifications do not exist, the community at large which occupies the space outside of the parentheses is not capable of traversing the non-binary space as its members often are unaware of the degree to which binary racial codes have been imbedded in their psyche; and, if they are aware, do not know how to operate outside of those codes. Therefore, the focus of twentieth-century critics on the ways in which racialized power and ways of understanding are active in the U.S. is necessary in order to help readers see, understand, and free themselves from those codes so that they are ready to interact in non-binary racial spaces. Morrison's texts show over and over again that the disabilities caused by the legacy of white patriarchal capitalism supremacy cannot be combatted unless people are made aware of those disabilities and, to echo bell hooks, believe in justice more than their "allegiance to race, sexuality and gender" (Castro).

Roberta's accusation that Twyla kicked a black woman and yet has the nerve to call her, Roberta, a bigot exacerbates readers' distrust of the characters' memories. Readers must try to recall whether Twyla did indeed call Roberta a bigot; perhaps readers will review the narrative for confirmation, having learned to question their own memory of the narrative. In fact, nowhere in the text does Twyla call Roberta a bigot. This further undermining of the readers' faith in the characters' memories—as well as their own—also complicates the readers' task of identifying the characters' races, because readers are likely to bring to the text an assumption about who bigots tend to be, who is more likely to accuse another of bigotry, and who is more likely to make a false accusation of bigotry. The problematic accusation also calls into question the completeness of Twyla's storytelling; perhaps she did call Roberta a bigot but failed to report it to her readers.

Despite the inconclusive reporting about bigotry, several of the "real readers" in the empirical study referred to it as a basis for their conjectures about the characters' racial identities. The ambiguity of the textual clues does not dissuade readers from drawing conclusions based upon them. Interestingly, no African American or Latino respondents in the empirical study cited their perception of a character's racism as evidence of Roberta's race, while the percentage of whites who mentioned racism was higher than that of any other ethnic group. At least among this group of readers, whites more readily assumed that racism signifies that a character is white, and also were more willing to excuse or ignore the fallibility of a narrator.[10]

In addition to dealing with conflicting memories, readers must fill narrative gaps and holes in order to make sense of the story. Unraveling the story's timeframe, as previously discussed, is one such puzzle; others require similar work from readers. For example, when Twyla launches a counter-protest across the street from Roberta's anti-busing demonstration, she produces a series of signs that "got crazier each day, and the women on my side decided that I was a kook. They couldn't make heads or tails out of my brilliant screaming posters" (258). Readers are not afforded the luxury of dismissing Twyla as a kook for she is their sole source of information; therefore, they must do the work of deciphering the signs. For example, in response to Roberta's sign that reads, MOTHERS HAVE RIGHTS TOO, Twyla makes a sign that reads, HOW WOULD YOU KNOW? To make sense of her statement, readers must recall that Roberta earlier had said that she had four stepchildren; Twyla is implying that Roberta is not really a mother.

Not only are internal aspects of the text confusing; the entire reading event itself baffles readers. As a first-person narrative, the text blurs the line between a written story and a spoken one. At times readers cannot help but note that they are reading a text, as when plot puzzles force them to review earlier passages (e.g., when faced with the question of whether Twyla had accused Roberta of bigotry). At other points in the narrative, the story maintains an unmistakable oral quality. The informality of Twyla's language leads readers immediately to the sense that they are listening to, rather than reading, the story.

The distinctively "oral" quality of "Recitatif" also contributes to the story's strategy of recruiting the reader in its mission to deconstruct race. To analyze this aspect of the text's rhetorical strategy, we find Robert B. Stepto's model of African American storytelling narratives helpful. In his essay, "Distrust of the Reader in Afro-American Narratives," Stepto argues that a characteristic feature of African American narratives is their implicit distrust of their readers, both black and white. The narratives typically feature rhetoric that resists a cavalier or "wrong" reading. Instead, creative communication takes place "when the reader gets 'told'—or 'told off'—in such a way that he or she finally begins to *hear*" (202–03; emphasis in original). Stepto intentionally uses phrases ("told," "hear") that signify a storytelling paradigm. He is specifically interested in African American authors who "choose to see themselves as storytellers instead of storywriters" (199) because he believes the prevailing reader-response theories, propounded by white critics, inadequately apply to this distinctive aspect of much African American literature. He therefore puts forth his own model of the various forms of such narratives. "Recitatif" exemplifies what Stepto means by an African American storytelling narrative.[11] Although the text is written, its structure mimics oral storytelling, a quality similar to Morrison's other works.[12]

Stepto describes four variations of the basic African American storytelling narrative, which

> is fundamentally a framed tale in which either the framed or framing narrative depicts a black storyteller's white listener socially and morally maturing into competency. In thus presenting a very particular reader in the text, the basic written tale squarely addresses the issue of its probable audience while raising an issue for some

or most of its readers regarding the extent to which they can or will identify with the text's "reader" while pursuing (if not always completing) their own act of reading [207].

One variation of the framed tale, which he labels a Type B tale, features a novice storyteller who only recently has achieved competence as a listener. A consideration of the four principal characteristics of a Type B tale reveals how well the model fits "Recitatif." First, "although the story's primary narrator is a novice teller (white or black), the black master teller is fully present as the teller of the story's tale," according to Stepto (209). Twyla exemplifies the novice teller. Her tale is little more than that of the event that led to her recently achieved competence as a listener to Roberta's story, namely, grappling with her challenged memory of the Maggie incident.

Stepto says that "the novice teller is seemingly still too close to the moment when competency was achieved and too overwhelmed by the teller, tale, and other features of that moment to author a story which is anything other than a strict account of that moment" (208). "Recitatif" *is* Roberta's story. Despite the fact that Twyla is the narrator of the framing story, it is Roberta who is the master storyteller. Although she eventually acknowledges she might be wrong about Maggie's race and definitely is wrong about kicking her, it is only with Roberta's confession that any resolution occurs. She controls the knowledge; only her telling can break the impasse. In contrast to Twyla's ignorance (e.g., her unfamiliarity with Hendrix; her confession that she failed to recognize the racial strife enveloping the nation despite nightly news reports), Roberta has had the knowledge and understanding all along (e.g., her statement, "Oh, Twyla, you know how it was in those days: black—white," and Twyla's confession to the reader, "But I didn't know" [255]).

Second, "although the novice teller may tell the tale of his or her previous incompetency to listeners situated within the tale's frame, direct address to the 'listener' outside the story (the 'outside' reader) is both possible and likely" (209). In "Recitatif," Twyla does not tell the tale to listeners within the frame, but does implicitly address the "outside" reader by speaking in first person. First-person speech implies awareness of a listener—in this case, the story's readers.

Third, "although the predominating autobiographical statement is still that offered by the master teller in the tale, the novice teller's self-history also has a place, sometimes a significant one, in the story as a whole" (209). Twyla's self-history—her enlightenment regarding race—certainly is significant. Roberta's autobiographical statement, however, dominates, especially her climb from illiteracy to affluence. It is Twyla's story only insofar as she tells of her maturation into a competent listener, and it is Roberta's story that she finally hears.

Fourth, "although the story is normally a framed tale, with this type we begin to see improvisations upon that structure, especially in those instances where the story is repeated and otherwise developed for the needs and purposes of novellas and novels" (209) and, we would add, short stories. "Recitatif" is, indeed, a framed tale. Twyla is telling the story of Roberta telling a story. There is another level, though: Morrison is telling the story of Twyla telling the story of Roberta telling a story.

Stepto actually offers two versions of the Type B story as he does for the other three types (A, C, and D) of storytelling narratives. For each narrative type that he delineates, each of which features a white listener listening to the framed tale within the framing narrative, he presents a corresponding type that differs only in the race of the listener. Thus, corresponding to narrative types A, B, C, and D are types A′, B′, C′, and D′, in which the listener is black rather than white. This dual feature of Stepto's model thus becomes especially problematic and especially interesting in relation to "Recitatif," for it is precisely the racial identity of the framed tale's listener (in this case, Twyla) that is at issue.

Is Twyla black or white? If Stepto's model fits "Recitatif" as well as we have argued it does, one must conclude that Roberta, as the master storyteller, is black and therefore Twyla is white. Corroborating this conclusion is Roberta's story of moving from illiteracy to knowledge, a well-documented African American literary theme dating back at least as far as Frederick Douglass's *Narrative*.[13] The significance of "Recitatif," however, lies in the open question of the characters' identities—not in its answer. The story, as Jan Furman notes, is precisely an "experiment in communicating without using racial codes as a shortcut" (108). Morrison herself states in *Playing in the Dark* that "Recitatif" "is an experiment in the removal of all racial codes from a narrative about two characters of different races for whom racial identity is crucial" (xi). But Morrison does not remove all racial codes from the narrative. She removes only *explicit* racial identifications of the two characters. There are, however, plenty of codes planted in the text that the reader is challenged to interpret. As Goldstein's empirical study demonstrates, readers eagerly, although divergently, interpret the text's codes. Trudier Harris's personal supposition on this matter yields a point that is similar to ours. She states Morrison "...positions readers with a racial discomfort that they either overcome, entering the text by the rules she creates, or that they consistently try to overcome by probing the text for blackness or whiteness, eagerly waiting and watching for the disguise to slip and the racial markers to reassert themselves" (*Fiction and Folklore* 110). What Harris and we take away from our experiences with Morrison's experiment in removing elicit racial codes is an intensified reader response experience that "heightens engagement [with the text] for readers conditioned by a racially constructed American social system" (*Fiction and Folklore* 110).

In addition to grappling with the enigmas—such as veiled racial signifiers—within the story itself, readers are confronted with issues about the reading experience itself, what we call *meta-textual enigmas*. Some of these meta-textual enigmas impose upon readers the shadowy presence of the author. For example, when Twyla describes Maggie's "stupid little hat," she adds, "Even for a mute, it was dumb..." (245), producing a pun on the double meaning of "dumb" that she apparently does not intend or even notice. Is this, readers might ask, a joke on the author's part?

Later, when recounting the episode of Roberta's unexpected appearance at the coffee shop in which Twyla worked, Twyla says:

> I walked over to the booth, smiling and wondering if she would remember me. Or even if she wanted to remember me. Maybe she didn't want to be reminded of St. Bonny's or to have anybody know she was ever there. I know I never talked about it to anybody [249].

Yet, Twyla is in the act of telling somebody—the readers/listeners of the story—about her experiences at St. Bonaventure. If she refrains from discussing with anybody—her husband, her son—even the fact that she lived for four months at St. Bonaventure, readers wonder why she is speaking to *them* about the experiences.

In fact, ostensibly, the sole basis for the encounter between her and the readers/listeners is Twyla's apparent desire to share intimate revelations about such events, some of which she acknowledges to be embarrassing, shameful, or painful to face.[14] By presenting this paradox, the author seems to be toying with the conceit of a first-person-narrated story. While some puzzles within the story disturb readers less experienced with wringing meaning from a narrative, this meta-mystery surrounding the reading experience itself appears to be aimed at readers more thoroughly trained and skilled, for they would be most likely to notice the incongruity of an ostensibly reticent yet thoroughly confessional narrator. Thus, some of the reader-disturbing tactics seem designed for one kind of reader, and others for another kind.

Besides listening to or reading the text, readers face another possible way to perceive it. Perhaps "Recitatif" is not a spoken or written tale but a sung one, combining speech and music. Even the title reflects the vocal foundation of Morrison's story. The *Oxford English Dictionary* defines "recitative," which comes from the French *récitatif*, as a "style of musical declamation, intermediate between singing and ordinary speech, commonly employed in the dialogue and narrative parts of operas and oratorios." By using the French word, Morrison not only alludes to the French phrase *faire le récit de sa vie*—to tell the story of one's life—but also connotes the term's meaning in music. Morrison is signifying on the notion of a recitation: a recitation is formal in Western music but, within "Recitatif,"

Twyla's storytelling appears casual. As a text itself, however, "Recitatif" can be viewed as formal if viewed from an African American aesthetic which includes standards for storytelling. Twyla is a character telling a story—in which she stars as a character—within the frame of Morrison's story.

Like the familiar African American folk figure of the front-porch storyteller, Morrison as author is once-removed from the story, letting the story play out as if Twyla were in control of it while Morrison, offstage, as it were, actually controls the tale. "Recitatif" clearly operates on more than one level and typifies the distinctly African American expressive strategy of "signifyin(g)" as described by Henry Louis Gates, Jr., in which the speaker (or writer-as-speaker) expertly disguises one meaning beneath a more apparent meaning (*Signifying Monkey*).

Morrison's connotation of an operatic recitative—a middle ground between verbal expression and musical expression—is particularly appropriate given the parallel significance of oral storytelling and musical signification in African and African American culture.[15] As Robert Palmer explains in *Deep Blues*, black slaves by the middle of the eighteenth century were forbidden from using drums and horns throughout North America except in French Louisiana. "Plantation owners had learned, sometimes the hard way, that such loud instruments could be used to signal slave insurrections" (33), Palmer writes. To express themselves, they "utilized mankind's most basic musical resources, the voice and the body" (33). Vocal expression, either spoken or sung, not only survived slavery, but perhaps enabled the slaves themselves to survive. With a one-word title, Morrison thus captures and honors four hundred years of African American expression. As Palmer states: "Through singing to themselves, hollering across the fields, and singing together while working and worshipping, they developed a hybridized musical language that distilled the very essence of innumerable African vocal traditions" (33). By connoting this tradition, Morrison consciously places "Recitatif" in an African American expressive tradition.

African and African American vocal traditions clearly are communal. Listeners are expected to participate. As a descendant of the African vocal tradition, "Recitatif" relentlessly perturbs readers to jar them from a position of relatively passive reception into one of active co-creation. This effect not only intensifies readers' attention to the story and their sense of stake in it, but also serves a broader, ideological purpose.

"Recitatif" thus exemplifies what Catherine Belsey calls an "interrogative text," as opposed to a declarative or imperative text. The interrogative text "disrupts the unity of the reader by discouraging identification with a unified subject of the enunciation. The position of the 'author' inscribed in the text, if it can be located at all, is seen as questioning or as literally contradictory" (91). In "Recitatif," the author's attitude is shrouded behind that of Twyla, and even Twyla's perspective is one of confusion, as she confesses her lack of understanding of contemporary race relations.

Belsey continues: "Thus, even if the interrogative text does not precisely ... seek 'to obtain some information' from the reader, it does literally invite the reader to produce answers to the questions it implicitly or explicitly raises" (91). "Recitatif" certainly invites readers to answer questions about the narrative itself, and, more significantly, about extra-narrative matters. Why do readers interpret clues in particular ways? What assumptions do they make about race and racism? Indeed, why do readers feel it is important to ascertain the characters' respective races in the first place? Beyond realizing their own predilection for racial labeling, some readers confront the prejudices that lead to *how* they categorize.

Belsey asserts, "The work of ideology is to present the position of the subject as fixed and unchangeable" (90). By presenting a text and the "reality" it depicts as *unfixed* and *changeable*, Morrison not only calls attention to an ideology that seems so natural that individuals fail to recognize it as such, but challenges that ideology. The text stirs up matters of race and racism, refusing to perpetuate oversimplified and unquestioned assumptions about racial categories and stereotypes.

Moreover, by guiding the reader into inferring the characters' races—in addition to demanding that the reader solve other sorts of textual and narrative puzzles—"Recitatif" forces the reader's complicity in the story's mission, which is to deconstruct race. Morrison states in *Playing in the Dark* that she wrote the story as an experiment in language, to see whether she could write a story without relying on the insidious linguistic shortcuts of racial categorization and stereotyping that she feels are so prevalent in American literature (xi). By making readers supply, from their imagination and experience, the missing information, the story encourages them to question the sources of those inferences. The reader is thus brought into the Morrisonian task of questioning racial categorization and stereotyping. In short, Morrison ingeniously works toward her ongoing mission of deconstructing race and racism by getting the reader to do so, a strategy that also pervades her novels.

Because it takes into account not only the experiential context of each reader that approaches a given text but also the historical and social context of each reading event, Mailloux's approach of rhetorical hermeneutics is a compelling one in analyzing Morrison's rhetorical tactic of using indeterminate racial codes. Readers come to the text with different assumptions and preconceptions that can best be understood in light of the "cultural conversations" about race and race relations that are both staged within the story and in which the story and its readers' interpretations participate.

In *Rhetorical Power*, Mailloux illustrates his approach by analyzing the discourse of race within and without *Huckleberry Finn*. A text, he says, "can be a topic in a cultural discussion or it can be a participant motivated by and affecting the conversation" (61). "Recitatif" on its own can hardly be seen as a topic in any cultural discussion. The small number of critical references to it evidences this fact. It most certainly is motivated by a conversation about race and prejudice, however. Morrison cites the story as an example of her goal to "free up the language from its sometimes sinister, frequently lazy, almost always predictable employment of racially informed and determined chains" (*Playing* xi). This mission stems from her practical concerns as a writer:

> I cannot rely on these metaphorical shortcuts [present in our language] because I am a black writer struggling with and through a language that can powerfully evoke and enforce hidden signs of racial superiority, cultural hegemony, and dismissive "othering" of people and language which are by no means marginal or already and completely known and knowable in my work [*Playing* x–xi].

By coupling "people" and "language," Morrison makes clear that her deconstruction of racial codes in the language of her works, most self-consciously in "Recitatif," is, to her, akin to deconstructing race. Her writing is the means by which she challenges the racism embedded in language and in society. Although "Recitatif" has not received the attention it deserves, it is a part of her oeuvre which, as a whole, is unmistakably "affecting the conversation" about racism and racial discord and the power of love to overcome them. Indirectly, then, "Recitatif" does participate in and does affect a cultural conversation. Furthermore, Morrison's work as a whole certainly is a topic in cultural discussion, as her citation by the Swedish Academy attests.

Mailloux further argues in *Rhetorical Power* that as a participant in cultural conversations about topics of the day, "literature can take up the ideological rhetoric of its historical moment ... and place it on a fictional stage" within the text (61). "Readers thus become spectators at a rhetorical performance, and sometimes, as in *Huckleberry Finn*, they also become actors in the drama they are watching" (61). As Mailloux argues (esp. 69–86), Twain's novel trains the reader to read appropriately the textual rhetoric. *Huckleberry Finn* depicts debates about slavery and abolition within the text, and characters actually hash out this debate among themselves. By becoming observers of this "staged" debate, readers are trained to read the rhetoric of the abolition debate in the society in which the novel is a participant. In other words, by observing (reading) the "staged" debate within the text, readers become better, more practiced interpreters of the rhetoric in the "real world" debate occurring in their society.

For all their differences, *Huckleberry Finn* and "Recitatif" share remarkable similarities. Not only are both first-person narratives by apparent innocents, but both exhibit this intriguing feature of staged debates. In "Recitatif," the debate about busing as a means of school desegregation, a topic that consumed Americans from the 1954 Supreme Court decision in *Brown v. Board of Ed.* through the 1980s (Troyna, esp. 53) is staged in the story itself. On one side of the street, literally and figuratively, is Roberta, who has joined other mothers in a demonstration against busing. "They want to take my kids and send them out of the neighborhood. They don't want to go," Roberta says (256). On the other side is Twyla, who, speaking through her car window after coming upon the demonstration, asks Roberta, "So what if they go to another school? My boy's being bussed too, and I don't mind." The argument escalates until it turns "racial": when Twyla says, "Well, it is a free country," Roberta replies, "Not yet, but it will be." When Roberta adds, "I wonder what made me think you were different," Twyla says the same thing back. As police officers pull Roberta's fellow protesters off of Twyla's car, Roberta turns her version of the Maggie incident into a verbal weapon, accusing Twyla of bigotry because she supposedly kicked Maggie (257).

Morrison does not take sides in this confrontation. Rather, by staging it—that is, by depicting the conflict like a theatrical drama in the text—she depicts the divisiveness of the issue of busing and simultaneously demystifies the racial motivation on both sides of the issue. By exposing the racial antagonism that, for Twyla and Roberta, lies beneath the surface of the busing issue, Morrison also exposes the racial prejudice for which the rhetoric for and against busing in the extra-textual narrative ("real life") has become a thin veil. However, Harris advocates a strikingly different interpretation from ours. She asserts that Morrison's baring of Twyla's and Roberta's "racial prejudices during the school desegregation incident … debunks … [Morrison's] initial thesis that race does not matter—or at least … severely calls it into question" (*Fiction and Folklore* 115). She states, "absence of racial markers aside, black and white human beings on American soil seem incapable of peaceful coexistence without tension based on race. *It is the norm,* and everyone seeks after the norm. Twyla and Roberta need the … [norm] in order to define themselves" (*Fiction and Folklore* 115–16, emphasis in original). We have mixed feelings about this. On the one hand, we agree that readers of "Recitatif" become spectators at this scene of rhetorical performance and, in Mailloux's terms, become actors in the drama they are watching to the extent that they accept the role and get "rehearsed" in reading the debate between Twyla and Roberta about the incident with Maggie, an issue on which the success of the story as a deconstructor of racism *in the reader's mind* depends.

On the other hand, by withholding the critical information not only of Twyla's and Roberta's racial identities but that of Maggie, too, "Recitatif" leaves it to the reader to complete the story. To do so, the reader is compelled to decide which character is black and which is white, which woman is correct about what happened to Maggie, and what the characters' acknowledged desire to harm Maggie signifies. (Is it racism?) To the extent that the reader accepts this role, for which Twyla's maturation as a hearer serves as a training exercise, readers confront the problem of having to use evidence not found in the text itself—conclusive evidence is simply absent—but in their own minds. If readers recognize this exposure of preconceptions about race, the preconceptions become problematic (e.g., "Why did I assume that Roberta's illiteracy meant she was black?" or, perhaps, "Why did I assume that Roberta's affluence meant she was white?"). When readers acknowledge and question these stereotypes, they contribute to the deconstruction of race. As we argue in the next two chapters, Morrison's novels feature this same characteristic strategy of reader involvement.

The issues raised by the readers in the empirical study evoke considerations of their expectations regarding a short story as a genre as well as of the prevailing attitudes of the society at the time of their readings, i.e., the contemporary United States. Hans Robert Jauss, a reception studies critic often considered a reader-response theorist, focuses upon "past historical readers within their specific horizons of expectations" (Mailloux, "Misreading" 5), emphasizing the mutable norms and conventions surrounding literature as well as the prevailing opinions and cultural debates of the period in which a given text is being read. Mailloux also advocates consideration of the cultural and temporal context of a given reading: "An act of reading is precisely the historical intersection of the different cultural rhetorics for reading such texts within the social practices of particular historical communities" ("Misreading" 3).

What most strikes me about these readers' responses to "Recitatif"— what is most revealing about contemporary social concerns—is that all but three of them were willing to conjecture about the characters' racial identities. Although the guesses themselves varied, as did the clues cited by readers as evidence for their guesses, only three of the sixty-seven individuals declined to guess, and even they expressed no feeling that it was odd or unreasonable to be asked to assign racial labels to the characters. Morrison often insists that race is an omnipotent force, referring, for example, to a "wholly racialized world" (*Playing* 4). This particular group of readers, in a particular period and place, certainly found it a normal, feasible, and appropriate task to read "race"—to interpret traits and behaviors in racial terms.[16]

The fact that readers cited both phenotypic clues, such as body shape and hair texture, and behavioral clues, such as religious piety and food preferences, as bases for their conjectures about the characters' racial identities also reveals much about contemporary American society. Going beyond phenotypic differences between races, which, although they are genetically minor, are quite visible (A. Appiah 21–22), many readers were willing to label a single individual "white" or "black" based on ostensibly *cultural* traits. When a person generalizes about the attributes of an individual based upon the individual's membership in a particular race, Henry Louis Gates, Jr., calls it "racism" ("Talkin'" 403). These readers have done something related: based on their generalizations about members of a race, they have inferred an individual's membership in that race. The practice of categorizing individuals by race is what John H. Stanfield II calls "racialism" (246), which he sees as a relatively benign component of racism. Morrison does not condemn readers for engaging in this practice; in fact, some of her most sympathetic characters (e.g., Stamp Paid and Baby Suggs in *Beloved*) do so. Rather, she wishes to call attention to the endemic use of racial generalizations in our language and our culture which, when they go unacknowledged, lead to discrimination and racial enmity. Morrison intends "Recitatif" to expose to readers their own remarkable willingness, ability, and tendency to make such racial inferences. Only by recognizing their racialist proclivity can readers transcend it.

These reader expectations—that race is meaningful and appropriate to consider; that the problem of the characters' racial identities are soluble and will be solved; that the plot will proceed chronologically; and that the narrator will be reliable—constitute part of what Jauss (esp. 22–24) calls the readers' *horizon of expectations*. Having been trained by previous contact with other examples of the short story genre ("a pre-understanding of the genre" [22]), as well as socialized to current attitudes and mores ("the wider horizon of experience of life" [24]), readers approached the text with a set of expectations which circumscribed their responses. In another time and place, readers' responses would differ because the readers' horizon of expectations would include different understandings of short story conventions and different systems of ethics. Juda Bennett points out that "the reader, black, white, or other, becomes a character or participant in the racialist complications that have been set up by the narrator and her ambiguous use of language" (212). As discussed in this chapter, the "real readers" of the empirical study found many of their expectations of "Recitatif" thwarted.

Wolfgang Iser's gap-filling theory of reading (*Act* esp. 167–70) focuses principally upon how a text controls the responses of its "implied reader" (*Implied Reader*, esp. xii). Peter J. Rabinowitz comments upon the great degree of authority Iser invests in the text, noting that "although he pays particular attention to the indeterminacies in the texts—the gaps that the reader has to fill in on his or her own—his reader remains very much controlled by the author, since those gaps are part of the strategy of the text" (Rabinowitz 606). As evidenced by the efforts of the "real readers" in this study to determine the characters' racial identities, Twyla's and Roberta's respective races constitute the most obvious and pertinent "gap" in "Recitatif." In the following chapters, we examine how and for what purpose the textual "gaps" (more specifically, what we call the *textual* and *meta-textual enigmas*) in *The Bluest Eye, Song of Solomon, Beloved, Paradise*, and *Home* are designed to influence the responses of the texts' "implied reader," a hypothetical construct that "incorporates both the prestructuring of the potential meaning by the text, and the reader's actualization of this potential through the reading process" (Iser, *Implied Reader* xii). In Chapter 5, we show how Morrison's 1997 novel, *Paradise*, recapitulates the themes and rhetorical tactics of "Recitatif" and her other novels.

2

The Bluest Eye

Thirteen years before publishing "Recitatif," Toni Morrison published her first novel, *The Bluest Eye*. Like "Recitatif," this novel features textual and meta-textual enigmas that characterize Morrison's entire oeuvre. Also as in "Recitatif," the gaps, puzzles, and problems in *The Bluest Eye* work to engage readers in ways and to an extent that a more traditional, linear, and "complete" narrative cannot. The effect of this narrative strategy is the same in both texts, as it is in her other works: it seeks to draw readers into its project of deconstructing race and recognizing and indicting racism. *The Bluest Eye* accomplishes these tasks by leading readers to reveal for themselves the pernicious effects of white values and standards of beauty upon blacks, principally, the development of an insidious self-hatred among African Americans.

Like "Recitatif," *The Bluest Eye* immediately challenges readers from its opening pages. The three-page prologue introduces two rhetorical tactics that recur throughout the main body of the novel: the author signifies on bits of a Dick-and-Jane reading primer, and an unidentified narrator begins to confide to readers his or her story. As readers soon discover, the narrative shifts without warning or explanation between this first-person narrator and an unidentified, third-person, omniscient narrator, leaving readers to figure out which is speaking at any given time and who the speakers are.

The Dick-and-Jane passage begins innocently: "Here is the house. It is green and white. It has a red door. It is very pretty" (7). This appears at first to be a benign and banal passage. After the paragraph-long passage, however, the text is repeated but without punctuation ("Here is the house it is green and white it has a red door it is very pretty…" [7]), producing in readers a sense of foreboding as it suggests a rushing torrent.

Immediately following that paragraph is another, even more mutated one, in which not only punctuation but even the spaces between words are omitted: "Hereisthehouseitisgreenandwhiteithasareddooritisverypretty…" (8). That something as apparently benign as a reading primer can go awry distresses readers, a feeling exacerbated both by the sensation of being carried away in a flash flood—a sensation caused by the omission of breaks in the words—and by the association of a reading primer with innocent children. As the text later reveals, the novel is, in fact, about unspeakably horrible things happening to a child.

Although the final version of the primer extract appears incomprehensible, it actually is not. The difference between the first and third versions of the primer passage "is that the third forces us to participate in the reading in a more active way by demanding that we identify individual words and supply from our own past experience of reading the first version the proper punctuation. The reader is once again, in the very act of reading, taught to read" (Gibson 161). (The idea of a text teaching a reader to read mirrors that of Steven Mailloux, as described in the Introduction.) Michael Awkward goes further, explaining specifically how this narrative technique based upon the primer furthers Morrison's task of racial deconstruction through her "attempt to alter the reader's perception of what should be viewed as normative and healthy" (62). He notes: "In her systematic analysis of an inversive relationship between pretext (the primer) and text (her delineation of AfroAmerican life), the author dissects, deconstructs, if you will, the bourgeois myths of ideal family life" (61, emphasis in original). Awkward argues that blacks' attempts to personify white standards create "not only an emotional barrenness similar to that of the primer family, but also intense feelings of failure and worthlessness such as those experienced by the Breedloves" (61). By showing readers that these feelings stem directly from African Americans' adoption of white standards of beauty, "Morrison attempts to break the spell of the hypnotic propaganda of an overly materialistic America" (61). In other words, the text attempts to render plain the hidden presumptions held by readers, to force readers to take a step back from their perceived world and to question what heretofore had seemed natural and unworthy of attention.

Moreover, the novel's deconstruction of the Dick-and-Jane primer underscores the outsider status of the Breedloves and other African American families. Presented as the quintessential American family, the white, middle-class characters in the primer series clearly do not represent the black community of Lorain. As Jervette R. Ward points out, the primer series, launched in 1927, attempted to respond to the Civil Rights Movement by introducing a black family in the stories, but neglected to diversify its characters in terms of socioeconomic status (24). Neither Pecola nor Claudia would recognize themselves in the primer; the black family does not look like theirs. As Jervette R. Ward notes, "The lack of diversity in regards to race and class made the Dick and Jane books unrealistic for minority children who tried to identify with the characters in their books" (19).

Timothy B. Powell contextualizes this effect by highlighting the contrast between the primer and the rest of the novel. He notes that Morrison's juxtaposition of the passage from the white primer with "her own black text" (750), she leads readers to question "not only the difference between the white and black text but also how we as critics are going to read what follows" (750). Gibson argues that Morrison deconstructs the white text, as evidenced by the eventual removal of all punctuation and spacing in the final version of the primer. Thus, "*The Bluest Eye* can be seen as a direct confrontation with the white logos, a necessary first step towards clearing the way for the (w)holy black text to appear" (752).

Shelley Wong, similarly, points out that "it is possible to locate a two-fold process which marks the trajectory of Morrison's narrative practice—i.e., the practice of taking apart and then pouring back together to form the ground of a new order of signification" (472). Only when white, bourgeois values, represented by the banal Dick-and-Jane text, are exploded for readers can the text lead them through a newly constructed perception, one not dictated exclusively by white standards and norms.

The Dick-and-Jane part of the prologue exemplifies the textual oddities that confront readers. The narration part of the prologue initiates the plotting gaps that readers must fill to make sense of the story—what we call *meta-textual* problems established in the reading process itself. The narrator begins, "*Quiet as it's kept, there were no marigolds in the fall of 1941*" (9, italics in original). As in "Recitatif," in which readers must figure out why a reticent narrator is confiding in them, readers of *The Bluest Eye* confront a narrator who presents to them information that is ostensibly secret. (Morrison returns to the phrase, "quiet as it's kept," again in *Paradise* [196]. J. Brooks Bouson notes that the phrase is one of Morrison's favorite African American expressions, and is a "phrase used by someone who is about to reveal what is presumed to be a secret" [358].) This one-page introductory narrative imparts to readers the knowledge that the narrator is speaking of times apparently long-past and that the narrator and the narrator's sister were participants in some ominous events: a girl named Pecola carried and lost the baby begotten by her own father, who is himself now dead. The narrator concludes this brief prologue by saying, "*There is really nothing more to say— except* why. *But since* why *is difficult to handle, one must take refuge in* how" (9, emphases in original). The text already notifies readers that the narrator is not entirely trustworthy. He or she is circumventing an admittedly difficult question—why the terrible events occurred—and offering only to explain how they happened. The narrator has just said that *why* is the only important question, but is not the question that he or she is going to address. *Why* is a question left to readers to answer, making it both the first gap (introduced at the novel's opening) and the last (lingering after the novel concludes as the most important question) that they must fill to complete the story.

The problematic identity of the narrator has generated discussion among some Morrison scholars. Gibson notes that Smith (whom he neglects to identify further) believes the passages built around the reading primer come via Claudia, but he himself believes they are related by an omniscient narrator (172). Awkward concurs with Gibson (68). Our own position is that the ambiguity of the narrator's identity is precisely the point; the question is not meant to be settled. In fact, those attempting to find "the" answer might be unwitting prisoners of a dominant Western critical paradigm in which ambiguity is discomforting if not intolerable. As in "Recitatif," in which the occasional ambiguity of the narrator's identity fits the text's overarching strategy of resisting readers' simple interpretations, this novel uses a problematic narrator to stimulate readers' thinking. Moreover, the use of the kind of ambiguity found in Morrison's fiction is a particularly African American storytelling technique. Specifically, what Henry Louis Gates, Jr., says about Zora Neale Hurston's *Their Eyes Were Watching God* applies equally well to both "Recitatif" and *The Bluest Eye* (except that "Recitatif" is not a canonical text):

> Free indirect discourse is represented in this canonical text as if it were a dynamic character, with shifts in its level of diction drawn upon to reflect a certain development of self-consciousness in a hybrid character, a character who is neither the novel's protagonist nor the text's disembodied narrator, but a blend of both, an emergent and merging moment of consciousness [*Signifying Monkey* xxv–vi].

Like Hurston before her, Morrison masters this African American storytelling tactic, thereby creating an appropriately authentic form for an African American story.

That readers by the novel's conclusion can be expected to answer the narrator's *why* question testifies, first, to the text's ability to provide sufficient but incomplete details so that readers must and can complete the story; and second, to Morrison's skill at indicting—and leading readers to recognize—the power of racism that can so crush a man that he can commit an atrocity. By the time readers reach the scene in which Cholly Breedlove rapes his own daughter, the text has prepared them to understand the enormity of his humiliation and rage. Although the text allows their horror, they finally are induced to answer the *why* question that the narrator declines to consider. Moved by linking the unspeakable act with the racism that beats the soul out of Cholly and eventually results in an innocent girl's insanity, readers are readied to join Morrison's campaign against racism.

In other sections of the text, Claudia is clearly the narrator. Whether or not the ambiguously narrated sections are attributed to her, Claudia is the principal narrator of the story; it is she who assumes the burden of relating the awful tale to the readers. In this regard, as well as in the case of the ambiguous narrator, Morrison maintains a self-conscious link to African American storytelling tradition. Trudier Harris describes Claudia's importance in this context, noting that she is the "active tradition bearer" who "can shape and tell the community's stories." Harris likens Claudia to a griot who "orders the events of a people's past, assigns values to them, and offers the possibility for future transformation." Claudia's tale shows, by negative example, the "detrimental effects of certain cultural beliefs upon unsuspecting individuals." The story thus has a beneficial, didactic effect, making clear "the implications and potential positive consequences of storytelling. The tale of Pecola Breedlove and Lorain, Ohio, then, is a narrative in the best tradition of an African-American interactive, communal event" (*Fiction* 15). Thus, Claudia figuratively transcends the text; she not only renders the tale, but also guides the reader/listener toward a contemplative understanding of its lessons.

The ambiguous relationship between character-as-narrator and the omniscient narrative voice—a tactic that also characterizes "Recitatif"— finds resolution at the novel's conclusion when the two voices merge. Awkward notes that the unification of narrative voices comes at Pecola's expense; it is just as Pecola's voice is fragmented in dementia that the narrative voices coalesce (94). Awkward points out that, at this point in the novel, "Claudia is privy to information which she clearly could have learned only from the omniscient narrator." Claudia thus merges with the omniscient narrator, assuming the omniscient narrator's voice and store of knowledge (94). By figuratively crucifying Pecola, the text frees readers from the confusing and discomforting double-voicedness of narration. Readers' relief comes only with the sacrifice of the character most victimized by black self-hatred.

The text's discomforting of its readers continues as the narrative begins: "Nuns go by as quiet as lust, and drunken men and sober eyes sing in the lobby of the Greek hotel" (12), an odd assortment of similes and metaphors. "Nuns go by as quiet as the wind," or some similar metaphor, might seem more appropriate; the juxtaposition of nuns and lust can do nothing but bemuse readers. The second half of the sentence also poses difficulty for readers: drunken men can certainly sing, but can sober eyes? Eyes might sing in a metaphorical sense (like Irish eyes that are "smiling"), but the text leaves as ambiguous whether the drunken men are literally or only metaphorically singing, and if the latter, what the metaphor might mean. As troublesome as this opening sentence is, it is appropriate in light of the motifs that will emerge later in the narrative: as the novel's title indicates, eyes recur as one motif; lust is another, and drunkenness is yet another. At this early point in the narrative, however, the text is only beginning to present problematic diction.

In *Race, Gender, and Desire*, Elliott Butler-Evans argues that the enigmatic opening lines of *The Bluest Eye* exemplify Morrison's tendency to privilege language, a tendency often cited as the basis of her writing's acknowledged lyricism. "Nuns go by quiet as lust" is a figure that is "meaningless within the context of the novel and seems almost arbitrary" (67), Butler-Evans writes. We agree that the novel's opening exhibits a typically Morrisonian lyricism that privileges evocative language. What Butler-Evans dismisses as meaningless and almost arbitrary, however, is doing, in his reading of it, precisely what it is meant to do. Mystifying readers enough that they question their own readings is one tactic within Morrison's strategy of stimulating self-reflection and consequent action among readers.

The text also forces readers to begin the formidable task of dealing with the narrative as a text. The text requires readers to surmise that the same narrator who addressed them in the prologue is doing so again; this is another first-person account. Two pages into this section, the narrator is identified as Claudia. Unlike the first-person narration in the prologue, however, this passage is presented in roman typeface rather than italics, as if to warn readers that textual clues that ordinarily indicate a switch from first-person narration to third-person narration—such as alternating typefaces—will be useless to them when dealing with this text. In fact, throughout the novel, some of the first-person narration is presented in roman typeface and some in italics. Readers must deduce by other means who is speaking at any given time. At times, the question of narrator remains inconclusive.

Claudia is speaking in this passage of an early childhood memory involving her mother's resentful caretaking of her sick children. Well into her recollection, she pauses and asks rhetorically, "But was it really like that?" (14). Just as "Recitatif" teaches readers to question the memories of the characters, this novel quickly lets readers know that they cannot rely on the memories as presented. Readers are reminded of the fallibility of memory near the end of the novel when the narrator acknowledges that "my memory is uncertain" (146). "So much for memory" (146), she says. Readers must reconstruct a story based on their own assessment of the veracity of the characters' statements. As with "Recitatif," readers must deal with what Catherine Belsey calls a disrupting, interrogative text (91).

In some ways, *The Bluest Eye* and Morrison's other novels are *not* like "Recitatif." In the short story, the racial identities of the characters are left to the reader to determine, a narrative tactic deliberately chosen by Morrison as a literary experiment. In her novels, the racial identities of the characters are obvious and crucial. Claudia, who narrates *The Bluest Eye*, not only exhibits keen awareness of race, but also a profound sense of its significance in her world. She thus resents Shirley Temple, who is adored not only by little white girls, but also by Claudia's sister, Frieda, and their new friend and temporary roommate, Pecola. Claudia says,

> Frieda and she [Pecola] had a loving conversation about how cu-ute Shirley Temple was. I couldn't join them in their adoration because I hated Shirley. Not because she was cute, but because she danced with Bojangles, who was *my* friend, *my* uncle, *my* daddy, and who ought to have been soft-shoeing it and chuckling with me. Instead he was enjoying, sharing, giving a lovely dance thing with one of those little white girls whose socks never slid down under their heels [19, emphases in original].

Even in her youth, Claudia understands the privilege of whiteness. She also understands how class marginalizes people like her family: "Being a minority in both caste and class, we moved about anyway on the hem of life...." (18). By referring to caste as well as class, Claudia indicates awareness of how her family's race determines its class. This perceptiveness distinguishes Claudia from the narrator of "Recitatif," Twyla.

Claudia's sophistication also sets her apart from Twyla. Twyla acknowledges many things she did not know. Her ignorance and naiveté contrast sharply with Claudia's insight, as when she explains why she destroyed the blue-eyed, white dolls she received every Christmas:

> Had any adult with the power to fulfill my desires taken me seriously and asked me what I wanted, they would have known that I did not want to have anything to own, or to possess any object. I wanted rather to feel something on Christmas day. The real question would have been, "Dear Claudia, what experience would you like on Christmas?" I could have spoken up, "I want to sit on the low stool in Big Mama's kitchen with my lap full of lilacs and listen to Big Papa play his violin for me alone." The lowness of the stool made for my body, the security and warmth of Big Mama's kitchen, the smell of the lilacs, the sound of the music, and, since it would be good to have all of my senses engaged, the taste of a peach, perhaps, afterward [21].

Yet, in keeping with Morrison's strategy of discomforting readers, Claudia's wisdom is tempered by an unreliable memory, and by meta-narrative problems similar to those in "Recitatif," as is again evidenced in the novel's next chapter. The narrator, describing a building in the town of Lorain, Ohio—the town in which the story is set and which also is Morrison's birthplace—states: "So fluid has the population in that area been, that probably no one remembers longer, longer ago, before the time of the gypsies and the time of the teen-agers when the Breedloves lived there, nestled together in the storefront" (30–31). The narrator, who apparently is Claudia but also could be a third-person, omniscient narrator—making it difficult for readers to distinguish between the narrator and Claudia-as-narrator, inasmuch as this passage includes no first-person pronouns that would indicate that Claudia is speaking—apparently *does* remember the building's history because he or she is relating it to readers. Readers are left to ask how this unidentifiable narrator can tell them the story if "no one remembers" its details.

Although many works of fiction feature omniscient narrators, this passage is particularly troublesome, partly because the narrator's identity (Claudia?) is already made problematic. Claudia clearly does remember these events because she participates in them as they unfold, and their gravity would render them unforgettable to anyone who witnesses them firsthand. If it is she who is speaking, her statement about events that no one remembers becomes a figure of speech—oral speech, in which a speaker might informally say that no one remembers such events. That the speaker remembers is obvious and understood. If such is the case with this passage, the implied figure of speech augments the "orality" of the storytelling because the understood exception of the speaker himself or herself is a more common feature of oral rather than written storytelling. On the other hand, if the narrator is a third-person, omniscient one, he or she provides unreliable information, for surely Claudia remembers the incidents described by the narrator. In fact, at the end of the novel, Claudia remarks that everyone who knew Pecola gained something from Pecola's ruin. To say that no one remembers the Breedloves is a dubious claim. Once again, readers face an unreliable narrator.

The meta-textual problem of the narrator's memory not only contributes to the destabilization of readers, but also contributes to the characterization of the Breedlove family. However problematic the claim might be, it would be fitting that no one remembers when the Breedloves occupied the ramshackle building because they were even more marginalized than Claudia's own family. In addition to being poor and black, the Breedloves were ugly, according to the narrator: "You looked at them and wondered why they were so ugly; you looked closely and could not find the source" (34). When it later becomes clear that, when Cholly and Pauline Breedlove were younger, they were attractive people, readers retrospectively determine that humiliating, demoralizing events—all directly or indirectly related to racial oppression—made them ugly, and that the internalized racism suffered by their daughter, Pecola, made her ugly, too. (James Robert Saunders sees Pauline's unnoticed tooth decay as symbolizing the hidden poison of the racist, sexist world that mars her self-perceived beauty, contributing to her contempt of her husband and her daughter.[1])

The story itself begins to unfold, but in a characteristically complex manner that requires more work of its readers. Like most of Morrison's fiction, *The Bluest Eye* begins *in medias res*, leaving it to readers to piece together the chronology of events. Had Morrison begun with the earliest events of the story—Frieda's and Claudia's early childhood—rather than with the narrator's ominous intimation that Pecola would carry her own father's baby, readers would be less interested in the events to come and, more significantly, might not labor through the text with the sense of foreboding that is crucial to the text's effectiveness. The scene in which Pecola's father, Cholly, rapes her does not occur until late in the text: pages 128 and 129 in the 160-page novel. The text initiates readers' horror of the event, however, on page 9.

Irony is often coupled with, and frequently accents, the novel's characteristic contrast of blackness and whiteness. The narrator's description of the girls' classmate, Maureen Peal, exemplifies Morrison's technique of ironic diction. Claudia, as first-person narrator, tells readers that Maureen is "a high-yellow dream child with long brown hair braided into two lynch ropes that hung down her back" (52). The loaded metaphor of lynch ropes contains connotations that readers must unravel. Claudia (and hence Morrison) could have said simply "ropes" but chooses to allude to the use of ropes to lynch blacks.[2] Maureen's high-yellow appearance highlights the color hierarchy in which society privileges lighter skin over darker, a hierarchy that is perpetuated even within the African American community represented by Lorain. The community does set Maureen apart. Claudia points out just how different Maureen is from the other black children:

> When teachers called on her, they smiled encouragingly. Black boys didn't trip her in the halls, white boys didn't stone her, white girls didn't suck their teeth when she was assigned to be their work partners; black girls stepped aside when she wanted to use the sink in the girls' toilet, and their eyes genuflected under sliding lids.... She even bought and liked white milk [53].

She even seems to escape the bitter winter that has stricken Claudia and Frieda: "There was a hint of spring in her sloe green eyes, something summery in her complexion, and a rich autumn ripeness in her walk" (53). As is typical in this novel, readers must complete what is only implied by the text: the other girls are not like Maureen because they are blacker, and her privilege in the neighborhood signals the internalized prejudice among African Americans.

Maureen, then, represents the self-destructive force of African Americans' acceptance of the color hierarchy, a self-hatred that is as deadly as lynch ropes. Because she lives among the black girls yet is considered superior because of her light skin ("Indeed, in 1941, Maureen would have been viewed as a black person worthy of imitation precisely because of her considerably toned-down black features," Harris points out [*Fiction* 48]); she is an unavoidable reminder to Claudia that, although she and Frieda were "nicer" and "brighter" than Maureen, they remained "lesser" than she (61).

Readers must consider why a girl so different from the *black* black girls has hair braided into "lynch ropes." By not spelling it out for readers, Morrison makes them read between the lines, as it were. This is, readers must remember, Claudia's perception. An astute observer, Claudia associates Maureen with pernicious discrimination based on phenotypes. Maureen's skin is nearly white, not black; her eyes are not dark; her hair is not black and kinky. Therefore, in the black world that Claudia so vividly depicts, Maureen has received every advantage, impoverishing further all the girls who are obviously and unmistakably black. The text ultimately reveals to readers the significance of Maureen's hair resembling lynch ropes: by emphasizing, through her contrast to the other black girls, their profound blackness, Maureen contributes to the figurative lynching of black girls like Claudia, Frieda, and especially Pecola, who, as Harris states, "has blindly, destructively internalized what Claudia is able to see about Maureen in a more analytical light" (*Fiction* 49). Claudia recognizes that the deadliness of Maureen's privilege derives from society's valuing of Maureen, not from Maureen herself: "All the time we knew that Maureen Peal was not the Enemy and not worthy of such intense hatred. The *Thing* to fear was the *Thing* that made *her* beautiful, and not us" (62, emphases in original). Claudia's recognition of this fact does not alter the power of skin-color privilege. Like the practice of lynching itself, which Stewart E. Tolnay and E. M. Beck say serves partly "to maintain a degree of leverage over the African-American population" (50), the skin-color hierarchy perpetuates white domination.

The self-hatred that such girls, and indeed all of the novel's black characters, develop because of internalized prejudice recurs as a theme throughout the novel. Black schoolboys taunt each other with the epithet "black e mo": "That they themselves were black ... was irrelevant. It was their contempt for their own blackness that gave the first insult its teeth" (55), the perspicacious Claudia notes. Innocent and ignorant Pecola, who enters a shop to buy some candy, also bears the shame of internalized prejudice. When the middle-aged, white shopkeeper regards little Pecola, she recognizes his disgust:

> She has seen it lurking in the eyes of all white people. So. The distaste must be for her, her blackness. All things in her are flux and anticipation. But her blackness is static and dread. And it is the blackness that accounts for, that creates, the vacuum edged with distaste in white eyes [42].

She tries to be angry, but instead succumbs to deep shame. Readers then encounter an irony that underscores the scene's poignancy: the candy she chooses are Mary Janes, from whose wrappers smile a white-faced, blond-haired, blue-eyed girl. In a world dictated by whites, Pecola has internalized the association between the blue-eyed, white image and sweet goodness. The self-hatred becomes her undoing, just as it becomes her mother's and father's.

Even the relatively high-bred black women in Lorain have learned to despise and repress their blackness; in fact, their haughtiness stems from having successfully extinguished, as much as possible, their blackness. The narrator's superficially nonchalant but actually quite bitter description of their comprehensive socialization process is worth quoting at length:

> They go to land-grant colleges, normal schools, and learn how to do the white man's work with refinement; home economics to prepare his food; teacher education to instruct black children in obedience; music to soothe the weary master and entertain his blunted soul. Here they learn the rest of the lesson begun in those soft houses with porch swings and pots of bleeding heart: how to behave. The careful development of thrift, patience, high morals, and good manners. In short, how to get rid of the funkiness. The dreadful funkiness of passion, the funkiness of nature, the funkiness of the wide range of human emotions [68].

In this context, funkiness denotes blackness. The narrator of this passage could have combined the penultimate sentence with the final sentence, which would have explicated the connection between funkiness (blackness) and presumably desirable elements of humanity such as passion, nature, and emotion. Instead, readers encounter the penultimate sentence about women learning to rid themselves of funkiness without yet judging such an exercise to be problematic. The narrator then appends a list of things sacrificed as part of the funkiness. Calling passion, nature, and emotion part of a "dreadful" funkiness puts an ironic twist on the way readers are meant to perceive these women's socialization. Rather than telling readers that these women give up part of their humanity in order to better serve white people, the narrator of this passage makes readers complete the connection, tipped off by the ironic use of the word *dreadful*.

Feminists (e.g., Elizabeth Atwood Lawrence 114) have long said that a sexist, patriarchal society commonly relegates women to the sphere of nature, to be controlled and dominated, rather than the sphere of civilization, where men consider themselves to be. Passion and emotion—those traits considered by men to be characteristic of women and signs of their relative weakness and inferiority—are indeed, from a masculinist perspective, "dreadful." In the midst of this novel's narrative, which illustrates with brutal clarity the insidiousness of women's oppression, the use of the word dreadful achieves a high degree of irony because the notion that passion and emotion—ostensible aspects of women's "nature," as it were—are "dreadful" clearly runs counter to the narrator's own attitude. This ironic statement spurs readers to consider their own attitudes toward women. Again, it is introspective readers, not the narrator, who are meant to conclude that to eliminate funkiness from themselves, these women suppress passion, nature, and the wide range of human emotions. Readers, then, are supposed to understand more deeply the self-hatred and self-denial that constitute a particularly insidious consequence of a racist society. While they are being trained to examine themselves for racial prejudice, they also are meant to begin to consider whether, and to what degree, they have internalized society's sexism.

The generational cycle of racial self-hate becomes evident when one such woman, Geraldine, an otherwise minor character in the novel, teaches her son racial self-hatred. The boy, Junior, seeks white playmates because "his mother did not like him to play with niggers. She had explained to him the difference between colored people and niggers. They were easily identifiable. Colored people were neat and quiet; niggers were dirty and loud" (71). This light-skinned boy "belonged to the former group" (71), the narrator tells readers. Junior, whom readers soon recognize as a boy ruined by internalized racism, lures Pecola into his house. Malevolently, he frightens Pecola by throwing a cat at her, and is angered when the cat takes to Pecola. (Foreshadowing the novel's conclusion, Pecola feels instant compassion for the cat: "The blue eyes in the black face held her" [74].) Junior grabs the cat and swings it above his head but accidentally lets go, fatally hurling it against a wall. When the boy's mother enters the room, the boy says Pecola killed the cat, and Pecola is thrown out of the house as the mother, herself black, calls Pecola a "nasty little black bitch" (75).

This scene becomes one more among several episodes that lead to Pecola's ultimate madness. All of the episodes, readers are expected to realize, are manifestations of the belief among whites and some blacks that white, bourgeois values—including discrimination based upon skin color—are normal and natural. In "Recitatif," such discrimination intervenes between Twyla and Roberta (e.g., when Roberta accuses Twyla of bigotry), although the characters otherwise had much in common. In *The Bluest Eye*, the utter disdain for African American traits and values results in Cholly's destruction of himself and others, Mrs. Breedlove's contempt for her own kin, and, most tragically, the immolation of Pecola. Although varying in degree, the condemnation of racial discrimination pervades both "Recitatif" and *The Bluest Eye*. By guiding readers to recognize and to condemn these manifestations of discrimination, Morrison advances her strategy of moving readers toward acknowledging their own prejudices and their complicity in oppressing those with less power. Anna Zebialowicz and Marek Palasinski note that strong community support could have prevented Pecola's madness, leading readers to acknowledge that they could do much more to act upon compassion for those who are oppressed: "Modern mental health research would indicate that [Pecola's] downfall would have been less likely if she had received more comfort from her family or friends..." (229).

The incident in Geraldine's home indicts middle-class African Americans who choose to adopt bourgeois, white values instead of traditional, shared values of the black community. Harris notes that, although self-improvement as a means to achieve middle-class status is unobjectionable, blacks often sacrifice "too much of themselves" in their pursuit of the white perspective. As Morrison shows, Geraldine's entry into the middle class alienates her from "the very roots she has used to grow her new status." The resultant haughtiness is an attitude "that Geraldine conveys to Pecola and that we can imagine her many twin sisters conveying to other unattractive little black girls who mistakenly intrude upon their sacred grounds" (Harris, *Fiction*, 29). Morrison's disdain for the portion of the black middle class that has abandoned its ties to the rest of African America is evident here, just as it is in "Recitatif," in which Roberta's bourgeois arrogance toward Twyla is linked to her moral near-bankruptcy. Roberta's egocentrism—a trait at odds with the traditionally communal orientation of African American culture that is, according to Jan Furman, "central to Morrison's epistemology" (8)—results in her alienation from the truth about Maggie, from

Twyla, and from herself. Only at the conclusion of the story, when she abandons her egocentric orientation and admits the truth about the incident in the orchard with Maggie, does Roberta redeem herself. (This interpretation of "Recitatif" relies upon our assertion that Roberta probably is black.)

Another such incident arises when Frieda and Claudia visit Pecola where her mother, Mrs. Breedlove, works as a domestic servant in a white family's house. When one of the white children asks, "Where's Polly?" Claudia is incensed. She says, "The familiar violence rose in me. Her calling Mrs. Breedlove Polly, when even Pecola called her mother Mrs. Breedlove, seemed reason enough to scratch her" (86). Moments later, when Pecola accidentally spills a blueberry cobbler, her mother disregards her child's burned legs and strikes her furiously. When the little white girl begins to cry at the violent scene, Mrs. Breedlove sweetly soothes her after angrily dispatching the three black girls. Claudia does not need to say to readers that Mrs. Breedlove's love should have been for Pecola. It would be better for Mrs. Breedlove to be devoid of love rather than to show affection for the white girl while withholding it from her own daughter. Readers are shown that, in fact, Mrs. Breedlove loves no one black.

This realization guides readers to reflect upon Mrs. Breedlove's seemingly misplaced affections. Why she seems to harbor so little affection for her daughter is answered shortly; why she kowtows to the little white girl is something that readers must then consider. It is clear that Mrs. Breedlove's economic survival depends upon her position in the white family's home. To show the least bit of animosity, or even indifference, to the white girl would constitute economic suicide. That Mrs. Breedlove is constrained in her behavior as a servant of the Fisher family is no accident. Mary R. Jackman illuminates the class-based roots of racial oppression, noting that

> the dominant members of society cannot afford to put subordinates in a position where they have nothing to lose. Thus, the institutions they establish are not designed to strip the weaker members of the community of *all* their resources. The purpose of expropriative institutions is to perpetuate exchange relations that are profitable to their dominant members [360, emphasis in original].

According to Jackman, the goal of the members of the dominant group is to give the members of the subordinate group "a vested interest while delivering the lion's share of resources to themselves" (360).

It is readily apparent, then, why Mrs. Breedlove must exhibit care and concern for the white girl. A more significant question is why the girl can call Mrs. Breedlove by her first name when no one else can. The text leaves readers to supply the obvious answer: because she is white. A white person, even a little girl, automatically invests in her the right to speak familiarly with Mrs. Breedlove, who is an adult but is black. Jackman notes how the economic exploitation of a minority group by the dominant majority is justified, maintained, and perpetuated through the codes of social relations between the two groups: "When the functional mechanics of the expropriation require sustained, intimate contact between groups ... the dominant group develops a more highly elaborated system of role segregation to demarcate the boundaries between groups" (161). Such demarcation fosters among the subordinate group members a feeling of cultural inferiority, making them believe that their inferior status is natural and appropriate:

> When role segregation constitutes an important basis of group differentiation, it is convenient for dominant-group members to depict the affected groups as sharply distinctive in their vital attributes in order to make the role divisions seem natural. The more central role segregation is to the conduct of the relationship, the more the dominant group feels moved to depict subordinates as sharply and categorically distinct and to explain group differences as self-perpetuating, either through biological or cultural processes [345–46].

From Jackman's perspective, even the affection shown by white employers for black servants emanates from self-interested and exploitative intentions. The members of the dominant group contrive "intimate relations between groups" so that they "are able to invade subordinates' day-to-day lives with institutional arrangements and ways of thinking that are profoundly coercive." The dominant group offers subordinates friendship and affection "on the strictly imposed condition that they comply with expropriative arrangements" (362).

Seen this way, the effects of Pauline Breedlove's position as a servant of the Fisher family are manifold. First, her economic survival is predicated on her acceptance of the social order in which she, as a black woman, remains inferior to whites, even to the extent that the little girl of the family is permitted to call the black woman by her first name. Second, the social order, based ostensibly on cultural differences but actually based on an economically exploitative relationship, is imposed so thoroughly upon Mrs. Breedlove that she internalizes the white-over-black hierarchy and expunges from herself any sign of affection toward another black person. Susan Willis notes of the black woman in the industrializing North: "Usually employed as a maid and therefore only marginally incorporated as a wage laborer, her alienation was the result of striving to achieve the white bourgeois social model (in which she worked but did not live)" (310). Thus, although Harris claims that Mrs. Breedlove "is getting as much from her white employers, especially emotionally, as they are getting from her in physical labor and devotion to their child" (*Fiction* 39), the mutuality of the relationship seen by Harris takes place in the amoral context in which Mrs. Breedlove believes—has internalized from the outside world—that humans are meant to be exploited. Third, the racial hierarchy extends beyond Mrs. Breedlove to include the entire black community. Jackman points out that, because of their disproportionate numbers, whites are less likely to encounter blacks in their daily lives than vice-versa, and when whites do encounter blacks, the latter are typically in an inferior position. "Thus, whites have been able to penetrate the black community to some extent while keeping the white community relatively insulated from blacks," she notes (163).

Jackman's analysis is borne out by the relationships depicted in *The Bluest Eye*. The white world represented by the Fisher family, the hunters who find the young Cholly in coitus, and the candy store owner who belittles Pecola are hardly affected by the black characters they encounter; they are largely indifferent. The blacks themselves, however, and the black community of Lorain as a whole, carry the profound burden of their supposed inferiority on a daily basis. The relationship between race and class, which is blurred in "Recitatif" in order to complicate the clues regarding the characters' racial identities, is in *The Bluest Eye* laid bare for readers as an element in its depiction of the mechanics and consequences of racial discrimination.

Switching from this first-person account to a third-person narration, the novel's next chapter begins (like "Recitatif," *in medias res*) to relate the story of a woman named Pauline Williams whose childhood was characterized by the shame of having a deformed foot. Interspersed throughout this chapter, first-person passages are quoted and italicized but unattributed. The text eventually reveals that Pauline Williams is Polly Breedlove; the quoted passages are her words. To whom she is speaking, however, remains puzzling. The casual chattiness of the passages suggests an intimacy with the listener, into which role readers appear to be cast as if they were sitting on Pauline's porch. The first such passage is short:

> "*When all us left from down home and was waiting down by the depot for the truck, it was nighttime. June bugs was shooting everywhere. They lighted up a tree leaf, and I seen a streak of green every now and again. That was the last time I seen real june bugs. They's something else. Folks here call them fireflies. Down home they was different. But I recollect that streak of green. I recollect it well*" [89; italics in original]

The intimacy becomes more acute later in the chapter, when Pauline begins speaking sweetly of lovemaking with Cholly in days gone by, before he became nothing but mean. The passage is deeply personal, prodding readers to feel they are eavesdropping on her private daydreams. Whether or not they are "meant" to hear Pauline's recollections, the ersatz intimacy between her and her "listeners" provides readers with insights into her character. Deepening readers' understanding of her feelings of betrayal and bitterness when Cholly becomes drunk and violent, the text offers readers another piece of the puzzle—a textual enigma—presented at the novel's beginning: why such terrible things happen to Pecola Breedlove.

The text leads readers to such understandings in a somewhat backward manner. Why Mrs. Breedlove shows no love to her daughter when she has compassion for a white girl is partially explained by her resentment of her husband, Cholly, who fathered the girl. The novel's next chapter provides readers the material with which to construct an answer to the question of why Cholly becomes drunk and mean. The text guides readers to begin to understand Cholly's rage so they will begin to understand why he rapes his daughter.

The chapter that backtracks to Cholly's childhood shows readers that his mother, who "wasn't right in the head" (105), abandoned the infant Cholly by the railroad and disappeared when her aunt caught her. The aunt, Aunt Jimmy, then raised Cholly. Cholly's father is long gone. When Cholly finally asks about him, Aunt Jimmy tells him that she thinks his father was a local boy named Samson Fuller who has since left town. When Aunt Jimmy dies, Cholly is left alone in the world.

It is at her funeral that a principal character-defining moment comes for Cholly. Ducking the reception with some distant cousins, Cholly playfully wanders into some tall grass with a teenaged girl. As darkness falls, he loses his virginity there. But the joy of the moment is shattered when two white hunters happen upon them and humiliate both of them by making Cholly continue coitus while they shine a flashlight on his buttocks, laughing and taunting. Rather than hate the men, Cholly suddenly hates the girl. Rendered impotent by fear, he can only simulate sex, but he "almost wished he could do it—hard, long, and painfully, he hated her so much" (117). Mercifully, the men leave and the two youths return to the reception. The incident is over quickly but its effects continue throughout—and beyond—Cholly's life.

The text communicates to readers the understanding that Cholly cannot hate the white men because they are too powerful. Hatred of the hunters "would have destroyed him. They were big, white, armed men. He was small, black, helpless" (119), the narrator explains. Instead, Cholly turns his rage against a helpless proxy, the young girl who moments earlier had charmed him. This insight into Cholly comes late in the novel. Readers are coaxed to reconsider, in light of this revelation, events presented earlier, such as Cholly's violent behavior with his wife and the rape of his daughter, the ultimate victim. ("In a society ordered by hierarchies of power based on race, class, and gender, no one is more powerless, hence more vulnerable, than a poor black girl," notes Cheryl A. Wall [3]). So imprinted with the humiliation at the hands of white men, Cholly can no longer distinguish among sex, love, and violence. The text does nothing to diminish readers' horror of his actions, but by this point in the novel the text has produced enough pieces to assemble an understanding of what makes him so horrible. As Gibson notes, Morrison makes no excuses for Cholly; "rather she says that what happens is very complicated, and that though Cholly is not without blame for what happens to Pecola, he is no less a victim than she"

(169). Morrison herself has noted that Cholly is not "just" a rapist and child molester: "He was that, but not just that" (qtd. in Madden 589).

Readers of the novel who are unfamiliar with the fundamental, feminist explanation of rape (see, for example, Brownmiller, *Against Our Will: Men, Women and Rape*, esp. 1–5) might not recognize as classic behavior Cholly's violent redirection of anger toward the only souls weaker than himself. Its painfully brutal depiction later in the novel drives home to them the purely violent—that is, not sexual—motivation for rape. Readers who already understand this essential truth about rape, though, see Cholly's crime not as a unique event but a typical—not to say excusable or inevitable—response of a deeply poisoned soul. This rape represents all rapes and thus universalizes its horror. Madonne M. Miner states:

> In depicting the effects of rape on one young woman, Morrison sets into motion a series of associations that take their cue from gender. Men, potential rapists, assume presence, language, and reason as their particular province. Women, potential victims, fall prey to absence, silence, and madness [181].

More significantly, the scene indicts readers for their complicity, however unintentional, in creating the kind of society that produces a Cholly Breedlove. The novel prods readers to consider how they have contributed to this most brutal facet of sexism, just as they consider their role in a racist society. The text leads them to connect bigotry and misogyny as well as their own culpability for each.

Armed with a bit of information provided by his Aunt Jimmy just before her death, Cholly immediately sets off to Macon to find his father. After a long bus ride and small disgraces, Cholly finds his father gambling in an alley. Feeling suddenly tender toward this man, Cholly is crushed when the man shouts, "Tell that bitch she get her money. Now, get the fuck outta my face!" (123). Deeply hurt, Cholly wanders away, only to suffer one final humiliation: "At the mouth of the alley where his father was, on an orange crate in the sun, on a street full of grown men and women, he had soiled himself like a baby" (124).

Toward the end of the chapter, the narrator sums up Cholly's life thus far. The figurative language used is significantly rife with metaphors from music—specifically, and appropriately, from jazz, the fundamental black musical form. The rich passage merits an extended quotation:

> The pieces of Cholly's life could become coherent only in the head of a musician. Only those who talk their talk through the gold of curved metal, or in the touch of black-and-white rectangles and taut skins and strings echoing from wooden corridors, could give true form to his life. Only they would know how to connect the heart of a red watermelon to the asafetida bag to the muscadine to the flashlight on his behind to the fists of money to the lemonade in a Mason jar to a man called Blue and come up with what all of that meant in joy, in pain, in anger, in love, and give it its final and pervading ache of freedom. Only a musician would sense, know, without even knowing that he knew, that Cholly was free [125].

Like a jazz musician, Morrison herself plays the disparate notes that constitute defining moments in Cholly's life. Ultimately, though, it is the readers who, trained and guided by the text, are invited to create the ensemble of notes, who are to become the musicians who know without knowing that they know. The text equips them to arrange the notes and give them meaning. Thus, readers are led to understand why, in the next three pages when the story returns to the fictional present, Cholly Breedlove rapes his daughter. Readers learn early in the novel (37) that this incident with the white hunters occurs, but the deep comprehension can come only after picturing the litany of ignominies described in this later chapter.

The curious use of the word *free* also instigates readers' reflection. Cholly at first appears to be as bound as any man can be. He is black in a society that values whiteness. He is poor in a society that values wealth. He has no steady work and, an apparent alcoholic, is a figurative slave to liquor. In what sense, readers are led to wonder, can he be free? Only by allowing themselves to succumb to the jazz riffs of the passage can readers make sense of the claim that Cholly is free. Like a jazz musician improvising within the accepted constraints of the artistic form, they are coaxed by the text to connect the "joy," the "pain," the "anger," and the "love" to render a picture of a man who once had dreams but lost them, who once knew happiness but never will again, and who now is relieved of the burden of caring about anything, himself included. Like so much of the novel, Cholly's freedom is ironic. Normally something valued—and, in a novel about African Americans, something that readers would expect to be especially prized, given the nation's shameful legacy of slavery—freedom in this case is perverted and dangerous.

Wong points out that "Cholly was free in the sense that he was not bound by responsibility (or response-ability) to anyone but himself" (476). This kind of freedom is deadly to Cholly, to his family (whose terrorized members bear out the narrator's claim that "the love of a free man is never safe" [159]), and to the African American community represented by Lorain. The text does not celebrate absolute freedom for individuals. Although it leads readers to indict the noxious fetters of white ideology as inflicted upon the African American psyche and community, it also depicts the destructive power of an individual alienated from the values and mores of the African American community. The freedom toward which readers are pushed is not an anarchic one, for that is dangerous and anathema to the traditional African American value of community (TuSmith viii, 21, 69; Coser 4). Rather, the text prods readers to move toward a freedom in which the norms of African America can work naturally and without distortion from racism to circumscribe the behavior of African American community members.

The theme of social culpability for aberrant behavior links Cholly with Bigger Thomas, the anti-hero of Richard Wright's *Native Son*. As Harris notes, Cholly's violence "cannot possibly be expected to form an ethical base for living in the world. Instead, like Bigger Thomas, he has accepted in part the animal status to which he was assigned" (*Fiction* 39). Even his neighbors conclude that "he had joined the animals; was, indeed, an old dog, a snake, a ratty nigger" (*Bluest Eye* 12), Harris points out (39).

The intertextuality between Wright's novel and Morrison's deserves further comment, particularly in light of the traditional intertextuality among African American literary works. (Henry Louis Gates, Jr., states, "If black writers read each other, they also revise each other's texts. Thereby they become fluent in the language of tradition" [*Signifying Monkey*, 124]). Moreover, as Claire Helene Joly notes, "Richard Wright was a highly reader-conscious writer who placed audience at the center of his poetics" (vii), as does Morrison. Robert B. Stepto notes that, just as Wright's work self-consciously follows in the tradition of predated texts, Morrison's work follows Wright's (147–48). We find it instructive, therefore, to refer to "How 'Bigger' Was Born," Wright's essay about the writing of *Native Son*, and to examine the similarity between the two characters.

Like Morrison's depiction of Cholly, Wright's character represents one (albeit pathological) response of a black man to a received social order in which he is automatically and thoroughly degraded. Wright notes that

> because the blacks were so *close* to the very civilization which sought to keep them out, because they could not *help* but react in some way to its incentives and prizes, and because the very tissue of their consciousness received its tone and timbre from the strivings of that dominant civilization, oppression spawned among them a myriad variety of reactions, reaching from outright blind rebellion to a sweet, other-worldly submissiveness [xii, emphases in original].

In Morrison's novel, Cholly represents "outright blind rebellion" of which Wright speaks. Wright, like Morrison, indicts the character's social milieu at least as much as the character's personal flaws, as is evident when he states:

> I felt and still feel that the environment supplies the instrumentalities through which the organism expresses itself, and if that environment is warped or tranquil, the mode and manner of behavior will be affected toward deadlocking tensions or orderly fulfillment and satisfaction [xvi].

Like the humiliating, racist atmosphere that fosters the tensions inherent in Bigger Thomas, the environment in which Cholly lives is poisoned by the omnipresent reminders that his blackness renders him ugly and impotent, a set of beliefs that he himself has internalized.

Perhaps most tragic for Cholly is his alienation from his own people, just as the power of racism cuts Bigger off from the community that could have restored his wholeness. Wright explains:

> I had also to show what oppression had done to Bigger's relationships with his own people, how it had split him off from them, how it had baffled him; how oppression seems to hinder and stifle in the victim those very qualities of character which are so essential for an effective struggle against the oppressor [xxvi].

Because his family and community have internalized white standards of beauty and value, they reject Cholly, and he rejects them. When, as a result of his alienation from family and community, he strikes out at both, he strongly resembles Bigger Thomas. Both Wright and Morrison take pains to show that such tragic, destructive reactions on their characters' parts are not inevitable but rather are instigated by their environments. Speaking about the black men who became his models for Bigger Thomas, Wright states that he had "better indicate more precisely the nature of the environment that produced these men, or the reader will be left with the impression that they were essentially and organically bad" (xi).

The text does not allow readers to dismiss Cholly as organically bad. He is extremely complex. For example, Cholly's confusion immediately after the rape is evident: "Again the hatred mixed with tenderness. The hatred would not let him pick her up, the tenderness forced him to cover her" (129). This moment of readers' deep understanding, mixed with revulsion, comes only because readers have participated in its construction. This short but climactic chapter is the quintessential example of Morrison's technique and purpose: readers themselves answer the *why* question—why Pecola Breedlove was tragically ruined as a human being—and their horror inspires an intense abhorrence of the racism that renders contemptible one of the two people most capable of and responsible for protecting and nurturing their daughter.

The novel's darkness does not subside with the rape scene, because readers have not yet co-created with the text Pecola's ultimate descent into madness. Immediately following the rape scene is the chapter in which Pecola receives the blue eyes she has unwaveringly desired. Throughout their engagement with the text, readers are guided to hope that Pecola's oft-stated desire for blue eyes would evaporate in an epiphany of self-realization. It is not to be.

From early in the novel, readers witness with sadness the innocent girl's association of blue eyes with beauty and value. How young Pecola must have been when the process of socialization taught her that a black girl's features were inherently ugly and were manifestations of her valuelessness. The narrator intimates to readers:

> It had occurred to Pecola some time ago that if her eyes, those eyes that held the pictures, and knew the sights—if those eyes of hers were different, that is to say, beautiful, she herself would be different.... If she looked different, beautiful, maybe Cholly would be different, and Mrs. Breedlove too. Maybe they'd say, "Why, look at pretty-eyed Pecola. We mustn't do bad things in front of those pretty eyes" [40].

So, when ignorant, lost Pecola visits a misanthropic town loner with a reputation for supernatural powers, he leads her to believe that poisoning his landlady's mangy dog, an annoyance to him, would bring her her blue eyes. Slightly mad himself, Soaphead Church writes in a letter to God:

> I, I have caused a miracle. I gave her the eyes. I gave her the blue, blue, two blue eyes. Cobalt blue. A streak of it right out of your own blue heaven. No one else will see her blue eyes. But she will. And she will live happily ever after [143].

The reality that belies Church's prediction about her "happiness" becomes gradually evident to readers in the novel's final section, ironically titled "Summer." This concluding chapter opens with a dialogue, alternating between two unidentified speakers. Their words are distinguished in the text by roman and italic type. Based on diction and banter such as, "I'm not being smarty. You started it" (150), readers are meant to surmise that the dialogue is between two children. When the conversation turns to the topic of one child's "truly, bluely nice" eyes (151), readers identify one of the conversants as Pecola. The identity of the other child remains unknown. Shortly, this exchange takes place:

> Where do you live?
> *I told you once.*
> What is your mother's name?
> *Why are you so busy meddling me?*
> I just wondered. You don't talk to anybody. You don't go to school. And nobody talks to you.
> *How do you know nobody talks to me?*
> They don't. When you're in the house with me, even Mrs. Breedlove doesn't say anything to you. Ever. Sometimes I wonder if she even sees you.
> *Why wouldn't she see me?*

Pecola does not have the answer to this question. The dialogue, however, reveals the answer to readers. They sadly realize that Pecola's friend is imaginary; Pecola now suffers from dementia. As with other crucial elements of the story, readers are left to supply this information, guided by the text. Similarly, readers' understanding of the situation is what completes the irony of the exchange that follows, when Pecola tells her friend that she no longer goes to school but does not know why:

> After that first day of school when I had my blue eyes. Well, the next day they had Mrs. Breedlove come out. Now I don't go anymore. But I don't care.
> *You don't?*
> No, I don't. They're just prejudiced, that's all.
> *Yes, they sure are prejudiced.*
> Just because I got blue eyes, bluer than theirs, they're prejudiced.
> *That's right.*

The text provides readers with the understanding that Pecola's perception is *not* right. Because, guided by the text, readers have come to understand the terrible consequences of racism, they have been trained to appreciate the irony of Pecola's statement about prejudice. They know that her schoolmates and teachers are not prejudiced because they are jealous of her newly acquired blue eyes; others do not even see the blue eyes because they do not exist. Those unspecified others are indeed prejudiced, but because of her black eyes, skin, and hair.

The text expects readers to supply the significance of other parts of the dialogue. At one point, Pecola's imaginary friend brings up the rape, saying it occurred on the couch. Pecola angrily responds, "See there! You don't even know what you're talking about. It was when I was washing dishes" (154). A moment later, the imaginary friend asks, "*Then why didn't you tell Mrs. Breedlove?*" (155). Pecola replies that she did, to which the friend says, "*I don't mean about the first time, I mean about the second time, when you were sleeping on the couch*" (155). The text thus directs readers to realize with repugnance that a second rape occurred.

In the novel's denouement, Claudia-as-narrator guides readers to some profound conclusions. "A little black girl yearns for the blue eyes of a little white girl, and the horror at the heart of her yearning is exceeded only by the evil of fulfillment" (158), she states, conducting readers to their own realization of the story's significance. The ultimate, crowning push from Claudia comes when she acknowledges what she and the others in Lorain took from Pecola:

> All of us—all of us who knew her—felt so wholesome after we cleaned ourselves on her. We were so beautiful when we stood astride her ugliness. Her simplicity decorated us, her guilt sanctified us, her pain made us glow with health, her awkwardness made us think we had a sense of humor. Her inarticulateness made us believe we were eloquent. Her poverty kept us generous. Even her waking dreams we used—to silence our own nightmares. And she let us, and thereby deserved our contempt. We honed our egos on her, padded our characters with her frailty, and yawned in the fantasy of our strength [159].

The intended effect of this passage upon readers is the novel's coup de grace. Its power lies in its ability to provoke readers' consciences as they realize that they, too, have drawn stronger from Pecola's demise. Her descent into insanity leads to their clear vision—of both the root cause of Pecola's tragedy and their own complicity in it.

Claudia's narration concludes the novel as she speaks of seeing Pecola, now mad, wandering among the town's garbage as if she has become garbage herself. Referring to the soil of her town, Claudia says, "This soil is bad for certain kinds of flowers" (160), invoking a metaphor for black girls like Pecola. Claudia once again leads readers to self-indictment when she switches to a first-person, plural pronoun, noting that

> when the land kills of its own volition, we acquiesce and say the victim had no right to live. We are wrong, of course, but it doesn't matter. It's too late. At least on the edge of my town, among the garbage and the sunflowers of my town, it's much, much, much too late [160].

Morrison, through Claudia, thus leaves it to readers to complete the implication of the passage. When Claudia qualifies her statement by saying that this is so at least at the edge of her town, readers must consider whether it is so in their towns, as well. Readers are led to appreciate that the land that "kills of its own volition" is not limited to Lorain, Ohio. The town in the novel serves as a microcosm of the greater American society.

Readers also are guided to understand that the soil is not poison for all of its "flowers," only particular kinds—the ones like dandelions, with which Pecola feels an affinity (41), which most people consider weeds. Even the black folk of Lorain, who make soup of the dandelion greens, dislike the sight of their yellow heads. Lastly, readers are meant to include themselves in Claudia's observation that we delude ourselves into blaming the victims. By so painstakingly and vividly depicting the deleterious effects of racism upon Cholly and upon Mrs. Breedlove, and how their resultant bitterness leaves no compassion in them with which to love, nurture, and protect Pecola, readers need not even accept blame from Claudia; they themselves have been prepared by the text to cloak themselves in culpability. The novel's initially dodged question—why Pecola Breedlove is destroyed—not only receives an answer from readers. When they complete the story, readers also know that they, inasmuch as they have knowingly or unwittingly contributed to the oppression of blacks, are part of the answer to the *why* question. Having thus implicated themselves after being guided by the text to do so, readers are prepared by the text to confront their own prejudices and to take up the banner of Morrison's campaign against sexual and racial oppression. Denise Heinze points out that Morrison suggests that "blacks are violated not only by bad whites but by all whites—and blacks—who tacitly or unknowingly support a society that is inherently racist" (153).

Claudia's role as an unreliable narrator who leads readers to moral judgment follows the model of "Recitatif." As Chapter 1 discussed, Morrison's short story contains the same tactic revealed by Mailloux's analysis of Hawthorne's "Rappaccini's Daughter." Mailloux finds that the unreliable narrator of Hawthorne's story tries readers' ability to discern the truth, and also tries their ability to assign moral responsibility (*Interpretive Conventions* 73–92). We pointed out in Chapter 1 that the same effect occurs in "Recitatif." The tactic is more pronounced in *The Bluest Eye*. Not only does the enigmatic narrator, Claudia, force readers to consider what is real and what is not; she also causes them to assign moral responsibility for Pecola's death and include themselves among the guilty.

The novel guides readers not only to a realization of their role as oppressors, but also to a vision of themselves as victims of the skin-color hierarchy. Having seen characters such as Mr. Yacobowski, the white candy store owner with an ugly contempt for Pecola, and the white hunters who find the young Cholly engaged in intercourse, even white readers[3] are prodded to recognize how their own natural inclinations toward human love and compassion are warped by prevailing racial categories and hierarchies. Their experiences as human beings are limited by damaging social values. Gibson notes: "The implication of the novel's structure is that our lives are contained within the framework of the values of the dominant culture and subjected to those values." To the extent that readers have internalized these values, "we are instruments of our own oppression" (162). Keith E. Bryerman shares Gibson's view that Pecola is not the only victim of blue eyes. The novel's readers "are both victimizer and victim," and, as the characters demonstrate, "the role of victimizer results from that character's own victimization by a larger society" (qtd. in Gibson 174). Analogously, readers are cast in the role of victimizer as a result of their own victimization by received standards of beauty and value.

Awkward points out that Morrison's first novel clears a space in American literature by challenging the received, Western model of a novel. The form of *The Bluest Eye* thus complements its content: both seek to challenge limited and limiting white values. Awkward notes that the novel is part of the African American "enterprise devoted to the denigration of the genre of the novel." He cites her merger of the narrative voices at the novel's conclusion, her manipulation of the "white" voice of the Dick-and-Jane reading primer, and her "apparent revisions of precursor texts" as evidence that Morrison has "added to the Afro-American literary canon another supreme example of a Genuine Black Book" (94–95).

"Recitatif" works toward the same end as *The Bluest Eye*—involvement of the readers in the destruction of prevailing attitudes that devalue African Americans—with a somewhat different tack. *The Bluest Eye* leads readers to embrace responsibility for their part in the perpetuation of racial oppression. The short story works on readers more introspectively by leading them to question their own personal prejudices and racial assumptions. As elements in Morrison's oeuvre, the two works lead readers to examine how previously unquestioned attitudes have led to complicity in a warped and alienating set of social values (principally in *The Bluest Eye*) and the roots of those social attitudes within each reader (principally in "Recitatif").

Like "Recitatif," *The Bluest Eye* is partly deconstructive. "Recitatif" seeks to deconstruct readers' internalized assumptions about racially ascribed traits. *The Bluest Eye* deconstructs an otherwise unrecognized and unquestioned set of beauty standards, particularly their destructive impact on girls (a theme that Morrison also addresses in *A Mercy*, as Susmita Roye points out). In both cases, the deconstruction serves to clear an ideological space for the creation of new attitudes about race (in the case of "Recitatif") and new, equitable standards of beauty and value (in the case of *The Bluest Eye*). Most significantly, both texts train readers to respond and expects them to carry into their world the mission the texts set forth, just as a griot expects her listeners to apply the lessons of her tale to their own lives. Harris puts it this way: "If the tale of tragedy is told/sung, rehearsed and replayed, perhaps, just perhaps, the listener/reader will be touched enough to move beyond the cathartic effect into a transformation of current conditions" (*Fiction* 27). Moreover, Jerome Bump values the emotional impact of *The Bluest Eye* and how it can move readers: "Suffering with [Pecola], knowing that pain consciously, *feeling* it, acknowledging it openly and directly, most of us will be less likely to inflict it on others, and more likely to take action against those who do" (162; emphasis in original).

The Bluest Eye and "Recitatif" both influence the course of American literature in that they challenge received, "white" notions of literary form. Both exhibit similar rhetorical approaches to themes of race and racism by mimicking African American, oral storytelling as a way of involving readers in the task of making meaning. Ultimately, these two works create an impact upon society at large, transcending their fictive worlds, by prodding readers to adopt the Morrisonian mission of exposing readers' unquestioned presumptions about race and confronting racial prejudice. Morrison's third novel, *Song of Solomon*, develops further the rhetorical tactics that characterize *The Bluest Eye* and "Recitatif" and is the subject of the next chapter.

3

Song of Solomon

Song of Solomon (1977) comprises an often-puzzling combination of myth, mystery, suspense, and magic. As Marilyn Sanders Mobley cites the "plethora of names,[1] the shifting chronology, the excessive dialogue, and the layers of individual and personal histories" as constituting "a mosaic of narrative that makes meaning seem elusive. In fact the reader's task is not unlike that of Milkman Dead, who must find the meaning in his complicated life story" (*Folk Roots*, 96–97). Readers gradually learn, along with the novel's protagonist, Milkman Dead, his family's history and its broad significance.[2] In locating and reclaiming his roots, Milkman discovers his own identity, which liberates him from his life of disaffection and alienation. He thus models for readers the kind of introspection engendered by Morrison's other literary works. For black readers implied by the text, such introspection should lead to reaffirmed connection to heritage (the past) and community (the present), insofar as Morrison's fiction, as Sanders puts it, "is a response to the loss of tradition, ways of knowing, and ways of perceiving oneself and the world. *Song of Solomon* bears witness to these lost and discredited traditions." (*Folk Roots*, 95). For white readers implied by the text, the novel encourages an embrace of aspects of America's African roots—especially orientation toward community—while surrendering some of the individualism supposedly at the core of American values.[3]

On the largest scale, the plot twists characterizing *Song of Solomon* constitute its most obvious challenge to readers. Laid out like a traditional mystery in which readers figuratively follow a protagonist detective, piecing together clues as they are discovered, *Song of Solomon* sends readers, along with Milkman, on false leads and dangerous trails as the "true" story gradually unfolds. Unlike its predecessor, *The Bluest Eye*, the conclusion of which seems inevitable, and its successor, *Beloved*, which slowly exposes for the reader its protagonist's horrifying past, this novel situates its protagonist in increasing danger; suspense engages the novel's readers. Forced to attend the text more closely, readers become more active "listeners," mirroring Milkman's transition from a blustering speaker to a liberated, wiser auditor.

Just as Milkman expresses frustration and bewilderment as his own story fitfully unfolds, readers are confronted with their own underscored ignorance. Passages such as "Milkman felt something missing from the conversation" (228), "The questions about his family still knocked around in his head like billiard balls" (294), and, even late in the novel, "Yet there were many many missing pieces" (304), hint to readers that they must remain receptive to conclusions they had never imagined. Like the symbolic Clearing in *Beloved*, this aspect of *Song of Solomon* works to open readers' minds so, when drawn to consider complex issues such as race, love, and history, they are less encumbered by ossified preconceptions.

Several aspects of the novel's structure and plot contribute to its ability to unsettle its readers. Like "Recitatif" and *The Bluest Eye*, *Song of Solomon* features an unreliable narrator, undermining readers' faith that they are obtaining a full, accurate story. Casting them in the same uncertainty facing Milkman, the narrator undercuts readers' and Milkman's revelations; the narrative's consciousness itself fluctuates. Wahneema Lubiano cites one example: Lena's and First Corinthians's perception of Macon's car "shifts to Macon's consciousness of it and ends in the consciousness of the people in the community looking at it" (104). In another example, at one instance seemingly omniscient with the ability to read Milkman's thoughts, the narrator immediately denigrates its own authority when it says of Milkman: "Sleeping with Hagar had made him generous. Or so he thought. Wide-spirited. Or so he imagined" (69). The resultant uncertainty carries great import, readers later realize, because Milkman's false consciousness early in the novel gives way to crucial self-knowledge at the novel's conclusion.

Even late in the novel, Milkman remains unsure of his senses, too distanced is he from nature and instinct: "Perhaps it was because the sun had hit the rim of the horizon, but Susan Byrd's house looked different" (320). The house's change in appearance reflects not an alteration of the house itself, readers are led to think, but rather a change in Milkman, and, by extension, in themselves. Milkman and readers following him are approaching the self-knowledge to which the novel has guided them, symbolized by the scene's sunset. In the novel's remaining pages, all will come together for Milkman and he will achieve peace.

Signifying, the characteristic wordplay in African American culture, adds a level of complexity and uncertainty to *Song of Solomon* by further undermining characters' and readers' certitude in their full comprehension of speech. Rooted in slaves' dire necessity to communicate with each other in ways that seemed innocuous to their masters, signifying entails speech (or its written representation) intended to be understood in one way by one's enemies and in a deeper, more meaningful, and typically opposite way by one's confidants. Readers struggling to ascertain the "true" meaning of characters' spoken words are warned away from confident interpretations, and likewise learn to distrust facile comprehension of the text itself. For example, Pilate believes she does not know her mother's name because she misapprehends the utterance of her father's ghostly presence, "Sing," as a command rather than a call to his wife. Multilayered, and often misunderstood, meanings throughout the text causes "truths to be withheld," as Lubiano notes (103). "Nevertheless, the text implies," according to Vikki Visvis, "that ... [Pilate singing an] old blues song allows her to reintegrate traumatic memory" (259) which means these truths are not withheld forever. While ensuring that readers feel uncertain that they comprehend all that occurs in the story, Morrison cannot afford to allow readers to feel completely alienated lest they decline the role she intends for them. She therefore balances tactics of lingual exclusion with those of inclusion. The text therefore admits readers, at carefully selected points, to "insider" status, a gesture particularly important for readers unfamiliar with African American forms of expression.[4]

Other tactics that create for readers a sense of familiarity and comprehension also involve language use. Many forms of African American expressive culture emerged out of necessity and have evolved in many quarters into an exceptionally sophisticated ability.[5] Survival for black Americans has depended for centuries on verbal facility with which one evens a score with an opponent without resorting to violence. Among other purposes, it provides a means for safely leveling a playing field. When directed against whites, such wordplay must leave its victim unaware that he has been bettered, while those within the non-dominant culture find some satisfaction in having fooled the oppressor. Lawrence W. Levine notes that related forms of African American humorous expression typically involve "the trivialization or degradation of ideas or personages normally held to be lofty or noble, and the advancement of those normally consigned to an inferior or inconsequential position" (300–01). For example, Pilate's shucking act, which frees Guitar and Milkman from jail, "puts one over" on the white police officer: "'Bible say what so e'er the Lord hath brought together, let no man put asunder—Matthew Twenty-one: Two. We was bony fide and legal wed, suh,' she pleaded" (207). The verse actually appears in Matthew 19:6; the citation she provides refers to a passage in which Jesus tells two disciples to seek out and release an ass from a nearby village. Pilate thus subversively communicates what she really thinks of the police officer and of the two foolish young men to whose rescue she is summoned. Morrison's self-conscious use of spelling that mimics a humble black dialect in depicting Pilate's routine, but which she eschews elsewhere in her writing, underscores her character's intentional signifying or, more specifically, "masking," the act of putting forth an artificial "face" to placate whites (Kubitschek 15). Witnessing Milkman's amazement at his aunt's craftiness, readers are shown the multiple levels of African American expression.

Two extended scenes featuring ritual insults, often called "dozens," exemplify Morrison's ability to bring even readers unfamiliar with this form of signifying—e.g., most white readers—into the loop. In the first instance, the tone turns from benign mockery to poignancy: After hearing Guitar's complaint that he and Milkman were refused a beer, Railroad Tommy launches into a hilarious catalogue of things the two young men will never have:

> "And *no* baked Alaska!" Railroad Tommy went on. "None! You never going to have that."
> "No baked Alaska?" Guitar opened his eyes wide with horror and grabbed his throat. "You breaking my heart!"
> "Well, now. That's something you will have—a broken heart." Railroad Tommy's eyes softened, but the merriment in them died suddenly. "And folly. A whole lot of folly. You can count on it" [60-61].

Although Guitar brushes off Railroad Tommy's underlying tone of sad sympathy, readers are led to consider what remains unsaid: the serious limitations placed on the lives of young black men in the early 1960s. Understanding Railroad Tommy's message even better than Guitar—who is a better talker than listener, as we shall see—readers are brought into the loop.

Later, a more serious, potentially deadly round of dozens occurs. The narrator begins by representing how Milkman appeared to a group of black men in rural Virginia: "Now one of them spoke to the Negro with the Virginia license and the northern accent" (266), highlighting the differences between him and them. The dialogue ensues:

> "Big money up North, eh?"
> "Some," Milkman answered.
> "Some? I hear tell everybody up North got big money."
> "Lotta people up North got nothing." Milkman made his voice pleasant, but he knew something was developing.
> "That's hard to believe. Why would anybody want to stay if they ain't got no big money?"
> "The sights, I guess." Another man answered the first. "The sights and the women."
> "You kiddin," said the first man in mock dismay. "You mean to tell me pussy different up North?"
> "Naw," said the second. "Pussy the same everywhere. Smell like the ocean; taste like the sea."
> "Can't be," said a third. "Got to be different."
> "Maybe the pricks is different." The first man spoke again.
> "Reckon?" asked the second man.
> "So I hear tell," said the first man.
> "How different?" asked the second man.
> "Wee little," said the first man. "Wee, wee little."
> "Naw!" said the second man.
> "So they tell me. That's why they pants so tight. That true?" The first man looked at Milkman for an answer.

"I wouldn't know," said Milkman. "I never spent much time smacking my lips over another man's dick." Everybody smiled, including Milkman. It was about to begin [267].

And so it does begin. The scene turns violent, and, with the jagged edge of a broken bottle, Milkman must defend himself against a knife until some women from the town enter the store and stop the fight.

The dozens entails verbal sparring in what Levine calls "a ritual of disrespect in which the winner was recognized on the basis of verbal facility, originality, ingenuity, and humor" (347–48). Through its strict, understood rule structure, the dozens provides a safe analogue for violent confrontation. In the second example cited above, the round of dozens spins out of control when the rural men's class-based resentment of the "uppity" stranger from the North overtakes their desire to adhere to the unspoken rules. Such outcomes are unintended and undesired (Levine 347); in this case, its occurrence signals to readers an increasing entropy in the plot and an accompanying sense of danger and suspense. As it does so, it carefully keeps readers "in the know": by alerting readers that Milkman "knew that something was developing" and that something "was about to begin," the text carefully includes readers—particularly white readers unfamiliar with the dozens—in its scope. Morrison thus balances the need to keep readers unsettled and the need to avoid alienating them entirely.

The mysterious Seven Days organization, whose purpose and membership the text reveals painfully slowly, further exemplifies the text's balance between allowing facile reading and presenting alienating textual and meta-textual enigmas. The organization's significance to the plot and to Milkman's self-education remains carefully controlled; the text reveals details piecemeal to readers as they and Milkman are prepared to understand and learn. Early passages in the text provide only hints about something potentially sinister:

> Guitar was halfway down the stairs. Already his thoughts had left Milkman and had flown ahead to the house where six old men waited for him.
> He didn't come back that night [120].

Guitar's destination, the identity of the six men, and their purpose remain unknown to Milkman and to readers.

Switching consciousness, the narrator later conveys Guitar's thoughts as he gazes at Milkman: "Guitar looked at him for a long time. Maybe, he thought. Maybe I can trust you. Maybe not, but I'll risk it anyway because one day…" (154). Guitar's unfinished thought, expressed in the text by an ellipsis, attains meaning only at the novel's conclusion, when Guitar attacks Milkman as the Seven Days' next victim. In this instance, readers are privy to more information than Milkman himself, who remains even more ignorant of Guitar's intentions than are readers. As the plot unfolds, readers confront the irony of Guitar's decision to distrust Milkman; they know Milkman speaks the truth when he denies stealing Pilate's "treasure." This knowledge leads readers to distrust a heavy reliance on appearances, a crucial step in deconstructing race.

The text further foreshadows the climactic scene between Guitar and Milkman by hinting at the former man's involvement in the Seven Days. When Milkman arrives in Shalimar, with Guitar on his trail, a local resident conveys a message meant to forewarn readers, if not Milkman:

> "No beer for sale on Sunday," the man said. He was a light-skinned Negro with red hair turning white.
> "Oh. I forgot what day it was." Milkman smiled [261].

A figurative nudge to readers, the passage leads them to recall that Sunday is Guitar's day; i.e., all violent acts to be committed on Sundays are his responsibility. If they connect that fact with Guitar's impending confrontation with Milkman, they experience increasingly heightened tension. The man in Shalimar continues, conveying, without understanding its grave significance, the message Milkman's "friend" has left for him: "Said to tell you your day was sure coming or your day ... something like that ... your day is here. But I know it had a day in it. But I ain't sure if he said it was comin or was already here" (262). Readers do not know, either, but they are prompted to speculate about what will happen to Milkman on this day, Guitar's day. Any certainty that Guitar's message is meant to be a threat gets undermined by Milkman's own thoughts, disclosed by the narrator: "There was no mistaking the message. Or the messenger. Guitar was looking for him, was following him, and for professional reasons. Unless.... Would Guitar joke about that phrase?" (262). Thinking about the message's meaning, Milkman concludes that his friend cannot mean harm; rather, "Guitar needed to find Milkman and he needed help" (264). Milkman is dead wrong, however, and the text thereby misleads readers. They later discover, when Milkman discovers, that Guitar means to kill him.

By linking mystery, danger, and foreboding to the underground Seven Days organization, the text leads readers to consider, when they are properly prepared to do so, the complex relationships among race, love, and violence. A key conversation between Milkman and Guitar provides that preparation. About midway through the novel, Guitar explains to Milkman the method and the rationale of the Seven Days. After reminding Milkman that whites commit random violence against blacks, he says he cannot sit idly by. "I help keep the numbers the same," he begins (154). He tells Milkman that a secret society of seven men retaliates against a randomly chosen white person every time, and in the same manner in which, a black person suffers violence. The society, the Seven Days, began in 1920. "I am one of them now," Guitar reveals (155).

Milkman struggles to understand Guitar's motives, resisting the idea that all whites are guilty of or capable of committing atrocities against blacks, and Guitar's belief that keeping the black-white ratio consistent is a noble and necessary endeavor. Most of all, Milkman questions and fears the hatred he ascribes to the Seven Days. He tells Guitar that such a life, one that precludes marriage and children, is devoid of love. Guitar retorts: "No love? No love? Didn't you hear me? What I'm doing ain't about hating white people. It's about loving us. About loving you. My whole life is love" (159). Milkman's pains to understand linkages among race and love and violence, constellations utterly foreign to Milkman, provide a model for readers to consider their own attitudes in new ways. Milkman's uncertainty—he never reaches conclusions about these issues—permits readers to think more deeply without feeling forced into final opinions. White or black, they are free to ask whether love of one's own "race" necessitates hatred of others; whether violence by a subordinated group can constitute racial self-defense; whether all members of a group that benefits daily from skin-color privilege are culpable for the oppression it causes. Consistently hopeful regarding race relations, Morrison constructs her text to suggest to black readers that a blanket indictment of whites, as modeled by Guitar, goes too far, but declines to decide the matter for readers. The text simultaneously suggests to white readers that, to a degree only they themselves can determine, bear responsibility for every lynched black body, every unfulfilled black life. Unsettling readers who likely believe they need not consider such questions is accomplishment enough for this text.

Dana Medoro, in fact, sees *Song of Solomon* partly as a conversation about justice in which Guitar and Pilate represent alternative orientations; "each informs—or exerts pressure on—the other's configuration of justice" (1). "Although the text does not ultimately sustain Guitar's eye-for-an-eye directive, as the scholarship on the novel concurs, neither does it entirely dismiss or discredit it," Medoro states (1). In her view, "Pilate stands for an ethical ideal, with an attendant ontological reconfiguration," while "Guitar stands for the reality of its absence in African American lives, announcing the force of law that often accompanies an ethical portal in an unjust world" (1–2). Although the novel holds up Pilate's loving approach to justice as heroic, the novel does not outright condemn Guitar's vengeance-based justice. In fact, Medoro argues, "Morrison's novel does not entirely throw out the function of enforcement or force in justice" (10):

> The scene in which Pilate wields the knife against the man who beats her daughter emblematizes this point. Coming up from behind him, Pilate aims the knife at his heart and has "a little talk" with him. Pilate then describes her position, asks the villain what

he thinks she should do, and then obtains a promise from him. "I won't never put a hand on her," he says, "I promise." ... Here, the knife seems to symbolize or sustain the possibility of consequence that laws enact and for which Guitar speaks; the promise Pilate secures introduces the ideal of justice that extends beyond retaliation or restitution [10–11].

The novel thus presents readers not a singular model of justice for which it advocates, but rather a complex pair of alternatives that at times seem contradictory and at others interrelated and complementary. For Horton, the Seven Days' retaliatory approach, because it is secretive, fails to restore justice: "Without this publicly acknowledged legitimacy, the wrong essentially remains unchallenged," he writes (82). Readers must wrestle with the moral questions themselves.

In addition to philosophical questions of morality, Morrison's use of the supernatural also works to unsettle most Western readers, who typically come from a rational tradition that distinguishes sharply between the "real" and the "magical." Like the ghost story of *Beloved* (discussed in the following chapter), *Song of Solomon* features several motifs and themes that defy readers' tendency to privilege what they see as rational or scientific while denigrating the magical or supernatural. By conflating the two perceived poles of the real-unreal continuum, the text works to blur the two in readers' minds by, for example, referring to ghosts as if they are common features of daily life (e.g., 109, 141, and 186). Following the example of Milkman, who comes to appreciate and believe the magical elements of African American culture through the stories he hears and the overarching story he himself completes, readers gradually abandon the real-unreal dichotomy. The text thereby opens readers' minds to new ways of knowing, a more spiritual phenomenology. Thus exposed, readers are better prepared to think more openly about the complex themes of life, race, violence, and love; they are less likely to cast the text's difficult questions in oversimplified, binary ways.[6] Although black readers are presumably more familiar with African and African American mythology, philosophy, and cosmology, such is not necessarily the case. Milkman himself, like his father before him, buys wholesale the received, Western manner of privileging the so-called "real." Milkman, according to Soophia Ahmad, "has been brought up without a native, ethnic cultural identity," just as his mother Ruth was (61). Milkman is *one* archetype of a black character, not an archetype of *all* African Americans, as Fatemeh Azizmohammadi and Hamedreza Kohzadi believe, just as Pilate is an archetype of *one* type of black woman, not *all* black women (2261).[7] The text therefore reminds black readers, as it teaches white readers, of an alternative way of knowing "reality."

The character of Pilate contributes significantly to the breakdown of the real-unreal dichotomy. Noble and enigmatic, strong, and resistant of stereotypes, she stands as one of Morrison's most compelling characters, which makes her a particularly effective model for readers. She alone harbors no fear of her brother, Macon, and balances his avarice (his name is roughly homonymous with "makin'," as in "making money") with an utter lack of materialism. If Macon represents wholesale belief in things worldly (money, prestige, and power), Pilate represents things spiritual and magical. When a man threatens her daughter Reba and Pilate stares him down and frightens him off, the narrator states that the neighbors knew he must be a stranger. A local man "would have known not to fool with anything that belonged to Pilate, who never bothered anybody, was helpful to everybody, but who also was believed to have the power to step out of her skin, set a bush afire from fifty yards, and turn a man into a ripe rutabaga—all on account of the fact that she had no navel" (94).

Somehow born without a navel and consequently ostracized in her youth, she becomes a stronger, more independent woman in adulthood, respected and feared because she is seen as supernatural. She practices a form of black magic, for example, using a voodoo doll to stop Macon from physically abusing his wife, Ruth (132). Her uncanny understanding of how to free Milkman and Guitar further attests to her preternatural wisdom; her magic makes all things possible: "Jesus! Here he was walking around in the middle of the twentieth century trying to explain what a ghost had done. But why not? he thought. One fact was certain: Pilate did not have a navel. Since that was true, anything could be, and why not ghosts as well?" (294). Readers thus are shown that magic laced with love brings power; she is stronger even than Macon or a white police officer. Speaking almost directly to readers, the narrator says of Pilate: "Even if you weren't frightened of a woman who had no navel, you certainly had to take her very seriously" (138). Like Milkman, readers are directed by their experiences with her to listen carefully to her.

As a figure representing the alienated black man, Milkman again might stand for the African American reader who has learned to disbelieve. Because, at this early stage of his development, Milkman clings to Western standards of rationality, the text must accommodate him, must address him in his own realm at first. The text thereby accommodates African American readers similarly situated, as well as white readers who perhaps always have been limited by Western "rational" thought.

As a teacher, Pilate takes on the role of griot, a storyteller and conveyor of cultural knowledge. As with an African village griot, Pilate is the vessel of accumulated cultural history and wisdom. As such, she has much to teach Milkman as well as readers. Most significantly, Milkman learns the skill of listening itself.[8] As Joyce Irene Middleton notes, "Milkman's immersion in this auditory experience awakens his dormant listening skills to new language experiences and ways of knowing" (35). Moving from speaker (a shallow, egocentric young man) to auditor (an open-minded, deeply empathetic member of a community), Milkman becomes mature and whole, ultimately modeling for readers a set of behaviors that would render them more open-minded, empathetic, and complete. He learns to trust his instincts more than his intellect, orality more than literacy. "Milkman's experiences—of the woods, hunters, killing—move him to use his preliterate imagination to reclaim his unlettered ancestors' skill for listening: an intuitive and sensual ability to converse with animals and with nature," Middleton states (35).

In the novel's climactic scene, Guitar accidentally shoots Pilate. Milkman "dropped to his knees and cradled her lolling head in the crook of his arm, barking at her, 'You hurt? You hurt, Pilate?'" (335). True to her characteristic strength and humor, she "laughed softly and he knew right away that she was reminded of the day he first met her and said the most stupid thing there was to say" (335). She asks Milkman to sing to her while she dies. Knowing no songs, he recites an old African American rhyme to her even after she dies in his arms, representing his ultimate entry into the spiritual world his aunt inhabited; Joseph T. Skerrett, Jr., refers to this act as Milkman's "recitation to the *griot*" (201; italics in orig.).[9] A bird snatches her recently removed earring, containing her written name, and carries it off. "Now he knew why he loved her so. Without ever leaving the ground, she could fly," the narrator states (336), providing his final lesson: the boundless love he learns from Pilate (Milkman loves even his would-be murderer, Guitar) enables Milkman himself to fly at the novel's extraordinary conclusion:

> Without wiping away the tears, taking a deep breath, or even bending his knees—he leaped. As fleet and bright as a lodestar he wheeled toward Guitar and it did not matter which one of them would give up his ghost in the killing arms of his brother. For now he knew what Shalimar knew: If you surrendered to the air, you could *ride* it [337; emphasis in original].

Hortense J. Spillers sees the evocative allusion to the African flying man myth as an illumination of attitudinal differences among three generations of Deads which are dialectically resolved in that stunning moment: "The transformation of the [flying African] myth to an alien place and its reidentification as a fictional motif form an economy of analogues which render the ... generations of the Deads synonymous in their American destiny. There is essentially no discontinuity now between fathers and sons" (695). Milkman's beautiful reconciliation of control and surrender in that moment collapses time (from Milkman's grandfather to himself) and distance (from Africa to North America) as well as history and myth[10] (697). "Enslaved Africans who flew back to their mother continent are the closest relational ties African Americans have to a tribal ancestry. They bear the tribal prestige of ancestors who at times may intersect with family enclaves and whose names and feats are known through personal knowledge or oral tradition," notes La Vinia Delois Jennings (114). According to Sanders, "Morrison sees myth in a broad sense, as usable past that she can consciously draw on to affirm the existential quest of the self as well as to affirm those folk processes that give coherence to black people as a collective entity or community" (*Folk Roots*, 93).

Knowing neither whether Milkman really flies, nor whether he or Guitar dies, readers are drawn to conclude that these questions are unimportant; Milkman's education and self-realization are the lasting point which they, too, are to learn. As Ahmad notes, it is Pilate who instills in Milkman "a craving to discover his true identity and roots—to go in search of his name—to trace his origins back to his rich African past so that he can shed the false illusions he has been brought up with, and be able to surrender to the air so that he can ride it" (68).[11] Ahmad also states that it is the genealogical guidance that Pilate provides Milkman that allows him to fly—"to emerge out of this Hades-like environment and breathe the free air of his sweet cultural heritage" (68).

Although Pilate is the principal channel through which Milkman learns, other characters contribute to his education, as well. Pilate teaches him the meaning of unconditional love of all individuals (her dying words are, "I wish I'd a knowed more people. I would of loved 'em all. If I'd a knowed more, I would a loved more" [336]), but Guitar teaches him to love and appreciate African American people—his people—in particular. Even his father, the hateful Macon, unknowingly teaches Milkman to understand individuals' faults and to appreciate the flawed human beings around him. For example, when Milkman learns from his newfound "people"—his extended family members and townsfolk—that Macon witnessed his own father's murder which resulted from white resentment of a successful black farmer, Milkman's view of his own father softens. The murder of his grandfather and the theft of the family farm two generations ago lead Milkman to understand his father's acquisitiveness, which he previously attributed solely to avarice. His father's drive, in fact, becomes a source of pride in the community he left before Milkman's birth. Milkman

> began to talk about his father, the boy they knew, the son of the fabulous Macon Dead. He bragged a little and they came alive. How many houses his father owned (they grinned); the new car every two years (they laughed); and when he told them how his father tried to buy the Erie Lackawanna (it sounded better that way), they hooted with joy. That's him! That's Old Macon Dead's boy, all right! [236]

One of them says of Milkman's father, "Can't nobody keep him down! Not no Macon Dead!" (236), a pointedly ironic statement given the novel's flying motif,[12] which includes the five-foot flight of the first Macon Dead when he was shot off of a fence on his own farm.[13] Through his kin's respect for his heretofore unrespectable father, Milkman begins to appreciate and learn from Macon, while connecting with his family's history and his own extended family. This set of connections constitutes one step in Milkman's self-realization.

In keeping with Morrison's concern with family and community, Milkman accomplishes his quest for personal identity and fulfillment only through making and appreciating ties to his people. These connections are further bound up in black history, so as Milkman finds his place in a historical narrative of black Americans, the novel leads readers to consider that history, as well. For example, as Milkman reverses the course of the Great Migration by traveling from his home in Michigan to his ancestral home in Virginia (a reverse migration undertaken by Frank Money in *Home*), he enters his people's Southern past: "All that business about southern hospitality was for real. He wondered why black people ever left the South. Where he went, there wasn't a white face around, and the Negroes were as pleasant, wide-spirited, and self-contained as could be" (206), the narrator states.

Having established Milkman as a model for readers, the text suggests that they consider the same question as he, opening them to reflect upon the complex social and economic forces that led millions of African Americans to the Northern states.[14] Moreover, Milkman's own observation that the Southern blacks are "wide-spirited" highlights his (Northern) lack of that trait; he had been described earlier as merely imagining himself to be so. Here, in the place of his family's past, he finds satisfied people. As Lubiano notes, "Milkman moves forward through the days and weeks of his journey through Virginia to the origins of his family's legends, to a time when history and geography coalesce. In Danville, Virginia, history and time are an overlapping of action, reenacted in modern times by Milkman, and history come to new (his) consciousness" (106). Aretha Phiri elaborates: "Milkman eschews what [Morrison] has described to Washington as the 'spiritually dangerous position of being self-sufficient, having no group that you're dependent on' (1994, p. 238). He matures to value his aunt Pilate's acquired 'deep concern for and about human relationships' (p. 149) by privileging instead existential substance, the intersubjective, communal and communitarian principles that traditionally inform black life (in the South) and that resonate thematically in all of Morrison's novels" (129). Only "consciously acknowledging, without necessarily historicizing, African-American history enables Milkman to subvert his former 'dead' self and navigate his black subjectivity with a living, embodied sense of existential agency," she notes (129).

As Milkman's consciousness develops to include the value of his past and his present, the text pushes readers to expand their own perspectives about race, place, and time, a crucial reclaiming of historiography, which, as Robert Holton notes, exemplifies much of African American literature, which "can be seen as an attempt to awaken from the nightmare of history, or to fan a spark of hope in the past by safeguarding the dead …

from a victorious enemy" (79). Phiri notes: "Milkman's material quest is transformed into a metaphysical journey of self-discovery informed by African-American mythology and folklore embedded in an Africanist cosmology and sensibility" (127).[15]

The interconnections among history, justice, personal and national trauma, and recovery so brilliantly developed in *Song of Solomon*, and especially Morrison's ingenious use of textual and meta-textual enigmas and gaps to lovingly ensnare readers, run through other Morrison novels. It might be worthwhile to consider at some length how, for example, *Love*'s textual enigmas, with readers' conventional aids such as a reliable narrator or a linear plot withheld, engage readers in extraordinary introspection as individuals and as agents in U.S. and world history. J. Brooks Bouson states:

> Morrison ... forces her readers to make wider sense of the larger historical and social—and also aesthetic—meaning(s) of the story she is telling, which creates, like other Morrison works, a world of vexed and vexing contradictions: a world where love transforms into hatred and hatred melds into love; where tenderness and innocence coexist with hatred and violence; and where the past is conflated with the present and where the dead—in particular Morrison's ghost-narrator, L, and the ghost of Bill Cosey—are both everywhere and nowhere [360].

Enlisting readers in a social justice mission as she has with her other novels, Morrison persists in *Love* to draw readers into engagement with the text and to inspire them to think, feel, and act to an extent unsurpassed by other writers. Whereas most of her novels primarily surface issues of racial prejudice and discrimination, *Love* in some ways privileges gender-based justice as its central focus. Heed, Junior, Celestial, and the narrator, L, all unapologetically commit crimes that stem from various forms of oppression but essentially escape punishment (Sweeney, 455) and express no feelings of guilt. For example, L expresses no regret over murdering Bill Cosey and altering his will insofar as her actions ensure that Heed, Christine, and May will avoid the further erosion of their agency and socioeconomic well-being in a patriarchal social structure (Sweeney, 458–59). Courtney Thorsson points out that the novel depicts the tragic loss of the love between Heed and Christine, a bond that would have saved both—and their community—decades of suffering (626–27).

Readers discover near the end of the novel that a strong love did exist between Heed and Christine when they were children, before patriarchy as represented by Bill Cosey interrupted and corrupted it; a "partial reconciliation" ensues between Christine and Heed, who "seem to call a truce before they die" and achieve a better understanding of one another, which Humann reads as a "small, hopeful note" by the novel's conclusion (260). Thus, despite rendering nearly the entire story as loveless, *Love* ultimately concludes with hope, leading readers to rewrite what they had perceived now that they realize that love was actually there at the story's outset, as Bouson evocatively captures:

> Replacing hatred with love in the novel's closure, Morrison counters the despairing vision of the perpetuation of shame and hatred in the lives of her characters with a hopeful vision of the healing power of love and the transformative potential of storytelling on an open and receptive reader who is held in a loving embrace by the author-storyteller [373].

Because unrelenting hopelessness would result in readers' despair, which would fail to motivate them to strive for social change, Morrison ultimately inspires readers to "break free of the cycle of unproductive memory" so they can "heal and look forward to the future" (Harack, 255–56).

For Susana Morris, the collective past that must be faced honestly includes the Civil Rights era that serves as a relatively subtle backdrop to the novel's action, a historical moment that many retrospectively see as dominated by African American men. "*Love*," she writes, "suggests that rejecting a narrow conceptualization of the time before and during the civil rights movement gives us not only a fuller understanding of the era but the apparatus with which to better understand our own present" (326). By encouraging readers to re-member the era—and the past in general—Morrison "reveals that although the past may not be pure, the present and the future need not suffer for it" (336).

As Harack puts it, the novel casts a fresh light on history (what Maria-Sabina Draga Alexandru refers to as "the historical slavery and marginalization trauma in Toni Morrison's writing" [192]) which enables the characters—and, by model, its readers—to face individual and collective trauma to provide "a new perspective, for both the characters in the novel and for Morrison's readers" (256). In the face of racism and sexism, love, based on affection, empathy, and respect rather than on sexual passion or normative romance, can heal societies as well as individuals. In that regard, James L. Mellard sees in this novel a continuity of Morrison's feminist theme: "[I]t is evident in all the novels from *The Bluest Eye* through *Sula* to *Song of Solomon*, *Tar Baby*, *Beloved*, *Jazz*, *Paradise*, *Love*, and *A Mercy*" that "[e]ven in a seemingly regnant patriarchal culture, there remains an unfathomable maternal power that rules it as much as does the paternal" (264). We might use the term "womanly" rather than "maternal," but Mellard is surely right to point out Morrison's insistence on the potential of women to foster progress and justice.

A master storyteller, Morrison draws upon and extends several narrative forms. As a novel about personal journey to a self-understanding, *Song of Solomon* has been characterized as a bildungsroman.[16] Similarly, Visvis sees the novel as a "quest narrative whereby the central protagonist ... finds himself and his place in society by engaging in a quest for his family origins—a quest that comes to fruition when he uncovers his family's genealogy" (256–57). The novel, however, goes beyond the typical Western bildungsroman in which a solitary hero matures through the trials of a personal quest. Aside from a relatively old protagonist (Milkman is thirty when he "flies" from Solomon's Leap), the novel presents a vivid, multivocal community rather than a monolithic entity with which a protagonist must contend.[17] Furthermore, *Song of Solomon* depicts the self-understanding achieved by several characters, besides its principal, through intercommunication and interdependence. When they help each other complete their individual and collective stories, the characters develop comprehension. None alone has the ability to complete his or her story.

Pilate, for example, learns a great deal on her own when she is ostracized by her community for being "unnatural" ("Her mind traveled crooked streets and aimless goat paths, arriving sometimes at profundity, other times at the revelations of a three-year-old" [149]), but she lacks omniscience ("Neither Pilate nor Reba knew that Hagar was not like them" [307]) and needs Guitar and Milkman to discover the truth about her father and mother. Guitar needs Pilate's storytelling to fire his imagination: "The boys watched, afraid to say anything lest they ruin the next part of her story, and afraid to remain silent last she not go on with its telling" (43).

On the other hand, Guitar demonstrates for readers the dire consequences of failing to listen, as when he disbelieves Milkman's truthful account of helping a man lift a crate onto a weighing platform. Guitar mistakenly believes Milkman has shipped gold to himself, cutting Guitar out of the proceeds. Relying on his fallible sense of sight rather than on the text-privileged act of listening, Guitar decides to kill Milkman (295–98). His reliance on sight fails him again when he later fires his rifle at Milkman but strikes Pilate instead.

The characters who listen actively and thus participate in communal storytelling invariably learn about themselves, their past, and their ties to kin, to the African diaspora, and to humanity at large. Phiri puts it this way: "As the expression of black subjectivity and invoking the relationship between black individual and communal identity, the Song of Solomon[18] is a self-reflexive ethnic form of story-telling that enacts an 'imaginative rediscovery ... [of] the history of all enforced [black] diasporas' (Hall 1990, p. 224)" (127). Mobley corroborates this view: "The achievement of *Song of Solomon* is that through the network of narrative that transforms Milkman, Toni Morrison takes on the role of griot and tells how we, her community of readers, could be transformed...." (*Folk Roots*, 133). We would add that the stories within this story collectively model for readers the path to self-understanding, making *Song of Solomon* a kind of meta-bildungsroman: the novel leads readers to mature along with the characters, relying on what Missy Dehn Kubitschek calls readers' "real-life processes of learning" in which they must listen and observe in order to piece together sensible narratives (73). As they are trained by the novel, readers are led to important, albeit unanswerable, questions about black and white, love and hate, and past and present. Readers need such skills, self-knowledge, and expanded worldview to participate in Morrison's metatextual mission to counter racism and other social injustices, a goal she continues with *Beloved*.[19]

4

Beloved

Toni Morrison's Pulitzer-Prize–winning novel, *Beloved* (1987), continues her use of African American cultural traditions and forms and her strategy of reader involvement in her mission to deconstruct race and combat racism. The novel's complex features include multivocality represented by shifting narrator identities, the insistent recovery of a lost or ignored history of slaves and slavery, the demonstration of the healing power of an African American community, the exposure of the hypocrisy of white liberalism and falseness of white conservatism, the challenge to Western literary and critical genres and forms, and the indictment of white Americans in the historical and contemporary oppression of blacks. Like its predecessors "Recitatif," *The Bluest Eye*, and *Song of Solomon*, *Beloved* explodes readers' expectations not only about the story itself but about memory, history, race, and their own attitudes and hidden assumptions and prejudices.

Innovating the traditional *in medias res* beginnings of her stories, Morrison launches *Beloved* in a way that intentionally mystifies readers to an extent even greater than that of its predecessors. In fact, even before the story itself begins, the novel's epigraph from Romans 9, "I will call them my people, which were not my people; and her beloved, which was not beloved," hints that things are not always as they seem, that they are always subject to radical change; this message is a warning to readers. Robert L. Broad points out that Morrison's choice of epigraph is even slyer than it appears: Paul is twisting the words of Hosea for his own purposes, a clue to readers to beware the use of history to oppress, a theme that becomes central in *Beloved* (194). Within the epigraph itself lies the blurred line between the individual and the group, which, Broad states, "rubs painfully against the grain of Western and American social mythology, and that is exactly the way Morrison wants it" (192). As the tale itself opens, the challenges to readers continue.

Its celebrated opening line, "124 was spiteful" (3), remains enigmatic until readers later find that 124 is the address of the house on Bluestone Road in which the principal characters live, a place that shapes the inner conflicts of its residents.[1] Morrison herself notes that she purposely delayed the identification of 124 as a house number ("Unspeakable Things" 32). That this textual enigma unsettles readers immediately is precisely the author's intention:

> The reader is snatched, yanked, thrown into an environment completely foreign, and I want it as the first stroke of the shared experience that might be possible between the reader and the novel's population. Snatched just as the slaves were from one place to another, from any place to another, without preparation and without defense ["Unspeakable Things" 32].

Even when readers learn several lines later that 124 is a house, the notion of a spiteful edifice challenges (Western) readers' conceptualized dichotomy of animate and inanimate objects. Thus, the text immediately leads readers to question and eventually to distrust previously understood cognitive categories. The novel is beginning to train readers to read the messages about race that it later delivers, when the scientific racism personified by the character called schoolteacher is shown to be even more heinous than the physical abuse endured by the slaves on the Sweet Home plantation. (Reflecting schoolteacher's inhumanity, he goes nameless in the text and his title is not capitalized.)

Contrary to the claim of Wendy Harding and Jacky Martin that Morrison desires comprehension (85), Morrison herself notes that she intended the novel to be "immediately incomprehensible" and "excessively demanding" for artistic and political reasons ("Unspeakable Things" 32). She expects her readers to feel confused, "without comfort or succor from the 'author,' with only imagination, intelligence, and necessity available for the journey" ("Unspeakable Things" 32). As she told interviewer Kay Bonetti, she wants to open a door for readers but it is up to them to step through (Morrison, *Toni Morrison Interview*).

The principal textual enigma in *Beloved* is the identity of the title character herself. Giulia Scarpa notes, "One of the most intriguing ways to access the depths of this novel is by exploring the identity of Beloved. This character embodies the essence of the narrative potential" (93). The fact that critics continue to debate her identity testifies to the complexity of the issue. As Broad states, "The question 'Who the hell is Beloved?' must haunt every reader of the novel, just as it hounds the characters Sethe, Denver, and Paul D" (190).

Making the readers as bewildered as the main characters is one tactic by which Morrison creates a powerful sympathy for the characters, a sympathy that opens the readers to the pain inherent in the story. The circumstances of Beloved's arrival are clear enough. After returning from a carnival, Sethe, Denver, and Paul D find Beloved, strangely childlike yet a fully grown young woman, waiting for them at 124 Bluestone Road. Beyond the facts of her arrival, she remains utterly mysterious. Critics have posed three principal explanations of Beloved's identity. The most obvious explanation is that she is the returned ghost of the baby whom Sethe killed nearly two decades earlier. Beloved knows of objects and events that only Sethe's own baby daughter could have known. Furthermore, her arrival comes shortly after Paul D exorcises from 124 Bluestone Road a haunting presence that has menaced its inhabitants for years, a presence understood by Sethe and Denver to be the spirit of the dead child. The text guides readers to the conclusion that, driven out of the house by Paul D, the spirit returns incarnate as Beloved. Calling herself Beloved is another significant clue: "Beloved" is the only word on the dead baby's tombstone. It also is clear that Sethe and Denver fully accept this explanation of Beloved's identity.[2]

This conclusion is meant to satisfy readers at first, but the text then unsettles readers' faith in their solution to the puzzle.[3] Complicating factors are introduced later, such as the stream-of-consciousness passage presented by Beloved in which she relates seemingly incomprehensible things, e.g., "I am always crouching the man on my face is dead his face is not mine his mouth smells sweet but his eyes are locked" (210).[4] Eventually, the text leads readers to realize that Beloved also possesses memories of a slave ship, of the Middle Passage, memories that predate by generations the murdered baby known as Beloved. The interminable crouching, the corpse on her face, the loss of her mother who chooses to jump overboard rather than be carried into slavery—such memories make Beloved more confusing than if she were "simply" a ghost, which in itself would constitute a stretch for Western readers trained to discount the supernatural.[5]

Hazy references in the text suggest a third possible identity of Beloved. Rumors that a white man who lived in the area (the outskirts of Cincinnati) kept a runaway slave as his sexual prisoner present to readers the tempting theory that Beloved is the escaped sex slave. Readers might desire this explanation because it allows them to dismiss the alternative, supernatural explanations.[6] As readers consider the possibility that Beloved personifies the lost souls of the Middle Passage, they are indeed drawn to contemplate the utter helplessness of a runaway slave, but the text does not rest there. Angelyn Mitchell reads Beloved "as a spirit who serves as the repository of memory and thus uses those memories to promote change in the narrative's other characters" (*Freedom*, 88).

Beloved, in fact, embodies all three suggested identities; the urge to conclude which of the three is Beloved's "true" identity stems from readers' inculcation in Western modes of thinking and is thus similar to readers' compulsion to categorize by race the two principal characters in "Recitatif." As Bao Jinping surmises, "Beloved ... [defies] all binary definitions and categorizations. She is neither absolute evil nor definite good" (6). Beloved's effect on readers is manifold, however. The text's resistance to readers' desire for a conclusion regarding her identity represents one element in the novel's strategy of exposing and exploding unquestioned categorization as well as revealing as a social construction readers' understanding of history.

The other principal textual enigma centers on how and why Sethe kills her baby. The details of this terrible event are revealed excruciatingly slowly to readers, just as they are to Paul D. It takes readers the length of *The Bluest Eye* to understand why Pecola Breedlove was destroyed, and readers of *Beloved* fathom Sethe's act only gradually. Again, the text puts readers into a position similar to that of a character such that greater sympathy is established: in this case, as Sethe physically circles Paul D in her house shortly after his arrival, gingerly dodging the details of the horrible deed she committed nearly twenty years earlier, the text does the same thing to readers. Philip Page notes: "Just as she cannot say directly what she did or why, so the narration does not tell the story directly. Just as Paul D only catches fragments, and must wait until she circles closer and closer, so must readers be content with fragments and wait until they are told enough" (35). Readers, of course, are not content with fragments, and they are driven onward throughout the story.

The text's withholding of information about Sethe's killing of her baby reflects the needs of the characters.[7] Sethe is unable to come quickly to terms with her action, and Paul D is unable to withstand an immediate revelation of what happened after both left Sweet Home so many years earlier. More significantly, readers cannot understand, without first being prepared by the text to comprehend the totality of slavery's evil, why Sethe kills her baby. Drawing a hand saw across her child's neck in a dark woodshed would be inexplicable behavior to readers unprepared to fathom its logic. Only by revealing small bits of the story at a time while simultaneously depicting the utter inhumanity of slavery, about which American readers "seem to suffer from an ongoing amnesia" (Broad 193), can *Beloved* make its intended impact upon its readers.[8]

Beloved ambitiously reveals to readers their ignorance and denial of the totality of slavery's horrors. Moreover, readers come to realize that their ignorance and denial stem from a falsified narrative that they call history, which has systematically deleted the experiences of "60 Million and more" victims. Thus are they complicit in the continuing oppression of those for whom slavery is an inescapable legacy. First, though, the text must lead readers to realize the extent to which slavery dehumanizes individuals, communities, and entire races—black and white.

It is not difficult to depict the brutality of slavery. The genius of *Beloved* lies in its ability to sneak up on readers, to open to them, without judgment, a sobering view of the institution such that the readers themselves conclude how horrifying it is. Morrison's approach is to implicate, not explicate. For example, instead of presenting readers with a straightforward depiction of slaveholders' treatment of slaves as chattel, the text figuratively places readers with Sethe as Paul D tells her what became of her husband, Halle, whom she had to leave on the plantation when she escaped. Having told Sethe that the sight of schoolteacher's nephews stealing her breast milk "broke" Halle, Paul D tells her about his last encounter with Halle before he, too, left Sweet Home:

> Carefully, carefully, she passed on to a reasonable question.
> "What did he say?"
> "Nothing."
> "Not a word?"
> "Not a word."
> "Did you speak to him? Didn't you say anything to him? Something!"
> "I couldn't Sethe. I just ... couldn't."
> "Why!"
> "I had a bit in my mouth" [69].

Paul D is not speaking figuratively, readers realize; he literally had a bit in his mouth like an animal. As silenced as Sethe is by Paul D's revelation, readers are stunned. Sethe, having experienced slavery, understands immediately and moves on. The text has figuratively slapped readers, however, and the sting is revisited repeatedly throughout the text—for example, when it reveals that Paul D for a time wore a spiked collar that not only made him unable to lie down to sleep but also humiliated him among the slaves at Sweet Home (227)—such that the cumulative effect is inescapable.

Indeed, Morrison goes well beyond depicting the physical cruelty endured by slaves, although she does this remarkably well. For example, Sethe's body, bearing the deep scars of the whip, "is the text upon which history has been written," as Dana Heller notes (111). The most heinous aspect of slavery, however, as the text shows readers, is its social and psychological toll.

Garner, the white owner of the Sweet Home plantation, is depicted not as a monster but as a relatively humane slaveholder. He is proud that his male "niggers" are not boys but men whom he trusts to run the daily business of the plantation and even to carry guns. The three Pauls, Halle, and Sixo are the "Sweet Home men." But as Paul D later realizes, "Garner called and announced them men—but only on Sweet Home, and by his leave. Was he naming what he saw or creating what he did not?" (220). Baby Suggs also notices: "The Garners, it seemed to her, ran a special kind of slavery" (140), but slavery nonetheless. That physical conditions at Sweet Home are better than at surrounding plantations does not diminish the fact that they are so solely because Garner so wishes. The slaves' fates lie entirely in his hands, such that when he dies, their lives change immediately and drastically upon the arrival of schoolteacher. Without Garner's life, "each of theirs fell to pieces. Now ain't that slavery or what is it?" Paul D asks (220).

Mrs. Garner, too, is depicted as relatively kind to the slaves, especially to Sethe. By fostering sympathy for her, the text then surprises readers with the realization that even she is an instrument of slavery's totalitarianism, as when Sethe tells Mrs. Garner that she wants to marry Halle:

> "Halle's nice, Sethe. He'll be good to you."
> "But I mean we want to get married."
> "You just said so. And I said all right."
> "Is there a wedding?"
> Mrs. Garner put down her cooking spoon. Laughing a little, she touched Sethe on the head, saying, "You are one sweet child." And then no more [26].

Although Mrs. Garner permits the slaves to choose their own mates, it is clearly only at her discretion. A proper wedding, the prerogative of white Christians, is never a consideration, as her chuckle reveals. As historian Orlando Patterson notes, black slaves in North America "had regular sexual unions, but such unions were never recognized as marriages" (6). Sweet Home is no different in this regard. Thus, although Heller acknowledges the relationship to Sethe as "exploitative" but finds between them "rarefied elements of a genuine love and sense of connectedness" (112), Mrs. Garner's love of Sethe is patronizing at best. We see much more emphasis in the novel on Mrs. Garner's exploitation of Sethe than on mutual love. Any connection between them because of their gender in a society as sexist as it is racist shrinks beside the unilaterally exploitative aspect of the relationship.

Even at Sweet Home, whites' authority over every aspect of slaves' lives is absolute. This fact again intrudes upon readers when, after Mr. Garner's death, Mrs. Garner sells Paul F and "lived two years off his price" (197). Although she does not want to break up the slaves' families, she can and does. Sweet Home, despite its relatively mitigated horror, fits the model of all slave plantations, including the one from which Baby Suggs's children are sold off, one by one. The novel illuminates for readers the institution's absolute ability to rend families. As Patterson notes of the black American slave: "Not only was the slave denied all claims on, and obligations to, his parents and living blood relations but, by extension, all such claims and obligations on his more remote ancestors and on his descendants. He was truly a genealogical isolate" (5). This "loss of ties of birth in both ascending and descending generations" is what Patterson calls "natal alienation" (7). As La Vinia Delois Jennings states, *Beloved* (as well as *Song of Solomon* and *Tar Baby*) "narrate more than the experiences of physical displacement by peoples of whole and part African descents. They address the psychological and religious reality of what it means for African Americans in the New World to be cut off from not only their living kin but also their dead kin, from knowing and calling their names, and from continuing their responsibility of reciprocity to them in the circle of life" (83). It is a particularly brutal aspect of slavery with which *Beloved* confronts readers.

By depicting Sweet Home as relatively benign, the text subtly, and therefore more effectively, drives home the comprehensive power of the slaveholder. Patterson notes: "Slavery is one of the most extreme forms of the relation of domination, approaching the limits of total power from the viewpoint of the master, and of total powerlessness from the viewpoint of the slave" (1). That Garner boasts of his male slaves being men—that he uses their status, granted by him, to improve his standing among the local planters—exemplifies Patterson's observation that "the slave became an extension of his master's power" (4). As Paul D recognizes, "Deferring to his slaves' opinions did not deprive him of authority or power" (125).

Having taught readers this lesson about slavery via a relatively humane slaveholder, the text then presents them with schoolteacher, a coldly sadistic man who takes over the plantation on behalf of the ailing Mrs. Garner after her husband's death. Rational only in a way that makes sense within the twisted logic of slavery, schoolteacher's cold, psychological abuse of the slaves crushes them. It is he who tells his nephews during a tutoring lesson to write Sethe's human characteristics in one column and her animal characteristics in another (193), and who, at another time, takes notes as one of them holds her down while the other suckles at her breast (70), an incident that nearly drives Sethe mad. She considers it much worse than the beating she received while pregnant (16–17) and the incident does drive her husband, Halle, mad because he witnesses it. Schoolteacher also sees Halle as chattel: "Maybe Halle got in the barn, hid there and got locked in with the rest of schoolteacher's stock" (224), the narrator speculates, reflecting schoolteacher's equation of Halle and stock. And using the ink that Sethe herself has made, schoolteacher records in his book the answers given by the slaves to his questions. Although the text refrains from revealing the questions to readers, it does imply that the questions are insulting and dehumanizing. "I still think it was them questions that tore Sixo up. Tore him up for all time," Sethe says (37).

In an attempt to draw readers' attention the contemporary relevance of slavery, the novel's critique of schoolteacher's manner also serves as a critique of scientific racism, the practice of perpetuating racial prejudice on ostensibly scientific grounds.[9] Morrison has acknowledged that she so named schoolteacher to point out racial discrimination perpetuated in social institutions such as science and theology.[10] Scientific discourse, while claiming to be dispassionate, disinterested, and objective, often masks racial preconceptions and prejudices. What Morrison calls the "master narrative" ("Friday on the Potomac") and the "official story" ("The Official Story") is the dominant, white culture's version of race, behavior, and history.[11] Purported to be objectively "true," this master narrative self-servingly casts blacks as incoherent, irrational, and animalistic. Schoolteacher personifies the master narrative: claiming to conduct coolly rational investigations into black behavior and traits as he studies, interviews, and experiments with the slaves at Sweet

Home, he is depicted by the text as monstrously cruel, not because he physically abuses them (although he does, even ordering the pregnant Sethe to be whipped), but because he denies them their humanity. Thus, the text reveals to readers that ostensibly objective analyses of race and racial objects are, in fact, among the master's tools for maintaining dominance. Readers are led to question not only their understanding of the past, but the ways in which they acquired that (mis)understanding.[12] The text thus directs readers to become less credulous of the version of history they have learned.

Sethe's act of infanticide, seen from the perspective of the white master narrative represented by schoolteacher, his nephews, and the sheriff's deputy—whom the text refers to as the "four horsemen" (148), evoking an apocalyptic vision as they approach Baby Suggs's home to reclaim, through the Fugitive Slave Law, Sethe and her children—is forever inexplicable. Surveying the bloody scene, one nephew asks, "What she want to go and do that for?" (150). Schoolteacher and his nephews, disappointed at the monetary loss represented by Sethe's act, ride away, "leaving the sheriff behind among the damnedest bunch of coons they'd ever seen. All testimony to the results of a little so-called freedom imposed on people who needed every care and guidance in the world to keep them from the cannibal life they preferred" (151). Blinded by their adherence to the master narrative, the whites cannot fathom Sethe's act.[13] Infanticide was rare among slaves, according to Eugene D. Genovese (497), so these white characters have no context for understanding her action. Even had they witnessed such acts before, their ideology would not permit them to comprehend. They dismiss Sethe's act as irrational behavior, evidence of the moral inferiority of blacks, which schoolteacher has studiously "proven" through his scientific inquiries. James Berger notes Morrison's position that "violence within the African American community cannot be understood without the recognition that law and science, power and official knowledge continue to violate African American lives" (411). The text thus guides readers to recognize that science, presumptively value-free, serves the white hegemony. Readers thus take another step toward deconstructing race, itself a social construction masquerading as scientific fact.

Similarly, readers are taught to question "white" education which perpetuates the socially constructed racial hierarchy. Toward the novel's conclusion, after Denver's successful mission into the community to save her family,[14] she undertakes to resume the education she aborted years earlier when a schoolmate silenced her with his reminder that her mother was a murderer. When Denver tells Paul D that Mrs. Bodwin "taught her stuff" (166), Paul D thinks to himself, "Watch out. Watch out. Nothing in the world more dangerous than a white schoolteacher" (166). Equating in the minds of readers the apparently benign Mrs. Bodwin with the malicious schoolteacher at Sweet Home, the text prods readers to consider that "white" education has played a role in the oppression of African Americans. As Heller notes: "While the formal institution of slavery may have become obsolete, the systematic structure of racial oppression and its denial of African culture, identity, and history continues in the socially and morally sanctioned institutions of education and language" (114). Considering the problematic stance of the white liberal Bodwins—who are abolitionists but also racists—readers are meant to be as concerned about Denver's education as is Paul D.

Morrison's impatience with white liberalism is evident throughout *Beloved*, in fact, especially as personified by the Bodwins. Depicted as well-meaning when confronted with the problems of an individual black person, they also appear to be insensitive to African American issues and concerns other than slavery. For example, they display in their home a statuette depicting a kneeling black boy with stereotypical features, including an exaggerated, coin-filled mouth. The inscription on the statuette's pedestal reads, "At Yo Service." This single item is, for readers, quite telling. Although kind to Denver and other African Americans, the Bodwins apparently see nothing offensive in their statuette celebrating black servitude.[15] The image leads readers to ascertain rather quickly that abolitionism is not necessarily equated with racial egalitarianism or even sensitivity. That the Bodwins regularly draw from the statuette money used in daily household commerce also symbolizes the Bodwins' exploitation of the African American servants in their home, gaining materially from them.[16] Indeed, readers might connect the white use of the black boy's mouth with Paul D's experiences on the chain gang when the white guards force the black men to perform fellatio (108).[17]

Such images in the text prod readers to consider the hypocrisy of much historical, white liberalism. Just as *The Bluest Eye* guides readers to consider their own present circumstances and attitudes about race through its presentation of a fictional past, *Beloved* alerts readers' consciousness to contemporary American society by highlighting an overlooked history. Sethe's attack on Bodwin near the end of the novel appears to be the act of a delusional mind; she believes he is schoolteacher returning for her and her children. Yet, like in so much of Morrison's work, the act is ambiguous. Readers at first might feel that Bodwin, who has worked all his life on behalf of the abolitionist cause, does not deserve Sethe's ire. The text complicates this view of Bodwin, however, by depicting him as insensitive to African Americans and self-serving in his abolitionism. In a passage recording his thoughts as he travels to Sethe's home, he thinks about his past in the abolitionist movement: "Those heady days were gone now; what remained was the sludge of ill will; dashed hopes and difficulties beyond repair" (260). He appears to regret the success of abolitionism for it left him without a cause for which to fight. The passage begins to depict Bodwin not as purely altruistic but also as egocentric (as well as Eurocentric). Bodwin becomes a much more complex character, whose good deeds as an abolitionist are credited by the text but whose racial attitudes are criticized.

Berger notes that the black characters' and the white characters' "histories are entwined" (417), as are the present circumstances of black and white Americans. He reads *Beloved* as a critique of contemporary white liberalism since the Moynihan Report of 1965, asserting that Morrison "links Bodwin here with a view of 1960s liberalism seen from the 1980s" (416). Just as twenty years have passed from Bodwin's abolitionist activism to his self-aggrandizing recollections, twenty years have passed from the Moynihan Report to the publication of *Beloved*. Berger believes that, at the time she published *Beloved*, Morrison had become increasingly critical of white liberals' self-congratulatory recollections of their civil rights activism in the 1960s. The novel, by equating contemporary white, liberal readers with Bodwin, thus robs readers of their smugness.

The liberal erasure of race has concerned Morrison into the 1990s. In *Playing in the Dark*, she notes that "the habit of ignoring race is understood to be a graceful, even generous, liberal gesture. To notice is to recognize an already discredited difference" (9–10). She argues that this liberal tendency to ignore race rests upon and perpetuates the assumption that, as she puts it in "The Official Story," her essay about the O.J. Simpson murder trial, "whites are the only ones who are unraced, neutral" (xx). This insistence among many whites that race no longer matters is plainly evident in the Simpson case: "There seems to be a universal sorrow that these proceedings were distorted, sullied by race," as if the defendant's race makes no difference in how he and the investigation are handled, she notes (xiv). With *Beloved*, Morrison re-races American history, such as with the repeated rhetorical tactic of referring to individuals by race—e.g., whiteman or coloredwoman—indicating that in the society depicted by the novel, race is inseparable from identity. Even children are identified by race, e.g., "whitebabies" (258). In her non-fiction, too, Morrison insists upon the inseparability of American identity and racial identity using the same compounding of racial adjective and noun, e.g., "whitemale" ("Unspeakable Things" 2). Only by acknowledging the force of race in history can readers begin to dismantle that force. As Morrison told Ntozake Shange, "moral resurrection … is possible only by confrontation with the dead past" (Shange 48).

While insisting upon the power of the social construction of race, the novel challenges the conventional dichotomy of black and white as well as the tendency of individuals in the Western cultural tradition to ignore differences among members of each half of the dichotomy. For example, the white character Amy Denver provides a sharp contrast to the evil schoolteacher. Through her selfless service to Sethe during her daring escape into freedom, Amy Denver represents hope for the future.

Denver "stands as the implied author's brightest ray of hope for black and white sisterhood," according to Bernard W. Bell ("*Beloved*" 11). Krumholz notes: "In *Beloved*, as in all of Morrison's novels, meaning is multiple; contradictions stand intact. For example, black people and white people are essentially and irrevocably different; they are also essentially and eternally the same" (398). Krumholz argues that, by challenging simplistic categories, the novel makes readers question what they have learned about racial difference, as "Morrison makes clear that race is not an absolute division either" (399).

The novel's symbolism, seen from the African American perspective (from which it is presented to readers), embraces complexity and ambiguity rather than the perspective of Western (European) tradition, which tends toward binary relationships and dichotomous categories of phenomena.[18] That is, as the novel reveals to readers the harm inherent in schoolteacher's belief in sharp, distinctive categories of human beings, it challenges not only the bases for racial categories but readers' tendency to employ categories. "Recitatif" exposes readers' assumptions about the characteristics of blacks and whites. *Beloved* builds upon that exposure to challenge readers' assumptions about the necessity of, the value of, and even the ability to categorize by race and, moreover, leads readers to question oversimplifying categorization of any social phenomena. Intolerance of ambiguity, readers are taught, is a Western trait and limits their appreciation of the richness of humanity and its art.

Although Morrison, in *Beloved*, shows no patience with white liberalism, she also uses the novel to critique the neo-conservative discourse of the 1980s. Berger notes that the rhetoric of Reaganism blames African Americans for their retarded socioeconomic progress. The argument from this perspective is that blacks' failure results from cultural insufficiencies; it denies "race as a continuing, traumatic, and structural problem in contemporary America" (408). The story, as staged in the novel, dismantles for readers this denial of the power of race. "Morrison's emphasis in *Beloved* on the systemic, structural effects of racism opposes the conservative view" (411), according to Berger. Readers are thus guided by the novel through a narrow channel of thought: they are shown the overwhelming power of race as a historical and social force, but also are directed—by the novel's depiction of the strength of black characters, especially women—to question the liberal assumptions that deny black agency and culture.

Beloved also calls on readers to question other aspects of contemporary racial rhetoric. In *Playing in the Dark*, Morrison demonstrates that American literary criticism has always figured blackness as absence and whiteness as presence while denying that the whiteness is figured against an unacknowledged image of blackness.[19] She sharply criticizes the presumption of American literary historians that "traditional, canonical American literature is free of, uninformed, and unshaped by the four-hundred-year-old presence of, first, Africans and then African-Americans in [what is now] the United States" (4–5). Although critics and literary historians have ignored what she calls an "Africanist" presence in three centuries of American literature, the literary tradition of North America has consistently constructed "Americans" as white, as opposed to the "savage" black.

Beloved first exposes for readers, including critics, the unacknowledged tradition of white Americans to define themselves against what Morrison calls an Africanist presence (the mythologized image of black people constructed by white people [*Playing* 7]), and then ironically and poignantly overturns the previously unquestioned racial definitions. In the novel, Morrison depicts the white slaveholders as defining themselves in relation to their images, however misguided, of their slaves. Calling grown black men "boys" makes Garner's fellow farmers feel manly (10–11). Labeling Sethe as crazy makes schoolteacher, his nephews, and the sheriff feel confirmed in their sanity and normality (148–50), although, as Stamp Paid points out, "She ain't crazy. She love those children. She was trying to out-hurt the hurter" (234).

While exposing the whites' practice of constructing themselves against their constructions of blackness, the novel subverts and reverses the definitions. For example, in the stream-of-consciousness passage in which Beloved seems to recall incidents aboard a slave ship, she mysteriously refers to "the men without skin" (211). Working through this difficult passage draws readers toward the realization that, to a black child recently kidnapped from Africa, white people would appear to be skinless. Her naive belief that skin is normally black strikes from some readers their assumption that skin is ordinarily white—that black skin is exceptional.

Beyond the realization that their assumptions regarding "normal" physical traits only artificially appear natural, readers face an even more intentionally disturbing lesson from the text: that white depictions of black behavior and morality are also socially constructed. The novel demonstrates this fact by coopting and reversing the attributes ascribed by the dominant culture to whites and to blacks. Contrary to white assumptions of black inhumanity, Baby Suggs says, "Those white things have taken all I had or dreamed" (89), and adds, "There is no bad luck in the world but whitefolks" (89). Later, Denver recalls Baby Suggs's statement that what whitefolks did "was a far cry from what real humans did" (244), contrasting white people and "real humans." Denver also knows that her mother's greatest fear is that Beloved will leave before Sethe can make her realize that even worse than her act of infanticide "was what Baby Suggs died of, what Ella knew, what Stamp saw and what made Paul D tremble. That anybody white could take your whole self for anything that came to mind. Not just work, kill, or maim you, but dirty you" (251). Agnieszka Łobodziec contends that through Beloved Morrison is representing "the African American response to Euro-American modernity [that] encompassed black people's reinterpretation and affirmation of their humanity, which white supremacy questioned, or even denied" (112).

Stamp Paid himself recalls a litany of white atrocities, from the burning of black schools to rape and lynching. When he finds a bit of a black child's scalp near a river, he asks, "What *are* these people? You tell me, Jesus. What *are* they?" (180, emphases in original). He does not attribute the implied atrocity to a single, mad individual, but to a race of people that has proven to him repeatedly that it (not his own race, as the whites claim) is subhuman. The text subtly shows readers that his blanket disgust of all whites differs ideologically and politically from whites' stereotypical attitudes about all blacks: in a racial caste system, whites have almost unlimited power, so their stereotypes of blacks are extremely injurious. The black characters' contempt for whites cannot significantly harm them. As Joe R. Feagin and Clairece Booher Feagin assert, discrimination refers to a dominant group's practices that have "a differential and negative impact on members of subordinate groups" (20–21). According to their definition, slaves cannot discriminate against slaveholders.

The apparent problem of Stamp Paid's essentialist language—generalizing about all white persons as if they are genetically and universally programmed to evil—is mitigated by the counter-example of Amy Denver, the simple, poor white girl who helps Sethe escape. Stamp Paid's negatively essentialist characterization of whites represents the converse of what Gayatri Chakravorty Spivak calls the "strategic use of a positive essentialism in a scrupulously visible political interest" (*Other Worlds* 205). That is, rather than to essentialize one's own group for political gain, the rhetoric here aims to reduce the relative power of the privileged group. In this case, the essentialist rhetoric is Stamp Paid's but the "scrupulously visible political interest" is Morrison's.

Readers uncomfortable with Stamp Paid's generalizations are relieved of the notion that Morrison shares his disdain for all whites. The attitudes of these two characters complement each other rather than conflict: readers come to understand Stamp Paid's hatred and distrust of all whites while learning to appreciate the power of Amy Denver's love, which so moves Sethe that she names her first daughter Denver.

Stamp Paid's revulsion, readers learn, comes from his understanding that whites project onto blacks their own ugly traits:

> Whitepeople believed that whatever the manners, under every dark skin was a jungle. Swift unnavigable waters, swinging screaming baboons, sleeping snakes, red gums ready for their sweet white blood. In a way, he thought, they were right. The more coloredpeople spent their strength trying to convince them how gentle they were, how clever and loving, how human, the more they used themselves up to persuade whites

of something Negroes believed could not be questioned, the deeper and more tangled the jungle grew inside. But it wasn't the jungle blacks brought with them to this place from the other (livable) place. It was the jungle whitefolks planted in them. And it grew. It spread. In, through and after life, it spread, until it invaded the whites who had made it. Touched them every one. Changed and altered them. Made them bloody, silly, worse than even they wanted to be, so scared were they of the jungle they had made. The screaming baboon lived under their own white skin; the red gums were their own [198–99].

Stamp Paid's certainty that every white person is infected by the jungle imagined by and created by whites leads white readers to a painful and serious self-evaluation. Just as *The Bluest Eye* prods readers to consider themselves among those who have benefited from Pecola's demise, *Beloved* asks readers to ask themselves if they, too, have projected their worst fears about themselves onto African Americans.[20] A crucial surprise for readers, especially white readers, is their realization of their own complicity—through previously unquestioned assumptions about race, black people, and white people—in the oppression of African Americans. Morrison makes this point clear:

> [M]odern life begins with slavery.... It made [Europeans] into something else, it made them slave masters, it made them crazy.... They had to dehumanize, not just the slaves but themselves. They have had to reconstruct everything in order to make that system appear true.... Racism is the word that we use to encompass all this. The idea of scientific racism suggests some serious pathology [Qtd. in Neal 257].

As *Playing in the Dark* does in non-fiction, *Beloved* does in fiction: both expose "the impact of racism on those who perpetuate it" (*Playing* 11). *Beloved* thus carries further the rhetorical strategy of *The Bluest Eye* to depict whites as victims of, as well as practitioners of, racism.

Beloved also inspires in readers a reconsideration of the institution of slavery inasmuch as their dismissal of it and its history contributes to the contemporary oppression of black Americans. Malmgren notes that "we readers must come to terms with our own ghost, the spectre of a ruthless and dehumanizing institution whose legacy we have yet to acknowledge fully" (100). The novel in this way collapses past and present. That the two can be sharply distinguished is, in fact, a notion peculiar to a Western concept of time. John S. Mbiti states, "The linear concept of time in western thought, with an indefinite past, present and indefinite future, is practically foreign to African thinking" (21). Karla F.C. Holloway notes that this story "demystifies time" ("*Beloved*" 522). The text, like "Recitatif" and *The Bluest Eye*, resists a linear representation of time. With phrases like, "As for Denver, the job Sethe had of keeping her from the past that was still waiting for her was all that mattered" (42), the narrative blurs the distinctions among past, present, and future. "Readers are placed generationally in a space that floats somewhere between an absent past and an absent future" (691), Pérez-Torres notes.

Also like *The Bluest Eye*, *Beloved* ends with the sacrifice of a black female. In the latter novel, the black women of the town exorcise the increasingly malevolent Beloved, whose presence is destroying Sethe and her relationships with Paul D and her daughter Denver. Gathering together outside 124 Bluestone Road, the thirty women begin to sing, fearlessly chasing the specter of Beloved from the home. The arrival of these women and their literally life-saving gift to Sethe is extraordinary, for these are the same neighbors who earlier, offended by the pride represented by Baby Suggs's huge feast for the townsfolk, refused to warn Sethe that schoolteacher was coming to steal her children.[21] Now, because Denver had reconnected the family to their community, the women come to rescue the family with their musical ritual.

Gradually, the community heals, forgetting Beloved altogether: "They forgot her like a bad dream. After they made up their tales, shaped them and decorated them, those that saw her that day on the porch quickly and deliberately forgot her.... Remembering seemed unwise" (274).

The reconception of family and the necessity of community are pressed upon readers by the novel's conclusion. Consistent with its challenge to Western modes of categorizing phenomena, *Beloved*, as Heller notes, "is a ghost story that challenges white-dominant culture's frame of reference for experiencing familial drama. Morrison's artistic narrative style, her merger of the powers of the past and the present, the living and the dead, the private sphere and the public sphere, unsettles the definitional boundaries of the Western European traditions of family romance and novelistic realism" (106–07).

While opening the definition of family, the novel testifies to its power: despite the horrors experienced by Sethe and Paul D, despite the intense conflict between Paul D and Denver instigated by Beloved, despite the burden of Sethe's infanticide upon Denver, the family triumphs at the end of the novel when Paul D and Denver offer one another civility and concern and, filled with love for Sethe, Paul D "wants to put his story next to hers" (273): "Sethe," he says, "me and you, we got more yesterday than anybody. We need some kind of tomorrow" (273).

This patchwork but loving and functional family contrasts sharply with the Breedlove family in *The Bluest Eye*. Although fitting the Western definition of a nuclear family, the Breedlove family is irreparably flawed; its members are alienated from each other and from the nurturing black community, while the middle-class, white notion of family as captured in the Dick-and-Jane reader—and in Geraldine's black family which has adopted white modes of behavior—is mocked. Sethe, Paul D, and Denver, however, lay out for readers a model of hope.

The family not only needs the community[22]; the reverse also is true. With the common enemies of a tragic past (slavery) and a difficult present (poverty, white racism, and the continuing threat of the Fugitive

Slave Law), the community needs the strength of each family. It is fitting, then, that the community not only survives, but apparently thrives, after Beloved's demise.[23]

The novel's illustration of mutual, communal support is reiterated in the scene depicting the escape of a black chain gang recounted by Paul D: without speaking, the forty-six men about to drown in their cages as the rain pours down drop together into the mud and, using the chain that binds them together, pull each other to the surface and to freedom. "For one lost, all lost" (111), states the narrator. This dramatic scene prepares readers to appreciate the community that reclaims and saves Sethe's family at the end of the novel.

Morrison lovingly preparing readers to understand the incomprehensible in other novels, as well. Just as readers are prepared quite gradually to understand the extreme, tragic trauma of Pecola's father's incestuous rape in *The Bluest Eye* and of Sethe's act of infanticide in *Beloved*—readers of those novels certainly are shocked, but are prepared to absorb the shock—readers of *Love* have been provided the cognitive and emotional preparation to make sense of Heed's underage marriage. They certainly are horrified, but they also understand how the final puzzle piece fits into the jigsaw narrative. What could have been taken by readers as nothing but a horrific fact if it were presented earlier in the text instead pushes readers to reconsider their assumptions about romantic love. Wyatt argues that the delayed revelation undermines the admiration for Cosey that the text had inspired ("*Love's* Time," 194). Because Cosey represents powerful masculinity, seeing his behavior as immoral and criminal undercuts readers' estimation of him and, by extension, leads them to recognize the toxicity of patriarchy. Stephanie Li observes that Heed and Christine "strive to identify themselves as the 'sweet Cosey child,' a term that brings both wealth and definition [through Bill Cosey's will] (*Love* 79). Once awakened to their ability to attract men, the girls experience one another as rivals rather than as friends. Competition for status and attention supplants their previous union as the two are unable to reconcile their sexuality with their original bond" (39), having internalized what Heather Duerre Humann calls "patriarchal capitalism" (250).

With this revelation, the novel leads readers to recast all they had read, from a story of heterosexual, romantic love between Heed and Cosey to a story about destructive patriarchy and, more importantly, a story about the love between two female characters, Heed and Christine, about which they were kept ignorant. They indeed have been rivals, but only because Bill Cosey warps their relationship. It takes readers about 180 pages, covering roughly fifty years, to gain this crucial comprehension.

Beloved's theme of community, also prevalent in Morrison's other novels, offers a potential salve for horrific trauma. Scarpa points out that

4. Beloved

Sethe is not isolated from her community because of her act of infanticide. Rather, she remains apart because of "her stubborn refusal to share her horror with the other women who witnessed it, who know and understand very well why she cut her baby girl's throat with a hand saw. Unless she shares it, she cannot be healed" (97). Without the readers' completion of the story—their figurative entry into the community that wants and needs to share the horror of Sethe's act—the characters and the readers remain unhealed in their isolation. Molly Abel Travis points out that readers "must deal with Beloved's otherness, recognizing her as a 'haint,' or the return of a repressed racial memory, and the spirit of Sethe's dead child. Yet there is Sethe's otherness as well, which is of a different order altogether—a murderous mother-love, simultaneously familiar and horrifying" (233). Readers must find a way to deal with this otherness in order to be healed.

Although the principal characters, having been healed, forget Beloved, readers cannot. Beloved figuratively leaves the pages of the novel and enters the world of the readers, haunting them with the memory of slavery and its legacy. Just as the tragedy of Pecola remains with readers after they complete *The Bluest Eye*, readers of *Beloved* cannot escape its personal call to them. As Malmgren states, readers "hold in their hands the very document that rehearses for them the story of slavery and its aftermath, thus memorializing Beloved's suffering and incarnating history's ghost" (100). William R. Handley notes that "Beloved's cultural memory is preserved in the text we read, even though Beloved vanishes" (684). In fact, Beloved and her story not only live on in the text, but are carried by readers to the extra-textual world where they—the story and the affected readers—can make a difference in this racialized society. "Thus, as the reader leaves the book, we [sic] have taken on slavery's haunt as our own" (397), according to Krumholz. Denise Heinze points out that the novel's success indicates that "readers feel the same need as Morrison to purge themselves; once again, writer, audience, and text engage in a dynamic of identification. Beloved, then, functions as supernatural memory relived for the sake of psychic and spiritual rehabilitation. Only through memory can the past be integrated into the present providing meaning to what it means to be human" (180).

Although coming to terms with the horror of slavery is difficult for readers, as it is for Sethe and Paul D, readers, like the characters, cannot move forward without confronting that ugly history. "As an eruption of the past and the repressed consciousness, Beloved catalyzes the healing process for the characters and for the reader" (Krumholz 397) as Pecola does in *The Bluest Eye*.

It is perfectly fitting that Beloved's exorcism is accomplished through communal singing and storytelling. Joseph T. Skerrett, Jr., states, "Storytelling is the primary folk process in Toni Morrison's fictional world" (193), and *Beloved* is rife with examples of the African and African American oral tradition, verbal and musical. Abena P.A. Busia confirms the connection between music and the griot tradition: "Storytelling, like song-singing, becomes cultural metaphor and the carrier of cultural meaning" (210). Trudier Harris notes that Morrison centers the form of the novel, as well as its content, around storytelling: "By developing her novel associatively, that is, by narratively duplicating the patterns of the mind, the way it gathers tidbits of experiences in *seemingly* random fashion, she achieves a structural effect that evokes the process of oral narration" (*Fiction and Folklore* 172, emphasis in original).[24]

All of the main characters of *Beloved* are storytellers, and, of course, the implied author is, as well. The implied author, as the master storyteller, is responsible for drawing readers into the communal circle. Thus, "the storyteller creates community, uniting, through narrative, the lives of the teller, the listener, and the greater world of experience from which the story is drawn" (704), states Pérez-Torres. The readers' sense of community with the characters is enhanced by the characters' shared and alternating roles as narrators.[25] Even when all have spoken, however, the story remains incomplete until readers participate in the storytelling circle, thus becoming part of the life-giving community.

We use the term *circle* advisedly. The figure of the circle, as Page points out, resurfaces continually in *Beloved*, especially in its evocation of a storytelling circle. Sterling Stuckey notes the connections among storytelling, circles, and listener participation in Central and West Africa:

> Since storytellers, or griots, focus mainly on the history of their people, ancestors are usually the principal subject of a particular chronicle of the past—the ceremony framed, as it were, by the listeners gathered around the storyteller. Depending on the demands of the narration, they either listen or, on signal from the storyteller, become active participants [14].

Stuckey also notes that the figure of the circle emerges in African funeral rites, in which "circular movement is used to represent themes of togetherness and containment" (14). Because *Beloved* focuses on black ancestors, stories, death, and community, Morrison's use of the figure of the circle is exceptionally apt.

Evidence that the text expects readers' participation in, and continuation of, the story lies in its celebrated and enigmatic coda. The phrase, "It was not a story to pass on," appears twice, followed by a variant, "This is not a story to pass on" (274–75). The phrase's ambiguity is evident in the various interpretations rendered by critics. Taken at face value, the phrase simply indicates the narrator's acknowledgment of the difficulty of telling and hearing the story's horror. As Jan Furman notes, "It threatens peace of mind and must be resisted" (80). Andrew Levy argues that the final phrase, "This is not a story to pass on," suggests that Morrison's "own narrative project is not altogether engaged in stomping out the past" (120). Not only is the text "not altogether engaged in stomping out the past"; it actively seeks to recover it for therapeutic purposes. Levy appears to have disregarded Morrison's command of irony.

Most of Morrison's critics allow for irony, and recognize that the phrase, in context, renders multiple meanings. Thus, Page points out that the narrator "*does* pass the story on. She [or he] and of course Morrison force readers to relive the country's past horrors and make them participants in the recreation of those horrors" (38, emphasis in original). Heinze addresses more specifically than Page the manner in which the passages make readers into participants, noting that the narrator accuses the characters, the narrator, and the readers of having "convenient memories"; the text thus "anticipates the inevitable and final reader response" (181). Heinze does not specify the response, however. Hardy and Martin believe that the intended response is that readers "discard the story and espouse the values at stake in the novel's symbolism" (94). Although we agree that the text invites readers to carry the story's lessons into their own lives, we doubt that the author intends such a moving story to be discarded. Marilyn Sanders Mobley's reading is the most complete, taking into account Morrison's use of irony which Hardy and Martin partially overlook. She states that the repeated declaration "is an ironic reminder that the process of consciously remembering not only empowers us to tell the difficult stories that must be passed on, but it also empowers us to make meaning of our individual and collective lives as well" ("Different" 363).[26] Finally, the phrase "to pass on" also evokes death, certainly a central theme in this novel.

The "not a story to pass on" phrase is still more complex than these critics recognize. If read with an emphasis on *pass* ("This is not a story to *pass* on"), the opposite of its originally apparent meaning becomes evident. Read this way, the phrase indicates that the narrator and, by implication, the story's readers, not to mention its author, are morally obligated and compelled to tell the story. Only Valerie Smith refers to this double-edged ambiguity: "'To pass on' might mean either to transmit or to overlook" (353), she notes. The capacity for the phrase to be read not only in diverse but even contradictory ways is typical in Morrison's work and helps to undermine the authority of the narrative voice, a practice described in our discussions of "Recitatif," *The Bluest Eye*, *Song of Solomon*, and now *Beloved*.

In telling the story, however, the implied author and the readers who take on the obligatory task of retelling the story distance themselves from its emotional toll. Valerie Smith notes the paradox of a written narrative: "To speak what is necessarily and essentially and inescapably unspoken is not to speak the unspoken; it is rather only to speak a narrative or speakable version of that event or thing" (349). She notes that "the act of telling the story of suffering, even one's own, requires one to position oneself outside that experience of suffering" (349). If, however, readers carry their new understanding of slaves' suffering into their own racist world and endeavor to change that world, then they move beyond the distanced empathy inherent in narrative to arrive at an affective sympathy and productive activity.

It is appropriate, in this novel of circularity, that *Beloved* ends with an ambiguous phrase, because it also features one at its outset. On the novel's first page, readers hear that Baby Suggs wondered that "her grandsons had taken so long to realize that every house wasn't like the one on Bluestone Road" (3). At first, the narrator appears to mean that the grandsons should have realized that not every house was like theirs (haunted), but a reconsideration of the passage shows that, literally, the phrase indicates not that some houses were different but that every house was different. This narrator, like the ones in "Recitatif" and in *The Bluest Eye*, resists readers' complete trust and belief. Readers' (listeners') distrust of the storyteller—as well as the storyteller's distrust of the listener, which Robert B. Stepto describes in *From Behind the Veil*—is a standard feature of the griot tradition.

Undermining the authority of the narrators teaches readers to beware the superficial meanings of words. In various places in the novel, readers are reminded of the multiple layers of meaning found in African American discourse. In the dangerous workings of the Underground Railroad, Ella helps Sethe's escape, outfitting her "as she listened for the holes—the things the fugitives did not say; the questions they did not ask. Listened too for the unnamed, unmentioned people left behind" (92). Similarly, the men of the prison chain gang cloak their messages: "They sang it out and beat it up, garbling the words so they could not be understood; tricking the words so their syllables yielded up other meanings" (108). At times, the black characters lie outright to protect themselves from whites, as when Stamp Paid tells a white man that he does not know the woman the man is seeking but then tells Paul D that he does know her (231–32). Even in relatively good times, between two intimates, words never communicate with precision and certainty, as revealed in this description of what Denver and Beloved share: "Sweet, crazy conversations full of half sentences, daydreams and misunderstandings more thrilling than understanding could ever be" (67).

The fragmentation of the narration itself further undermines of the narrative's authority. Like Faulkner, Morrison uses multivocal narration to complicate the text, simultaneously presenting multiple, sometimes conflicting perspectives, and forcing readers to participate in meaning-making. Moreover, Morrison's text calls readers to question the "master narrative" or "official story" by opening themselves to alternative interpretations of texts.

Bell notes the complexity of the narration in *Beloved* and what it helps to accomplish as a tactic to instigate readers' responses:

4. Beloved

Occasionally, the implied author's consciousness merges with the narrator's, the narrator/protagonist's with the characters,' the past with the present, and the black female's with the male's. These techniques compel the reader viscerally and cerebrally to fill in the gaps in the text of the fragmented, yet complementary, embedded stories and memories of Baby Suggs, Nan, Sethe's mother, Ella, Stamp Paid, and Paul D. The implied reader is moved by these illustrative comparisons and contrasts to reconstruct and reconsider the unspeakable human cost of American slavery, racism, and sexism, then and now—to whites as well as blacks, to men as well as women—, and to sympathize with Sethe, black mothers, and black families in their struggle against while male hegemony to affirm their self-worth as a racial group [11].

Page also notes that the narrative fragmentation requires readers' active participation in building the story, pulling them deeper into it, such that "the cumulative effect of the intensive exploration of the characters' memories is profound" (37).

Even the ostensibly omniscient narrator poses problems for readers. In the scene in which Sethe kills her baby, the narrator says of Sethe, "And if she thought anything, it was No. No. Nono. Nonono. Simple" (163). Ordinarily, an omniscient narrator would know what Sethe thought. Readers of *Beloved*, however, find themselves unable to count on the narrator. In fact, the narrator indirectly warns readers against credulity, as when the narrator speaks of Denver: "Years of haunting have dulled her in ways you wouldn't believe and sharpened her in ways you wouldn't believe either" (99). The narrator's teasing of readers forces them to consider which is more untrustworthy: the narrator or their own belief. That is, perhaps their disbelief is well-founded because the narrator is not trustworthy, or perhaps their disbelief is a sign of their own inability or refusal to comprehend the horrors Denver has endured. Either way, readers find no assurances in the text, just as readers of "Recitatif" and *The Bluest Eye* are led by unreliable narrators to question their own powers of understanding of and empathy with oppressed peoples.

Also like "Recitatif" and *The Bluest Eye*, this novel features an enigmatic narrator who tests readers' ability to discern the truth as well as their ability to make moral judgments. As we discussed in earlier chapters, this tactic also characterizes Hawthorne's "Rappaccini's Daughter" (Mailloux, *Interpretive Conventions* 73–92). Like Claudia in *The Bluest Eye*, the narrator of *Beloved* pushes readers one step further, causing them to include themselves among the culpable.

Like the narration, the symbolism in *Beloved* is fragmented and ambiguous.[27] Paul D recalls, many years later, the day on which young Sethe chose Halle among the Sweet Home men to be her mate, a choice for which the men waited a year. Halle and Sethe finally consummate their relationship in the cornfield at Sweet Home. Paul D remembers:

> Halle wanted privacy for her and got public display. Who could miss a ripple in a cornfield on a quiet cloudless day? He, Sixo and both of the Pauls sat under Brother [a tree]

pouring water from a gourd over their heads, and through eyes streaming with well water, they watched the confusion of tassels in the field below. It had been hard, hard, hard sitting there erect as dogs, watching those corn stalks dance at noon. The water running over their heads made it worse [26–27].

Paul D's and the third-person narrator's voices blend as the recollection continues in evocative, poetic language:

> As soon as one strip of husk was down, the rest obeyed and the ear yielded up to him its shy rows, exposed at last. How loose the silk. How quick the jailed-up flavor ran free.
> No matter what all your teeth and wet fingers anticipated, there was no accounting for the way that simple joy could shake you.
> How loose the silk. How fine and loose and free [27].

Noting that critics often misread the scene as representing a coming-together of Halle and Sethe and, two decades later, of Sethe and Paul D, Harding and Martin criticize "the practice of judging a work according to conventional patterns derived from Western models" (87). "The corn is obviously a highly erotic image, but it is made into a symbol of harmony and closure only through an extremely selective reading" (87–88), they assert. They note that, as a tale conveyed through multiple storytellers, the episode in the cornfield comes to readers from the distinct memories of Sethe and Paul D. Only by ignoring the contradictions in the recollections can one conclude that the corn symbolizes harmony, they claim. Rather, they note that the

> parallel courses of the couple's remembering do not merge, as we might expect, with the "he" or "she" converging on the plural pronoun "we" or "they"; instead, in the last line of the passage the associative pronoun "you" invites the reader to participate in the ambivalence of the experience [90].

Readers succumbing to the Western tendency to reduce the scene's significance do so at their own peril. Accepting an oversimplified and inaccurate explanation of the scene puts readers in the same position to be mocked by the text as is Mr. Garner, who thinks the broken corn stalks "was the fault of the raccoon" (27). Like much of the novel, the cornfield conveys multivalent meanings to readers open to them. In fact, the complexity of the scene—its problematic composition and frustrating gaps in the characters' memories, such as the fact that "Paul D couldn't remember how finally they cooked those ears too young to eat" (27)—clues readers to refrain from the Western tendency toward either/or interpretations. This is not a Euro-American narrative; it is an African American narrative. Pérez-Torres recalls the argument of Henry Louis Gates, Jr., that "the signifying of black narratives—the linguistic playing, punning, coding, decoding, and recoding found in African American texts—emerges from the pressing necessity for political, social, and economic survival" (694), which is clearly evident within the story itself in the slaves' discourse and also is true of the novel as a text.

The text presents readers with symbols bearing multiple potential meanings. Moreover, the symbols derive from African, African American, European, and Euro-American sources, which is appropriate for a complex, African American work. Bao notes that, rather than confirming storytelling "as a singularly authentic form of communication," Morrison's "reliance upon collective thinking and impersonal memory, the telling and interpretation of stories through multiple voices ... engages with the numerous ways—official and unofficial, central and decentralized, privileged and marginal—narratives function in multicultural spaces" (4). Noting how *Beloved* bridges Africa and America, Handley notes that the novel which "so deeply mourns the past in a Western sense is also a novel that seeks to create a future in the African sense" (684). Schmudde points out that "Morrison's references to the Ohio River and to the stream behind 124 blend [European] Christian and African water symbolism" (410). Indeed, Beloved herself links Africa and America, bearing cultural and symbolic characteristics of both continents.[28] It is appropriate that Beloved, a mystical link between the West African homeland and the American tragedy of slavery, is doubly called into existence in *Beloved*: within the narrative, she is called into being by Sethe, who needs to heal (her name means "atonement," Horton points out [88]), and extra-textually by Morrison, who seeks to recover a history that is lost, repressed, or both, so that the nation can heal.

Beloved's corporeal existence is a manifestation of the West African concept of *nommo*, "the magic power of the word to call things into being, to give life to things through the unity of word, water, seeds, and blood" (Handley 677). Morrison certainly is aware of this concept; she writes, "I sometimes know when the work works, when *nommo* has effectively summoned, by reading and listening to those who have entered the text" ("Unspeakable Things" 33). Through the power of *nommo*, Morrison empowers the "60 Million and more" who have vanished from history. It is crucial to note that, as her own comment reflects, *nommo*'s effectiveness depends upon readers' responses. The unheard word has no power; the heeded word—in this case, the forceful story of *Beloved*—can transform nations. Handley asserts that Morrison, through the *nommo* represented by the novel, "calls a racialized readership to hear things it does not know and an African American community to discover what it may become" (701). Scarpa also believes that "Morrison offers a form of therapy to the haunted Black psyche with the construction of a text whose complicated structure mimetically reproduces the journey toward recovery of its hurt characters" (103). Thus, in structure and narrative tactic of conjuring *nommo*, *Beloved* validates African American culture and history on behalf of its readers.

In addition to her use of *nommo*, Morrison also employs the African American trickster tradition, in which a character thought to be relatively weak outwits a stronger character, thereby shifting power relations in his favor.[29] The minor character Sixo clearly fits this description. Twice he gets the better of schoolteacher. The first time is when schoolteacher catches him with bits of gristle on his plate and a piece of meat in his hand:

> "You stole that shoat, didn't you?"
> "No. Sir." said Sixo, but he had the decency to keep his eyes on the meat.
> "You telling me you didn't steal it, and I'm looking right at you?"
> "No, sir. I didn't steal it."
> Schoolteacher smiled. "Did you kill it?"
> "Yes, sir. I killed it."
> "Did you butcher it?"
> "Yes, sir."
> "Did you cook it?"
> "Yes, sir."
> "Well, then. Did you eat it?"
> "Yes, sir. I sure did."
> "And you telling me that's not stealing?"
> "No, sir. It ain't."
> "What is it then?"
> "Improving your property, sir."
> "What?"
> "Sixo plant rye to give the high piece a better chance. Sixo take and feed the soil, give you more crop. Sixo take and feed Sixo give you more work." [190].

His cleverness leads to a beating, but schoolteacher's stature is diminished when he takes Sixo's bait. The second incident is Sixo's final act: Tied to a tree and burning after being caught trying to escape, Sixo laughs and yells, "Seven-O! Seven-O!" (226). Baffled by his riddle and frustrated by his courage, the white men shoot him. Paul D understands Sixo's joke, for he knows, as the text leads readers to conjecture, that Sixo's lover, the Thirty Mile Woman, is pregnant with his son. Ultimately, although the whites destroy Sixo, he lives on in his progeny, having inverted the power relations between him and the white men. Sixo's triumph as a trickster is an extreme example of restructuring power: Sixo, a slave, is essentially powerless, a "social nonperson" (O. Patterson 5), and schoolteacher, a slavemaster, wields nearly absolute power, yet Sixo transcends the worst that the whites can inflict upon him.

Along with *nommo* and the trickster figure, Baby Suggs's preaching also infuses *Beloved* with elements of African American culture. Baby Suggs' sermons in the Clearing subvert white Christian doctrine with African American standards and modes of behavior and belief. "Uncalled, unrobed, unanointed, she let her great heart beat in their presence" (87), the narrator says of her spiritual leadership of the black townsfolk. The narrator continues:

> She did not tell them to clean up their lives or to go and sin no more. She did not tell them they were the blessed of the earth, its inheriting meek or its glorybound pure.
> She told them that the only grace they could have was the grace they could imagine. That if they could not see it, they would not have it [88].

Her exhortations are pragmatic and healing; her sermons are based not on dogma or doctrine but on love. She celebrates, not shames, human bodies and feelings, restores them after they have been desecrated by whites: "No, they don't love your mouth. *You* got to love it. This is flesh I'm talking about here. Flesh that needs to be loved" (88, emphasis in original). The magical scene concludes with Baby Suggs saying, "More than your life-holding womb and your life-giving private parts, hear me now, love your heart. For this is the prize" (89). The narrator tells readers:

> Saying no more, she stood up then and danced with her twisted hip the rest of what her heart had to say while the others opened their mouths and gave her the music. Long notes held until the four-part harmony was perfect enough for their deeply loved flesh [89].

Baby Suggs's message is that to restore themselves, blacks must rely not on anything whites can give them, or even on God, but on their own great capacity for love.

Baby Suggs also is an agent of community, drawing together the black folks of the town. Her role is one that was common: Genovese states that during slavery and Reconstruction, "rather than preachers somehow usurping community leadership, the natural leaders of the community, as defined by the slaves themselves, felt the call to preach and knew that preaching was their road to prestige, power, and deepest service within the black community" (258). Levy associates Baby Suggs with Morrison herself. Baby Suggs's preachings, "like Morrison's novels, repudiate the standard norms of responsibility and salvation, earthbound or otherwise" (121), he argues. Levy notes, "Only Baby Suggs's call for creative vision really matches the narrative project attempted by Morrison in *Beloved*: an invocation to seek creative recombinations of the past that thread confidently through the dynamics of salvation and destruction that a rich, if painful, history can offer" (121). Similarly, one of this volume's co-authors has stated elsewhere: "Like Baby Suggs preaching in the Clearing, Morrison clears an ideological space, stripping old, unquestioned, and unproductive thinking about race and races. Also like Baby Suggs, she counts on her auditors to build with her, upon the newly cleared space, a new vision of a society in which all members, regardless of age, gender, race, and class, are liberated" (Goldstein-Shirley, "Preacher"). Like she does with "Recitatif" and *The Bluest Eye*, Morrison with *Beloved* effectively deconstructs received standards of beauty, faith, responsibility, and love in order to inscribe on a tabula rasa a new ideology that does not oppress African Americans or deny their history and culture.

Beloved, again like "Recitatif" and *The Bluest Eye*, challenges received concepts of proper artistic form as well as theme. Readers cannot be certain that *Beloved* is a novel at all; it mimics an oral tale. Even taken as a novel, however, its genre is indeterminate. On one level, it obviously is a ghost story. Schmudde points out, however, that it is no ordinary ghost story because

> in contrast to most conventional ghost stories, suspense and terror are created not by the supernatural per se but by the effect on the main characters of confronting the undead past in the context of the present, and by the effect on the reader of confronting the historical past through the mythic past of fiction [409].

Beloved might be a ghost story, but it is a problematic, unconventional one.

Beloved also contains features of historical slave narratives. Scarpa notes some similarity between Harriet Jacobs's well-known narrative, *Incidents in the Life of a Slave Girl*, and *Beloved*, such as the assertion that death is better than slavery (Scarpa 103 n5). As Furman notes, however, Morrison's narrative goes beyond traditional slave narratives, which tend to suppress anger and avoid offending readers who, as Frances Smith Foster explains, "were, after all, members of the society being criticized" (14). As Wilfred D. Samuels and Clenora Hudson-Weems comment, "The caution practiced by the slave narrator was inevitable" (97). Of Morrison's narrative, which does not suffer the same restrictions as slavery-era narratives, Furman states: "The reader should not merely *know* about the horror of slavery but *feel* what it was like" (77, emphases in original). *Beloved* thus does not fit neatly in the slave narrative genre; it revises and transcends the genre.

Bell refers to the novel this way: In addition to being a ghost story and "new-slave narrative," it is a "postmodern romance that speaks in many compelling voices and on several time levels of the historical rape of black American women and of the resilient spirit of blacks in surviving as a people" ("*Beloved*" 9). Pérez-Torres also sees *Beloved* as a postmodern text: "At a very basic level, this engagement with postmodernism manifests itself in the aesthetic play of the novel" (689). Because of its manner of undermining its own authority and of intentionally and reflexively calling attention to itself as a text, the novel does bear postmodern traits. Even so, as Pérez-Torres notes, the text "profoundly challenges a postmodernism which values reified alterity" (707). By insisting upon a material "presence premised upon a historical, cultural and political absence," the text counters this reification, he states.

Where Bell and Pérez-Torres see postmodern impulses in the text (albeit, in the latter's case, qualified and complicated postmodernism),

Krumholz sees modernism. She claims that "Morrison adapts techniques from Modernist novels, such as the fragmentation of the plot and a shifting narrative voice, to compel the reader to actively construct an interpretive framework" (396). Perhaps in its fragmentation of plot and of narrative voice, *Beloved* bears elements of modernism, and in its reflexive tendency to call readers' attention to its problems as a text it appears postmodern.

In any case, whether oral tale, ghost story, slave narrative, modernist novel, or postmodernist novel, *Beloved* defies categorization.[30] That the text resists a categorization of form is fitting, given the text's thematic challenge of categories that derive from Western notions of reality. In one more way, then, the novel defies readers' attempts to trust this—and by extension, any—text.[31] Having learned to distrust narrative authority and received, naturalized taxonomies of form and content, readers are better prepared to judge for themselves the racial realities they confront.

Having thus cleared an ideological space for the story (after leading readers to come to terms with America's shameful history so they can heal from it) and for the text itself (by challenging received notions of artistic form), the novel creates a new hope. As the novel ends, Denver again takes up literacy lessons. Although silently warned by Paul D that a white schoolteacher can be dangerous, Denver hopes to become a teacher herself. Armed with a hard-earned understanding of her mother's story and the lessons of her grandmother ("There is no bad luck in the world but whitefolks" [89]), Denver will take over the task of teaching the past to her own people. She thus represents a potentially liberating future, a culmination of what Angelyn Mitchell calls a "paradigm of metaphysical liberation" in "the context of Black womanhood" (88). Moreover, if Baby Suggs can be read as representing Morrison,[32] Denver can be read as representing readers. Having learned a fuller, more accurate (and certainly more painful) history, they go forth to teach and to change. Like "Recitatif," *The Bluest Eye*, and *Song of Solomon*, *Beloved* relies on its power to alter readers as a way of altering American society, exemplifying the ways in which "Morrison's narratives contribute importantly to [the] long process of bearing witness, and testify to the continuity of a historical (and historiographical) struggle," as Horton notes (89). Ultimately, as Angelyn Mitchell puts it, "the narrative's characters—and perhaps the readers—are empowered to confront the metaphysical dilemmas of their personal and collective pasts in terms of slavery, effecting a liberation from the historical pain and shame of slavery" (88).

5

Paradise

A marvel of intertextuality, *Paradise* (1998) draws together several narrative techniques and thematic concerns of Morrison's earlier works, providing a capstone for the end of the previous millennium. *Paradise* returns to the extraordinary tactic of omitting racial information about key characters, an experiment she began fifteen years earlier in her short story, "Recitatif." The jarring, present-tense first line of *Paradise* reads, "They shoot the white girl first" (3)—an exemplar of Morrison's tactic of textual enigmas that constitute her strategy of disarming readers—which instantly entices readers to wonder about her identity.[1] Indeed, the first paragraph omits not only who is shot and by whom, but also where, when, and why the shooting occurs. At the novel's end, more than three hundred pages later, readers have developed intimacy with several female characters, none of whom is identified by race, just as "Recitatif" never reveals the racial identities of Twyla and Roberta. The question of which is shot first, then, remains as unanswered as the one that haunts readers of *The Bluest Eye* (why must Pecola be destroyed?).

Like the rest of Morrison's narratives, *Paradise* features various forms of an unreliable narrator that undermines textual authority and thereby guides readers to interact more fully with the text. Almost every chapter ends with an obvious factual omission, teasing and prodding readers to speculate about the plot and consider the implications of its potential directions. The "Grace" chapter, for example, closes with this passage, containing a non-sequitur and a deliberately withheld fact:

> What postponed the inevitable were loves forlorn and a very young girl in too tight clothes tapping on the screen door.
> "You have to help me," she said. "You have to. I've been raped and it's almost August."
> Only part of that was true [77].

Readers must infer that the girl has lied about being raped, an ironic reversal from Pecola's silence, in *The Bluest Eye*, about her own violation.

The succeeding chapter, "Seneca," opens as cryptically: "Something was scratching on the pane" (81). The text never reveals the thing's identity;

5. *Paradise* 115

rather, readers are led to another mystery: the identity of Dovey's "Friend," a ghostly figure reminiscent of the one who led Zechariah, generations earlier, to the spot on which Haven was to be built (97–98). The chapter concludes just as enigmatically, creating rather than filling a gap in the readers' comprehension of the narrative:

> The sobbing—or was she giggling—woman was gone now. The snow had stopped. Downstairs, someone was calling her name.
> "Seneca? Seneca? Come on, baby. We're waiting for you" [138].

Neither the departed woman nor the speaker is identified.

In some instances, the omitted information underscores for readers the import of the given passage. The chapter titled "Divine," which, readers discover, bears its own irony in light of the earthly, humanly flawed characters on which it focuses, opens with a two-page monologue by an unidentified speaker. When the text finally identifies him as the Reverend Pulliam, readers find the irony compounded, for his sermon argues that humans are "capable of learning how to learn, and therefore interesting to God, who is interested only in Himself which is to say He is interested only in love" (142). Pulliam and his followers demonstrate their own inability to learn as they prefer to maintain their old prejudices, and they, as executioners of the Convent women, sacrilegiously occupy God's role as judge but without His love and mercy. The text thereby establishes a deepening contrast between Pulliam and his rival, the Reverend Misner, setting up alternative models for readers' potential attitudes and actions.

Appropriately, Pulliam's parishioners understand his message in conflicting ways (145–47), and Misner, thinking silently to himself, completely contradicts Pulliam's message as he holds a wooden cross, "urging it to say what he could not: that not only is God interested in you; He *is* you." He wonders of his townsfolk: "Would they see? Would they?" (147). The text thus prods readers to ask themselves whether *they* see what Misner wants his townsfolk to see: a conception of God as loving and merciful. As the rivalry between the two clergymen intensifies, the text leads readers to side with Misner, associating him with hope and potential: "Senior Pulliam had scripture and history on his side. Misner had scripture and the future on his" (150).

Elsewhere in the novel, the narrator eschews narrative authority by presenting readers with alternative explanations of events or phenomena. When, for example, Grace (who, like several other characters, also has a nickname, "Gigi") arrives in Ruby, the narrator temporarily occupies the perspective of the young men watching her immodest form: "Either the pavement was burning or she had sapphires hidden in her shoes" (53). Readers, forced to dismiss either explanation as rhetorical, are meant to conclude instead that the young woman's apparently suggestive walk arouses the interested gaze of the men.

The narrator also declines authority when presenting another of the novel's pairs of characters, hiding behind a passive voice but warning readers that communication and meaning sometimes elude: "The Morgans always seemed to be having a second conversation—an unheard dialogue right next to the one they spoke aloud" (62). A similar passage appears later:

> It had long been noticed that the Morgan brothers seldom spoke to or looked at each other. Some believed it was because they were jealous of one another; that their views only seemed to be uniform; that down deep was a mutual resentment which surfaced in small ways.... In fact the brothers not only agreed on almost everything; they were in eternal if silent conversation. Each knew the other's thoughts as well as he knew his face and only once in a while needed the confirmation of a glance [155].

These passages prepare the reader for the twins' eventual falling out while disinclining them to believe a single point of view.

The enigmatically inscribed Oven in the center of Ruby provides another source of various interpretations. Like Morrison's texts themselves, the inscription is read by the novel's characters through the lenses of their individual experiences and prejudices, as if the Oven were the townsfolk's own unreliable narrator. Typically, Pulliam and Misner represent opposing interpretations of the words that Zechariah chiseled onto the Oven decades earlier. At a town meeting, Misner states that the issue at hand is to clarify the Oven's "motto."

> "Motto? Motto? We talking command!" Reverend Pulliam pointed an elegant finger at the ceiling. "'Beware the Furrow of His Brow.' That's what it says clear as daylight. That's not a suggestion; that's an order!"
>
> "Well, no. It's not clear as daylight," said Misner. "It says '...the Furrow of His Brow.' There is no 'Beware' on it."

The men of the town join the debate:

> Destry, looking strained and close to tears, held up his hand and asked, "Excuse me, sir. What's so wrong about 'Be the Furrow'? 'Be the Furrow of His Brow'?"
>
> "You can't be God, boy." Nathan DuPres spoke kindly as he shook his head.
>
> "It's not being Him, sir; it's being His instrument, His justice. As a race—"
>
> "God's justice is His alone. How you going to be His instrument if you don't do what He says?" asked Reverend Pulliam. "You have to obey Him" [87].

The text again, by declining to settle the issue for readers, leaves them to focus on a more important issue than who is right. In this case, the text leads readers to appreciate the irony that Pulliam and his men claim to be righteous followers of God's will but take it upon themselves to wreak vengeance on a group of women because they cannot face their own flaws and frailties.

Regarding the interpretation of the Oven's inscription, readers find a model in Dovey, Steward Morgan's wife: "'Beware the Furrow of His Brow'? 'Be the Furrow of His Brow'? Her own opinion was that 'Furrow of His Brow' alone was enough for any age or generation. Specifying it, particularizing it, nailing its meaning down, was futile" (93). The town's historian, Pat Best, also wisely notes that the inscription can mean more than any of the men understand because they wish to impose a singular definition upon it:

> So the rule was set and lived a quietly throbbing life because it was never spoken of, except for the hint in words Zechariah forged for the Oven. More than a rule. A conundrum: "Beware the Furrow of His Brow," in which the "You" (understood), vocative case, was not a command to the believers but a threat to those who had disallowed them. It must have taken him months to think up those words—just so—to have multiple meanings: to appear stern, urging obedience to God, but slyly not identifying the understood proper noun or specifying what the Furrow might cause to happen or to whom. So the teenagers Misner organized who wanted to change it to "Be the Furrow of His Brow" were more insightful than they knew [195].

The narrative thus trains readers to interpret with open minds and to be sensitive to alternative meanings and perspectives, a crucial lesson if the text is to prepare readers for interaction with individuals from different backgrounds in an increasingly diverse society. The passage also helps train readers to read the narrative with an open mind, warning them not to impose a singular meaning on an intentionally ambiguous text. Like the repeated passage in *Beloved*'s coda ("This is not a story to pass on") which resists any singular interpretation, *Paradise* assertively insists upon open-ended readings. Morrison recognizes that readers wedded to their own perspectives alone make poor progressives in race relations. The narrator's reference to the headline in the *Herald* that brought Haven's founders out west—"Come Prepared or Not at All" (13)—might as well be meant for readers of Morrison's work.

Morrison returns in *Paradise* to another literary technique used effectively in previous work: the doppelganger, or double. Like Sula and Nel in *Sula*, Milkman and Guitar in *Song of Solomon*, and Twyla and Roberta in "Recitatif," Morrison pairs characters in *Paradise* to analyze individually some particular aspects of an otherwise single, complex consciousness. This fragmentation of what might have been a unified personality entails "the splitting up of a recognizable, unified psychological entity into separate complementary distinguishable parts represented by seemingly autonomous characters," according to Robert Rogers's classic definition of the literary doppelganger by division (5). Two critical doppelgangers in *Paradise*, the Morgan twins and the two clergymen, enable Morrison to explore the psyches of complex, imagined individuals and, moreover, to provide readers with alternative models of behavior. Pulliam and Misner as components of one doppelganger pair represent the impious touched by holiness and the godly touched by the earthly, respectively. Deacon and Steward

Morgan represent the egocentric and closed-minded and the penitent and open-minded, respectively. Steward's contempt for whites, for example, contrasts Misner's graciousness toward them:

> "Who all is that?" asked Steward.
> "Just some lost folks." Anna handed him a thirty-two-ounce tin of Blue Boy.
> "Lost folks or lost whites?"
> "Oh, Steward, please."
> "Big difference, Anna girl. Big. Right, Reverend?" Misner was just stepping back in.
> "They get lost like everybody else," said Anna.
> "Born lost. Take over the world and still lost. Right, Reverend?"
> "You just contradicted yourself." Anna laughed.
> "God has one people, Steward. You know that." Misner rubbed his hands, then blew on them.
> "Reverend," said Steward, "I've heard you say things <u>out</u> of ignorance, but this is the first time I heard you say something <u>based</u> on ignorance" [122–23].

Misner also deeply loves black folks, as is evident when he bemoans his fellow citizens' loss of heroism and communal storytelling (160–61). The narrative clearly favors, as models for readers' behavior, both Deacon's introspection and subsequent repentance, like Milkman's in *Song of Solomon*, and Misner's capacious love of humanity, regardless of race.

Both pairs of characters, however, transcend simple binary divisions.[2] All four characters, considered even without their doubles, constitute complete and complex human beings; *Paradise* is no simple allegory. Rather, by presenting various ways of responding to the same set of circumstances, these characters serve as models of behavior from which readers may choose. Furthermore, although the text clearly leads readers to favor one behavioral choice over the other in each doppelganger pair (i.e., Misner's over Pulliam's and Deacon's over Steward's), the novel also invites readers to embrace both kinds of response as human. That is, the novel does not lead readers to reject completely the less-favorable behaviors, but to recognize them and the characters who exhibit them as complex and ultimately human.

As in all her previous work, Morrison here encourages readers to abandon simplistic dichotomies of good and evil. While holding out Misner and Deacon as preferable models, her novel refrains from complete condemnation of Pulliam and Deacon. Consolata, in a mystical moment near the end of the novel, makes this point—albeit enigmatically—when she speaks to the troubled women who have become her informal charges:

> My child body, hurt and soil, leaps into the arms of a woman who teach me my body is nothing my spirit everything. I agreed her until I met another. My flesh is so hungry for itself it ate him. When he fell away the woman rescue me from my body again. Twice she saves it. When her body sickens I care for it in every way flesh works. I hold it in my arms and between my legs. Clean it, rock it, enter it to keep it breath. After she is dead I can not get past that. My bones on hers the only good thing. Not spirit. Bones.

No different from the man. My bones on his the only true thing. So I wondering where is the spirit lost in this? It is true, like bones. It is good, like bones. One sweet, one bitter. Where is it lost? Hear me, listen. Never break them in two. Never put one over the other. Eve is Mary's mother. Mary is the daughter of Eve [263].

Consolata's insistence that body and spirit, like *yin* and *yang*, are incomplete without one another recalls Baby Sugg's remarkable sermon in the Clearing in which she implores her congregants to honor their flesh as well as their spirit (*Beloved* 88–89). Like many of the text's important messages to readers, Consolata's dream-like utterance resists easy comprehension. Indeed, Consolata's own listeners fail to understand her (263), just as a citizen generations earlier eluded his auditors ("Royal, called Roy, took the floor and, without notes, gave a speech perfect in every way but intelligibility. Nobody knew what he was talking about and the parts that could be understood were plumb foolish" [194]). Readers must decipher Consolata's statement by recalling disparate incidents in her past and cross-referencing them with her speech. The effort that this exercise requires ensures the readers' deeper comprehension of the paradoxical nature of human existence which they are to embrace.

The paradoxes in *Paradise* in large part work upon Morrison's use of African ritual inheritances[3] with which she seeks to "expose the reader's own politics"—as Morrison so aptly puts it in her essay titled "Home"—while making other kinds of perception not only available but inevitable (7). Readers discover that Morrison provides only partial knowledge; the rest of the knowledge they need for accurately reading her texts comes from culture, particularly the African ritual inheritances in American culture. As Juda Bennett affirms, *Paradise* "asks its readers to examine the importance they place on fixing racial identity, hardly allowing them to remain passive readers or disingenuously uninterested" (213). However, *Paradise* also asks readers to examine the importance they place on confining spirituality to western modes of interpretation. Just as Maggie with legs like parentheses represents what readers must find buried in the text of "Recitatif," so are African ritual inheritances buried between the colonization of western modes of Christianity; to understand Morrison's characters in all of their complexity, readers must ferret out these African ritual inheritances.

African ritual inheritances, as noted by religious historian Margaret Washington Creel, were the metaphysical practice of nearly all Africans transported to the Americas during slavery (69–97). Morrison's works tend to focus on African rituals as practiced within the new world boundaries of the Americas. We maintain—as encapsulated in the words of Judika Illes—that in African American ritual inheritance novels like the works of Toni Morrison, "Africa is always the touchstone, the persistent and tenacious ancestral mother wisdom and spiritual foundation that refuses to fade away" (ix). Consequently, Morrison is leading readers to think of *Paradise* in particular as part of a community of healing stories—the transatlantic version of Ethiopian healing scrolls[4] whereby the authors are the healers (*dabtaras* or *debtaras* in Ge'ez, Tigrinya, and Amharic) creating the literary equivalent of healing scrolls with the potential of healing readers through visual rhetoric.[5]

The knowledge of the traditional indigenous cultural medicine of Africa is in danger of extinction because of the prejudices rooted in colonization, a process represented by the Convent outside of Ruby. Morrison's texts call for the informing power of these spiritual and botanical medicinal systems to be taken seriously, not just as myth or legend. They are a site where art, faith, science and prayer meet: the synergistic energy of medicine, mystery, power, spirits and the miraculous. This is why many of Morrison's points often appear to be enigmatic: Readers often fail to heed the guidance she gives, such as in the foreword of her first novel, *The Bluest Eye*. Morrison states that full comprehension for readers lies in the codes embedded in black culture (*Bluest Eye* xii-xii). If readers are unfamiliar with or disregard the translation guides provided by the codes, they will not fully comprehend Morrison's messages. In fact, the reclamation of African cultural heritage is at the center of all of Morrison's novels, as is rewriting the dominant white perspective on the value of blackness.

The techniques and thematic concerns Morrison employs in her writing mimic the healing properties of Ethiopian healing scrolls. Telling stories helps Morrison as well as her readers to heal. Therefore, when Morrison "reads" the text of her body[6] and writes that text, she is healed, and consequently, her readers are, as well. Since ills such as pernicious racism perpetuate collective trauma, Morrison's literary remedies are appropriately communal.

The story arcs of African ritual inheritance novels, including *Paradise*, represent the various African healing processes that are used to cure a range of reader ailments. For example, in Toni Cade Bambara's *The Salt Eaters*, the narrative voice can be seen as the prayer language that accompanies the images on a healing scroll. Within the novel—the transatlantic version of the scroll—this prayer language helps the protagonist, Velma, and by extension, the readers, to translate the images, the visual rhetoric of the novel. Part of Dabtara Bambara's healing prayer for Velma, as well as the reader, is to "tap the brain for any knowledge of initiate rites lying dormant there, recognizing that life depended on it, that initiation was the beginning of transformation and that the ecology of the self, the tribe, the species, the earth depended on just that" (247). The prayer declares "the thunderous beginning of the new humanism, the new spiritism [that could be created] if only attention could be riveted on the simplicity of the karmic law—cause and effect. There were choices to be noted. Decisions to be made" (248).

Channette Romero declares:

The Salt Eaters suggests that remembering "dormant" belief traditions will allow people of color to be initiated into a higher state of consciousness that transcends limited notions of nationalism and hold the power to transform "the self, the tribe, the species, the earth." However, this quote indicates that the power to transform the self and the earth is possible only if people recognize the larger effects of their choices, and act accordingly. The novel alerts its readers to *ideological choice*, and the moral implications of their ideologies [132].

Romero's assessment resonates with Morrison's view that readers are the most important repository of knowledge about their illnesses—their political positions, assumptions, presumptions, and racial codifications and their participatory role in the perpetuation of such a system—and about what is needed to heal that illness. Once readers recognize what is needed to complete their healing story and share that story with other readers with similar illnesses, the story then has the potential power to heal the entire community of readers suffering from that collective illness.

Similarly Consolata and all of the women at the convent in *Paradise* undergo a spiritual metamorphosis when Consolata is freed from the oppressive spiritual practices of her colonizers and opens herself up to the old world practices of her ancestors. The story arc in *Paradise* incorporates the prayer language—the narrative voice in the novel—as well as the talismanic images—body outlines on the cellar floor—that are found in Ethiopian healing scrolls. Consolata had the Markan healing gift of touch referred to as "stepping in" in the novel. When Scout Morgan dies in a car accident, the narrator states:

> Consolata looked at the body and without hesitation removed her glasses and focused on the trickles of red discoloring his hair. She stepped in. Saw the stretch of road he had dreamed through, felt the flip of the truck, the headache, the chest pressure, the unwillingness to breathe. As from a distance she heard Easter and July kicking the truck and moaning. Inside the boy she saw a pinpoint of light receding. Pulling up energy that felt like fear, she stared at it until it widened. Then more, more, so air could come seeping, at first, then rushing rushing in. Although it hurt like the devil to look at it, she concentrated as though the lungs in need were her own.
> Scout opened his eyes, groaned and sat up [245].

Consolata had been taught to view such things as practicing witchcraft and for a long time was unable to accept her ability to heal. However, Lone Dupree (the town of Ruby's dabtara) made it clear to her that it was not witchcraft but a gift from God she was fool to despise (246–47). Consolata "came to terms with it in a way she persuaded herself would not offend Him or place her soul in peril. It was a question of language. Lone called it 'stepping in.' Consolata said it was 'seeing in.' Thus the gift was 'in sight.' Something God made free to anyone who wanted to develop it" (247). Not only is Morrison a dabtara of the Paradise healing scroll (the novel); Consolata acts as a type of dabtara within the scroll allowing the women in the

Convent to obtain a wholeness that was impossible before the healing ritual in the cellar, saying to them, "I call myself Consolata Sosa. If you want to be here you do what I say. Eat how I say. Sleep when I say. And I will teach you what you are hungry for" (262).

The narrator continues:

> In the beginning the most important thing was the template.... When each found the position she could tolerate on the cold, uncompromising floor, Consolata walked around her and painted the body's silhouette. Once the outlines were complete, each was instructed to remain there....
>
> That is how the loud dreaming began. How the stories rose in that place. Half-tales and the never-dreamed escaped from their lips.... And it was never important to know who said the dream.
>
> ...The templates drew them like magnets.... They spoke to each other about what had been dreamed and what had been drawn.
>
> ...With Consolata in charge, like a new and revised Reverend Mother, feeding them bloodless food and water alone to quench their thirst, they altered. They had to be reminded of the moving bodies they wore, so seductive were the alive ones [their templates] below [262–65].

As the dabtara within the scroll, Consolata exposes the vile spirits torturing the women at the Convent, drives them out, and seals each woman's spiritual entryway to prevent the evil spirits from returning. Readers struggle with the way their cultural, racial, and gender assumptions and identities affect their reading of the story as it is through those assumptions and identities that Morrison leads readers to see "...that all knowledge is partial and everyone reads out of their own identity.... In asking us to become participants in the creation of story, in both the delineation of character identities and in what their racial complexion signifies, ... we begin to see through our own cultural beliefs and conditioning" (Bennett 212). Bennett concludes, "If we are as generous and wise as Morrison, we challenge others to do the same" (212). Such a participatory mode of reading allows readers to challenge "traditional" wisdom and begin the process of understanding and accepting the multiple perspectives of their reader identity.

In order to be whole, the women at the Convent must know their stories through esoteric knowledge, as is revealed by Connie's comment to Mavis: "Scary things not always outside. Most scary things inside" (39). To help readers experience an equivalent sense of this interiority, Morrison gives them access to secret wisdom and knowledge that is only available to readers who come ready to transcend the limits of dominant, white worldviews.

Morrison uses this secret wisdom to unfold *Paradise* and her novels in a nonlinear fashion to engage the reader in the hopes of bringing them to an understanding that "what liberates us is," according to Theodotus the Gnostic, "the knowledge of who we were, what we became; where we were, whereunto we have been thrown; whereunto we speed, wherefrom we are redeemed; what birth is, and what rebirth" (Clemens Alexandrinus, Excerpta ex Theodoto 78.2). In other words, the reader finds salvation through gnosis, or esoteric knowledge. According to Aoi Mori, "Morrison ... never feeds the readers with specific information. She simply shows a glimpse of the ... fact[s] and leaves the readers to explore the background of the incident. By doing so, Morrison encourages the readers to participate in the novel, respecting their intuition and sensitivity" (41). Thus, the reader is bringing a living experience to the text and completing its meaning as an active agent, which equips them to read the counter-text to hegemonic Eurocentric ways of knowing that Morrison wishes to deconstruct. Morrison's persistent, uncompromising use of ambiguity on multiple levels pushes the reader to relinquish the obvious sense of her words and to find the hidden meaning of individual statements and of the novels as a whole. Morrison thus leads the reader into questioning what they believe and why. This destabilization leads readers to investigate their beliefs, particularly about themselves or a particular group of people, without questioning why they believe it. As readers consider the historical facts related to Morrison's novels, including *Paradise*, they began to understand that many of the hegemonic beliefs they hold are untrue, but often terribly destructive.

In addition to the admonition that readers embrace all aspects of their contradictory selves, *Paradise* returns to and augments themes in earlier works of Morrison's. In some cases, as with the theme of skin-color privilege, Morrison signifies upon herself, revising in ways that reinvigorate preceding lessons for readers. As discussed in Chapter 2, Pecola Breedlove succumbs to madness brought on by her community's promulgation of skin-color hierarchy, which makes her yearn to be what she cannot be. Leading readers to own their complicity in maintaining skin-color hierarchy, *The Bluest Eye* depicts the exorbitant price of privileging lighter skin. In *Paradise*, Morrison twists the idea of skin-color hierarchy, pulling readers to the realization that privileging dark skin similarly rends a community—in this case, the all-black town of Ruby, Oklahoma.[7] In Ruby, the so-called 8-rock black folk, dark as the blackest "8-rock" coal, are doubly prideful—that is, both proud of their accomplishments and guilty of the sin of pride.[8] As Pat realizes, this arrogance, this blind adherence to the notion of blood purity, helps destroy her own lighter-skinned daughter, Billie Delia, and contributes greatly to the ruination of the town, a sad irony given that 8-rock blood purity "was their recipe. That was their deal. For Immortality" (217). If the town's most powerful citizens see a threat to the 8-rock bloodlines as a threat to the town itself, it stands to follow that they perceive women—the childbearers—to be the primary source of danger. This misogynistic line of reasoning leads to the extreme act of extermination that opens and closes the novel. In the novel's nearly essentialist characterizations of men and women,

Ruby's men seem much like *Song of Solomon*'s Macon Dead and the women, especially the maternal Consolata, seem much like Pilate.[9]

Readers, especially those who also have read *The Bluest Eye* (and *Tar Baby*, in which the issue of dark-skin privilege becomes a metaphoric wedge between Son and Jadine), thus confront the spiraling evil of skin-color hierarchy, no matter which shade is privileged. *Paradise* provides a provocative expansion of this theme, moving beyond the powerful but incomplete notion that prejudice derives exclusively from white oppression. The narrative voice, expressing Pat's private thoughts, states that

> for ten generations they had believed the division they fought to close was free against slave and rich against poor. Usually, but not always, white against black. Now they saw a new separation: light-skinned against black. Oh, they knew there was a difference in the minds of whites, but it had not struck them before that it was of consequence, serious consequence, to Negroes themselves.... The sign of racial purity they had taken for granted had become a stain [194].

The dangerous and ultimately destructive attitude inherent in black-against-black discrimination strikes readers as particularly ironic, given the treatment meted out to their own ancestors in the Disallowing, when the impoverished but proud migrants were turned away by the citizens of an all-black town:

> Their horror of whites was convulsive but abstract. They saved the clarity of their hatred for the men who had insulted them in ways too confounding for language: first by excluding them, then by offering them staples to exist in that very exclusion. Everything anybody wanted to know about the citizens of Haven or Ruby lay in the ramifications of that one rebuff out of many [189].

The painful irony stems from the fact that Ruby's current residents vividly remember, but refuse to learn from, the Disallowing, which recalls the refusal of Mercy Hospital to admit blacks in *Song of Solomon* but reverberates more disturbingly because it is perpetrated by other black citizens rather than by a white institution.

The novel's astounding conclusion, exemplifying Morrison's attention to the complexities of intersectionality, caps the two primary themes of Morrison's oeuvre: racism and sexism. As Misner and Deacon represent moderation, tolerance, and love ("It was Deacon Morgan who changed the most. It was as though he had looked in his brother's face and did not like himself anymore" [300]), the Convent's women represent transcendent sisterhood. Like the love between Nel and Sula which transcends the death of the latter, the bonds among the women of the Convent cannot be severed by circumstances, however violent. The Faulknerian blending of their stories (264) represents their unity in suffering, a point underscored by Morrison's refusal to identify which is the white woman who gets shot.[10] An assault against one of the women is an attack upon all of them. In the chaotic raid scene, readers note that Steward shoots the white woman (285), three women fight the attackers (286), and Steward shoots Consolata (289). Witnesses tell Roger Best that three women lie dead in the grass and two in the house, but he finds no bodies upon his arrival at the Convent (292). In the denouement, Mavis, Grace, Seneca, and Pallas seem to be unharmed (310-17). Their appearances, however, remain strange and ghostly. Having learned that Morrison eschews divisions between the natural and the supernatural, readers remain unable to resolve the mystery of who survives and who dies. In Morrison's fictional world, all of the women live, whether in body or in spirit.

Paradise ends hopefully[11]:

> Suddenly Richard Misner knew he would stay. Not only because Anna wanted to, or because Deek Morgan had sought him out for a confession of sorts, but also because there was no better battle to fight, no better place to be than among these outrageously beautiful, flawed and proud people [306].

Misner's conclusion urges a response from readers. Acknowledging the weaknesses in himself and his neighbors, Misner chooses not to turn away but to make a difference. *Paradise*, Morrison's endnote to the twentieth century, asks readers to do the same. For white readers, the difference might stem from a self-understanding that includes culpability for the racist history that engendered mass migrations of black citizens. For black readers, the difference might arise out of refusal to reverse, rather than transcend, a skin-color hierarchy. In any case, the text, like all of Morrison's previous work, demands from readers coalition and action.

6

Home

Just as her protagonist, Frank Money, comes full-circle in Toni Morrison's tenth novel, *Home* (2012), the author returns to numerous themes that run through all of her work: community, masculinity and femininity, the power of love to transcend unspeakable evil, and, of course, "home" as a place and a concept. Again, she masterfully guides her readers' cognitive and emotional responses through ingenious techniques that belie the apparent simplicity of the tale itself, told in a scant 147 pages. In this chapter, we examine how *Home* moves its readers, largely in light of her earlier novels, especially *Paradise* and *Love*, whose themes, we argue, find emphasis and nuance in *Home*.

The titles of Morrison's novels typically contribute to Morrison's mission to train readers, encapsulating some of the "lessons" she imparts in the novels' texts. In this case, there is no home for Frank until he undergoes his own transformation. Moreover, the novel's title itself disrupts simple understandings of what constitutes a home. Just as the Convent in *Paradise* belies simple interpretations of the novel's title, and just as readers find almost no examples of love in *Love*, "home" is a complex concept in *Home*. Insofar as Morrison's novels' titles are intentionally multilayered, we find it worthwhile to examine here how previous novel titles influence, intertextually, potential understandings of the title *Home*, using, as an example, Morrison's earlier novel, *Love*. As Angelyn Mitchell points out, Morrison "often questions idealized notions of love: maternal, paternal, fraternal and sororal (whether biologically or in terms of friendship), sexual, passionate, platonic, self, racial, etc." ("*Love*").

By titling her 2003 novel *Love*, Morrison begins to set a (humane) trap for readers for whom the title calls to mind heterosexual, romantic love. (The word *love* appears only seven times in the novel.) Readers learn early in the novel that two female characters vie for the love of Bill Cosey, a competition apparently won by Heed. Such a conflict, especially when it features a powerful man, seems conventional, if not downright trite. Morrison, of course, subverts readers' expectations yet again. Quite late in the novel, readers finally discover that the "winner" of Bill Cosey, Heed, was a child when she married him. Wyatt states that the scene of Heed's honeymoon with Cosey "comes as a shock to the reader, who through the first 127 pages of text has been led to assume that Heed's marriage was age-appropriate—that it was, indeed, all that a romantic marriage could be (62). The conflation of honeymoon with paper dolls and coloring books emphasizes the temporal contradiction condensed in the figure of child-bride" (Wyatt, "*Love*'s Time," 196).

All of Morrison's novels in some way connect justice and love. Megan Sweeney, for example, observes that "as Morrison's novel [*Love*] deconstructs myths about love, it also deconstructs myths about justice; indeed, *Love* might just as well be titled *Justice*" (445). (In fact, Morrison had stated two years before her death that her next novel was tentatively titled *Justice* [Kaiser and Manyika].) Moreover, Morrison herself, in her seminal essay "Home," states that "the term domesticates the racial project, [and] moves the job of unmattering race away from pathetic yearning and futile desire; away from an impossible future or an irretrievable and probably nonexistent Eden to a manageable, doable, modern human activity" (3).[1] She hopefully imagines a dissolution of the power of race but demands practical action to effect that change.

Morrison's anti-racist project therefore requires readers, of course. Judylyn S. Ryan remarks upon Morrison's ability to motivate readers to action: "Morrison reveals the world as it is with such clarity that readers are prompted to consider what needs doing, what must be done" (161). In *Love*, however, Morrison never lays out a clear path for readers to follow, as they must find their own, symbolized, perhaps, by Junior's befuddled wandering through town in the novel's initial scene. Indeed, Mary Paniccia Carden states that *Love* "suggests that the best possibilities for finding a comfortable, equitable place require leaving well-worn paths and going along uncharted ways, where the established streets do not and cannot go" (143). Ultimately, although *Love* in some ways is about the absence of love among its characters, we would argue that, ultimately, it *is* about love in what it endeavors to inspire among its readers: the drive toward social justice. In that sense, as Anissa Janine Wardi suggests (202), we should read the title *Love* as a verb, not a noun. We would go further to say that its readers ought to take it as Morrison's *command*.

We return now to *Home*. Like *The Bluest Eye* and *Beloved*, *Home* launches with an intentional disorientation of the reader, textual and meta-textual enigmas that make what should be a familiar place—a home—into a disconcerting mystery. The epigraph, presented in the form of an eleven-line, free-verse poem Morrison originally wrote as part of the lyrics of a score that she co-authored with André Previn, opens with three questions that become key ones for Frank as well as for the reader:

> Whose house is this?
> Whose night keeps out the light
> In here?
> Say, who owns this house? [Previn and Morrison, vii]

The poem's speaker seems troubled at his[2] inability to identify the house, whose interior is dark and sinister. Although Morrison originally wrote these words nearly a decade before publishing *Home*, the poem perfectly prefigures Frank's discomfort with his estranged hometown of Lotus, Georgia, which he recalls as "the worst place in the world" (83). The poem turns out to be even more appropriate as it concludes: "Say, tell me, why does its lock fit my key?" (vii). When first encountering the epigraph, however, readers are unaware that by the novel's conclusion, Frank will not only have reclaimed Lotus as his home—answering the metaphoric question of why the home's lock fits his key—but also come to terms with the "night" that had kept "light" out of his own memory, his own soul.

In typical Morrisonian style, the speaker confounds expectations by reversing "lock" and "key"; one might more naturally say, "Why does my key fit its lock?" By reversing "lock" and "key," however, Morrison privileges the part not controlled by the speaker, rendering the speaker that much more powerless while confronting what is even more disturbing than the mystery of the house's ownership: the fact that the speaker is unknowingly its owner. Analogously, readers at first are likely to believe the narrator when he says of the house, "It's not mine" (vii), but even in the space of eleven lines, Morrison has undermined the narrator's credibility when the narrator acknowledges that his key fits the lock. As in her previous novels, Morrison puts readers on notice: Suspend credulity—do not trust the master narrative—and think for yourselves.

Although every one of Morrison's novels features an unreliable narrator of one form or another, *Home* takes the technique one step further. From its first chapter, in the first person from Frank Money's point of view, Morrison's protagonist speaks directly to and sometimes even argues with the narrator. He is reluctant for his own tale to be told: "Since you're set on telling my story..." (5), he says, implying that he would just as soon have it remain untold, reminiscent of the final lines of *Beloved* in which the narrator says, "This is not a story to pass on" (274–75). This odd and brilliant conceit establishes a kind of conspiracy in which the narrator relates to readers what appears to be a private, perhaps confessional tale, piquing readers' interest. In subsequent chapters, Frank's relationship with the third-person narrator becomes increasingly complex, bemusing readers. At times, Frank admonishes the narrator: "Don't paint me as some enthusiastic hero [for heading back to Lotus to rescue my sister]" (84). Elsewhere, he challenges the narrator: "You never lived [in Lotus] so you don't know what it was like" (84); he says of Korea, "You can't imagine it because you weren't there" (93); and, describing summer heat in the South, he says to the unseen narrator, "Describe that if you know how" (41).

Most bewildering, Frank even contradicts the narrator, with whom he alternates chapters. For example, in chapter five, he tells the third-person narrator that what the narrator had written earlier was untrue, chastising the narrator: "I don't think you know much about love. Or me" (69). Having a protagonist directly challenge the third-person narrator certainly undermines readers' credulity, to say the least. Moreover, if one imagines Morrison herself as the narrator, the irony is multifaceted: A literal figure of Morrison's imagination and invention is accusing Morrison of knowing little about him, and also little about love, although one would be hard-pressed to find a writer more sophisticated about various forms of love than Morrison.

Like all of Morrison's novels, *Home* presents a tale of individual and collective trauma and inchoate recovery from it. In *Home*, this theme engenders the unusual, ingenious structure of a story dictated by the protagonist to an unnamed narrator of limited omniscience. Evelyn Jaffe Schreiber has cited "the importance of verbalizing trauma and the need for an empathetic witness to hear the trauma story if one is to recover" (2), noting characters' "hard-won personal victories available through verbalization of trauma and community sharing" (31). Although Frank has not completely healed by the end of the novel—and might never be fully healed—he is on his way, having verbalized his story to the narrator.

By having "heard" his story, readers, too, participate in Frank's recovery, their empathy having been elicited by Morrison's tale. Insofar as they are complicit in the micro- and macro-aggressions Frank faces upon his return from Korea, readers are called upon by Morrison to contribute to his healing and to the nation's. Aitor Ibarrola states that "it could be argued that *Home* is a joint enterprise in which trauma victims, who offer their testimony, and a scribe ... cooperate to give shape and meaning to stories that had remained previously silent" (117). He writes, "The presence of somebody willing to bear witness and to assist in the recovery of those [suppressed] memories is crucial for the victim's reconstruction of a sense of self" (117). Lakeisha Meyer goes further, suggesting that readers can learn to process their own traumas through narratives like Morrison's (242). The narrator of *Home*, however, is a medium, an imperfect scribe, an implied auditor. In a sense, then, Morrison must enlist living readers in the real world to "hear" Frank's story to enable his journey toward recovery. Figuratively, Frank's tale remains dormant until readers open the book and co-create the story, guided by the text.

The first chapter is Frank's, in his own voice, with which he recounts a dramatic, formative moment in his and his little sister's childhood. He (before readers have identified the speaker as Frank) starts off: "They rose up like men. We saw them. Like men they stood" (3). Soon readers realize he is speaking of a pair of battling stallions.[3] In presumably telling the narrator this story, Frank begins to recall that he and his sister witnessed the ignoble, hasty burial of a man's body while lying hidden in the grass. "I really forgot about the burial," he states. "I only remembered the horses" (5).

Morrison thereby immediately establishes themes of repressed memory. Moreover, in what seems at first encounter a minor aside from Frank, collective—a community's and, by extension, society's—forgetfulness also emerges in this chapter, as Frank recalls that the adults were too distracted to notice, let alone punish, the two children for returning home late: "Some disturbance had their attention," he states (5). Like a prestidigitator, Morrison distracts readers from what later turns out to be crucially important—the "disturbance" bound up with what the children saw—with the pageantry of the warring horses. As she has done with her earlier novels, she sets the protagonist up as a model for readers to follow, placing them in the same position of confusion. Like Frank, readers have crucial information withheld from them, and learn the difficult truth only when they are prepared for it, analogous to Frank's own journey "home" to a truth that, readers later learn, he possessed all along but was ill-prepared to face.

The horses, of course, are significant themselves. "They bit each other like dogs," Frank states, "but when they stood, ... we held our breath in wonder" (3-4). He continues: "They were so beautiful. So brutal. And they stood like men" (5). In this complex constellation of similes, Morrison connects the masculine, noble image of stallions with, on the one hand, the savage depiction of dogs, and on the other, the upright, civilized image of men, who themselves are capable of both iniquity and sublimity. The evocative trope, "they stood like men," also anticipates the sign that Frank nails to a tree at the novel's conclusion: "Here Stands a Man" (145).

The structure of the novel itself furthers Morrison's intent to disrupt readers' expectations. The novel comprises seventeen chapters—seventeen signifying a balance of spirit and order in Christian numerology (Levend Water), as well as being a prime number, which suggests irreducibility (this being a remarkably compact tale, as concentrated as a *haiku* which [coincidentally?] always comprises seventeen syllables)—which alternate in the first dozen chapters between first-person narrations by the protagonist, Frank, and a (partly) omniscient third-person narrator. Rather than switching back to Frank, however, chapter thirteen retains the omniscient narrator's voice. This syncopation comes at the novel's climax, as Frank finally finds his sister, Cee, whom the women's community of Lotus patiently and lovingly heal from horrific sexual experimentation perpetrated upon her by her employer, Dr. Beauregard. Then, at the novel's denouement, Frank narrates chapter fourteen, a continuation of the climax, in which he realizes and confesses that it was he, not his fellow soldier, who shot a young Korean girl in the face after experiencing the overwhelming shame of arousal at her sexual advance. Frank then has the final say in chapter seventeen, wherein he recounts, in ten brief lines, his healed sister inviting him, restored from his own trauma, to "go home" (147). With that satisfying resolution, readers, too, have productively transcended the pain of witnessing Frank's recollection of wartime horror, assuaged by the feminine love of Lotus, and are ready to move on, although the healing journey is finished for neither Frank nor the novel's readers.

Like several of Morrison's novels, *Home* elaborates a theme of a recovery *of* memory that enables a recovery *from* memory, another instance of what Morrison famously calls "re-memory" in *Beloved*—"the way subjugated [individuals or] peoples reconstruct histories which have been destroyed by oppressive practices such as colonialism" (Boswell 32).[4] Just as *Beloved* subtly but powerfully persuades readers to remember, and reconcile themselves to, the national trauma of slavery's brutality rather than to succumb either to the unhelpful and irresponsible elision of or, on the other hand, the neoliberal tendency to wallow in guilt over Americans' national trauma, *Home* invisibly cajoles readers to cope with the toll of the Korean War nationally and globally. Left with self-destructive bitterness after the war, Frank models for readers the gradual reconciliation that comes from first facing the suppressed truth and then coming to terms with it by accepting and returning the love of one's family and community, one's regenerative, emotional home.

In Morrison's world, love and home are intertwined. As one would expect, the titular theme of "home" in this novel is rich and complex, as it is throughout Morrison's oeuvre. In Morrison's work, "home" is a fluid state of mind as much as a physical or geographical site. Claudia Drieling notes: "From a writer's perspective, Morrison proposes 'home' as a continual process of creating subversive narrative concepts and forms of language that aim to reconcile positions of exclusiveness and inclusiveness, of defiance and affirmation.... '[H]ome' is revealed in Morrison's concept as fundamentally ambivalent" (16). From one's home, one imagines the world outside; while outside, one imagines the world at home. Both worlds bear the markings of oppressive societal and cultural narratives, such that individuals must recast narratives to feel at home when they are at home. Quoting from Yi-Fu Tuan's seminal work in cultural geography, *Space and Place*, Drieling states: "It is through 'routine activity' that human beings transform unfamiliar space into familiar place. As a result of this process, '[h]ome is an intimate place' (Tuan, 1977, 144), and as such, it is a place that 'a person knows and constructs [as] a reality' (Tuan, 1977, 8), so that from it, argues Tuan, individuals derive a sense of emotional attachment and rootedness" (14). Through his reunion with his sister Cee, and his ultimate appreciation for the feminine community of Lotus, Frank begins to remake his mental image of the town from "the worst place in the world" (83) to "home."

It takes a while for Frank to recognize the real reason he hated Lotus and rejected it as his home. It is not the town's lack of sidewalks or indoor plumbing, but the racial violence represented by the burial of a lynched African American man that he and Cee had witnessed but he had forgotten. "As a pivotal, defining childhood memory, it [the lynching] speaks volumes about the sense of danger and instability that is wrapped up in Frank's ideas of nature and of home," writes Valerie Smith (133). What has changed by the end of the novel, such that Frank's feelings toward the town have softened, is not Lotus, but Frank, and with him, *Home*'s readers.

All of Morrison's novels "partake of both the illusion of realism and the artifice of metaphor," notes Cheryl Wall (54). She writes, "The illusion of realism enables us to know the places in the novels, while the artifice of metaphor cautions us that we do not know them as well as we think. By attending to the metaphorical, we confront the moral domains that are central to Morrison's art. These obligations, in turn, inform our reading protocol" (54). As *Home* insists that readers reconcile its sites represented with verisimilitude, such as Seattle and Chicago, with its fantastic, fictional sites, such as Lotus (whose very name evokes the exotic), they begin to release their mental dichotomies of "real" and "imagined."

Indeed, places—even "real" ones—actually are socially constructed, as are the meanings we attach to them. "America" is as much an imagined place as Lotus. Yet, like the concept of "race," social constructions can bear powerful consequences. How we use them—how we craft stories of and about them—determines whether they are regressive or progressive. Wall says of *Home*:

> Readers get a sense of the social interactions in black communities of Chicago and Atlanta in the 1950s, but that sense depends as much on what readers bring to the text as what the text represents. To be sure, many come with an understanding of life in segregated America.... Although readers may rue the gaps [in Morrison's depictions of locales], they can fill them in. As they do, they might recognize how the absences put the moral questions that the novel raises in bold relief. What does it take to be a man? What obligations do people have to one another? [63]

Smith elaborates, in a passage that bears extended quotation, on the metaphorical concept of home in the novel's historical context:

> *Home* invites readers to think not so much about the significance of literal houses, but rather, about the broader meaning of home. More specifically, it asks us to think about the meaning of home during the 1950s, a decade for which many late twentieth- and twenty-first century Americans have become nostalgic. Contemporary US culture often associates the 1950s with an idealized vision of postwar prosperity and intact nuclear families and evinces a fascination with the fashion, architecture, and design

of the period. Indeed, despite its association with the waning days of Jim Crow segregation, African Americans will also often romanticize this period as a time when black communities were more unified both socially and politically, and when people watched out for each other's children. Within the context of the failure of public education in this country and the broken promise of the 1954 *Brown vs. Board of Education of Topeka* decision, some will even yearn for a return to the pre–Brown era as a time when primary and secondary schools were safer, and public education was more effective. *Home* suggests that these idealized images of the 1950s depend upon a willed act of forgetting the complexities and contradictions of the period. In this novel, Morrison revisits that era in order to reflect on the complicated ways disenfranchised African Americans might have experienced it. By examining the idea of home from a variety of perspectives, she casts the '50s as a time when the notion of home was under assault [132].

By leading readers to remember the 1950s in all its complexity—including the unsavory and in fact traumatizing events of the era[5]—Morrison points the way toward collective recovery.

As she has done in all of her previous novels, Morrison uses textual gaps to enlist readers in the co-creation of the story, pulling them in intellectually and emotionally such that they undergo their own transformation along with the characters. Again, rather than spelling out key aspects of the plot and their implications, she provides only hints, such that the deeper meaning takes shape not on the page but in readers' minds.

Sometimes the gaps seem small, but pack a wallop. For example, after escaping the hospital where he awoke, utterly confused and amnesic, furtively making his way south in response to a cryptic message about his gravely ill sister, he gets off the train and sees a gasoline station: "He wanted to get into the bathroom, pee, and look in the mirror to see if he had an eye infection [because he had been seeing disturbing visions], but the sign on the door stopped him" (23). Rather than tell readers that the sign said something like, "Whites Only," Morrison guides readers to supply the humiliating truth themselves.

In other cases, the textual gaps are significant and consequential, but their impact comes much later when the text finally reveals crucial information. In the same scene in which Frank is denied the use of a restroom by dehumanizing Jim Crow segregation, he thinks to himself about his former lover, Lily, who had soothed his self-incriminating flashbacks to the war in which he witnessed the deaths of his two best friends:

> Only with Lily did the pictures fade, move behind a screen in his brain, pale but waiting, waiting and accusing. Why didn't you hurry? If you had gotten there sooner you could have helped him. You could have pulled him behind the hill the way you did Mike. And all of that killing you did afterward? Women running, dragging children along. And that old one-legged man on a crutch hobbling at the edge of the road so as not to slow down the other, swifter ones? You blew a hole in his head because you thought it would make up for the frosted urine on Mike's pants and avenge the lips

calling mama. Did it? Did it work? And the girl. What did she ever do to deserve what happened to her? [21–22].

Unbeknownst to readers, this casual mention of a girl seems to be a minor enigma. As the story continues, however, readers discover who the girl was (a young Korean girl offering sex, a behavior suggesting that she had been sexually abused, perhaps by other American soldiers), what happened to her (she was shot to death), and at whose hands (Frank's), but only after being continually misled by the unreliable first-person narrator—Frank himself—and the novel's fallible, third-person narrator.

This central, textual enigma unfolds gradually through the entire novel. In chapter nine, Frank first begins to elucidate the incident, describing how a fellow soldier, his relief guard, encounters the little Korean girl who shocks him by touching his crotch and saying something that sounds like, "Yum-yum." Frank recalls, "As soon as I look away from her hand to her face, see the two missing teeth, the fall of black hair above eager eyes, he blows her away" (95). As Frank recalls his horror, readers believe they finally have arrived at the truth regarding the protagonist's demons. "Thinking back on it now," he says, "I think the guard felt more than disgust. I think he felt tempted and that is what he had to kill" (96). He bitterly adds, "Yum-yum."

By expressing some degree of empathy for his comrade, despite his horror, Frank lays the groundwork for his own rehabilitation, modeling for the reader what turns out to be a profoundly difficult self-forgiveness. Like Frank, however, readers are not ready for the ultimate truth. First, Frank must learn to keep the ghosts, the memories, at bay. About two-thirds of the way through the story, as he recalls the rage he felt after witnessing his two best friends' battlefield deaths and the guard's killing of the little Korean girl, he "suddenly realized that those memories, powerful as they were, did not crush him anymore or throw him into paralyzing despair" (100).

Readers need not wait long to discover "what else was troubling him." As chapter fourteen begins, Frank speaks again directly to the third-person narrator to drop a bombshell, as it were:

> I have to say something to you right now. I have to tell the whole truth. I lied to you and I lied to me. I hid it from you because I hid it from me.... My mourning was so thick it completely covered my shame.
> Then Cee told me about seeing a baby girl smile all through the house, in the air, the clouds. It hit me. Maybe that little girl wasn't waiting around to be born to her. Maybe it was already dead, waiting for me to step up and say how.
> I shot the Korean girl in her face.
> I am the one she touched.
> I am the one who saw her smile.
> I am the one she said "Yum-yum" to.
> I am the one she aroused.
> …

> How could I let her live after she took me down to a place I didn't know was in me?
>
> ...
>
> You can keep on writing, but I think you ought to know what's true [133–34].

Like Sethe and Paul D in *Beloved*, who could not carry on with their shared future until they dispatched the ghost of Beloved by confronting their own histories, Frank—who earlier had criticized a police officer for shooting the then-eight-year-old son of a newfound friend, saying, "You can't just shoot a kid" (31)—cannot find peace until he settles up with the ghost of a young girl he himself had shot. Moreover, it takes the powerful, triumphant love of a women's community to make that possible, just as it does in *Beloved*.

The healing has begun, but clearly has not concluded. Frank needs—and readers need—to learn and process more. As he watches Cee recover from her own horrific trauma, aided by the stern, loving women of Lotus, Frank realizes that she "was gutted, infertile, but not beaten. She could know the truth, accept it, and keep on quilting. Frank tried to sort out what else was troubling him and what to do about it," the third-person narrator states (132).

Frank's inchoate healing is enabled only because he is learning gradual lessons. His circumstances are preparing him to face his past only when he is ready. Morrison employs this strategy of delaying characters'—and readers'—understanding in other novels, as well. As perhaps most easily recognized in *Beloved*, *Love* also features a plot structure described by many critics as circular. Katrina Harack connects the structure to trauma, which, as in *Beloved*, must be approached carefully to avoid alienating readers at the outset:

> The form of Morrison's novel is inherently connected to issues of memory—circling around primal scenes of trauma, the story is narrated by L (who was a cook at Cosey's resort, but is now dead), and the reader has access to more information than L would have had while she was alive [259].

As we argue in our chapter on *Beloved*, "spiral"—if not "whirlpool"— might be a better descriptor than "circular" regarding the shape of Morrison's plots. The stories gradually pull readers toward an awful, central truth for which the text has prepared its readers; in the case of *Love*, the slowly revealed truth centers on Heed's and Christine's estrangement and on Bill Cosey's murder. Cynthia Wallace notes that

> many of the most revealing pieces of the puzzle arrive near the end of the novel, suspending even partial understanding of the narrative and undermining our confidence in our own knowledge: we have to learn to wait for the text, submit to it, trust it to catch us up in its own good time as it teaches us humility and submission to its mystery.
>
> ...Even the question of which woman dies at the end—Heed or Christine—is obscured by a mix of signifiers that seem to point to both women [385].

Humann elaborates further:

> [T]he fragmented narration affects how readers perceive these characters, in part because it defers the moment when readers learn the circumstances that led to Heed['s] and Cosey's marriage. One effect of this is that readers of the novel may not initially sympathize with Heed as much as they would have if they had, instead, learned early on that her family forced her into marrying Cosey, a man who had already sexually molested her. Moreover, by delaying the moment when this information is revealed, Morrison builds suspense regarding the reasons that have caused Heed and Christine to become adversaries [261].

The construction of *Love*'s plot thus prepares readers to respond deeply and personally: "The narrative structure gives this love story an ethical dimension, as readers are prompted to confront, revalue, revise, and expand their notions of love," according to Jean Wyatt ("Love," 261).

By implicitly advocating reconciliation and self-forgiveness in *Home*, Morrison is not suggesting forgetting. As a model for readers, Frank remains troubled as he reflects upon how his dogged mourning for his dead friends "let him off the hook, kept the Korean child hidden. Now the hook was deep inside his chest and nothing would dislodge it. The best he could hope for was time to work it loose" (135). The narrator adds, "Meantime there were worthwhile things that needed doing" (135). Analogously, Morrison urges the collective American conscience to acknowledge the untold suffering of the Korean War—and all wars—in order to come to terms with it and move on, productively and communally.

In addition to her extraordinary use of an unreliable narrator—in the case of *Home*, *two* unreliable narrators—Morrison also masterfully infuses the story with symbolic systems that provide depth and structure to the novel. Most prevalent and crucial is a tree motif, which Morrison actually establishes before the book is even opened. The first hardcover edition of *Home* features on its cover an embossment of a detail from a Roman altar dating to the first century CE in which two birds—which here suggest Frank and Cee—alight upon the branches of a bay tree, a doubly fitting symbol: first, the altar belonged to a ten-year-old girl, perhaps roughly the same age as the girl Frank kills in Korea; and second, laurels made of bay leaves represent victory (Hall and Clark), suggesting that, by the story's conclusion, Frank and Cee together, figuratively and literally, conquer death.

Within the novel, the first reference to a tree comes early and laden with violent tragedy. As Frank runs in the snow away from the hospital at the beginning of the novel, he recalls how, at age four, his and other black families on the edge of town were chased out of their homes by white racists, but one elderly man refused to leave. Beaten to death, his body was tied to the magnolia tree planted by his great-grandmother in his front yard. "Maybe it was loving that tree ... that made him so stubborn," Frank supposes (10).

In dark of night, several evacuees return to furtively bury the man beneath his beloved magnolia, a symbol of dignity and magnificence, but also—as Daniel J. Martin notes in his discussion of Billie Holiday's haunting song, "Strange Fruit"—a symbol that evokes lynching (95).[6] This poignant burial beneath a tree foreshadows another at the novel's conclusion.

A bit later, under the care of a kind minister he encounters on his way to Georgia, Frank tries to remember what he had done to get picked up by police, which led to his incarceration in the mental hospital: "Perhaps he started a fight with a stranger or started weeping before trees—apologizing to them for acts he had never committed," states the narrator (15). This thought on Frank's part is ironic: His troubles actually stem from acts he *had* committed but had subconsciously repressed. Perhaps this irony works subconsciously upon readers, who cannot know, upon their first reading of the novel, that it foreshadows Frank's gradually and painfully recovered memory, especially in light of the narrator's subsequent statement, "Back was the free-floating rage, the self-loathing disguised as somebody else's fault" (15), hinting at the later revelation that Frank's blame of a fellow guard for killing the young girl disguises his own guilt.

Trees offer both cover for and protection from danger, making this motif more nuanced and demanding greater consideration from readers. For example, in a scene that deepens the novel's characterization of Frank's and Cee's relationship, a young Cee distractedly watches her brother play baseball. She is puzzled when Frank walks away from the baseball game and disappears into the trees, circling around toward and beyond her, she later learns. The narrator states, "Suddenly he was behind the tree she was leaning against, swinging his bat twice into the legs of a man she had not even noticed standing behind her" (51). When he explains that the man—a stranger—was flashing her and what that meant, she begins to tremble, but, revealing a sweet tenderness, the young Frank calms her: "His fingers, like a balm, stopped the trembling and the chill that accompanied it" (51–52). In this instance, the tree, like Frank himself, harbors both danger and succor.

Readers are first introduced to the tree that, figuratively, stands at the center of the novel when Cee is recalling how, in their youth, she and Frank often "sat by the stream, leaning on a lightning-blasted sweet bay tree whose top had been burned off, leaving it with two huge branches below that spread like arms" (52). Morrison often uses traditional symbols in extraordinarily rich ways, as she does here. The lightning-split tree[7] evokes a Christian cross, suggesting death and redemption, important themes in *Home*, as well as the physically and psychically separate but connected siblings who share familial roots.

The pastoral beauty of Southern trees later strikes Frank when he finally returns to Lotus, signifying his restored appreciation of his hometown: "Had these trees always been this deep, deep green?" (117). He then fondly recalls the lightning-cleft sweet bay tree on the bank of the stream. Soon he is there, with his sister, having come full circle (132).

In the novel's final scene, Frank and Cee return again to the bay tree to re-bury the bones of the man they saw unceremoniously interred twenty years earlier, when they were children. Frank then nails to the tree a sign that reads, "Here Stands a Man" (144–45), signaling a restoration of the dead man's dignity and masculinity, but also Frank's own, appropriately symbolized by the tree itself: "Wishful thinking, perhaps, but [Frank] could have sworn the sweet bay was pleased to agree. Its olive-green leaves went wild in the glow of a fat cherry-red sun" (145). Frank is thinking of the anonymous African American man he has interred when he writes, "Here Stands a Man," on a board, but what readers "see" in their mental image of the scene is *Frank* standing; Frank stands before us as a man. It is then that Cee meaningfully and poignantly says to Frank, "Come on, brother. Let's go home" (147).

It is significant that going home for Frank must involve Cee. Reuniting with Cee—his only sibling and the only person he has loved his whole life—at least in part represents the end of Frank's alienation from himself and from his community. "Frank returns to Lotus to save Ycidra, called Cee, an act so selfless and loving that it would seem to ensure his moral heroism," notes Cheryl Wall (63). "Moreover," Wall writes,

> as Frank sees how the townswomen have saved his sister, and as he observes the bonds among the townsmen, he begins to change his view of Lotus.... Still, Frank cannot be at home in Lotus until he has confronted his own wrongdoings. The novel performs a delicate shift here. It does not downplay the social wrongs of segregation or the questionable politics of American involvement in global wars. Frank Money is imbricated in the complex histories of his time. Yet the novel turns on his vulnerable humanity [63].

As Manuela López Ramírez says about Frank, "Saving his sister is saving himself.... Only through his sibling can Frank improve his self-esteem, reconnect with his community and acquire a sense of direction and achievement" (140). In his restored wholeness at the novel's end, as he begins to reconcile the worst and the best of himself,[8] he serves as a model for readers, particularly American readers, who can embark on a collective progress only when they acknowledge the worst and the best of American history and culture.

Returning "home" does not mark the end of Frank's journey toward recovery, however, but rather the beginning of the healing process. Ibarrola points out that "while it is undeniable that, on a personal level, Frank succeeds in rescuing his sister and quieting many of his own demons by the end of the journey, it is much more difficult to argue that the cultural and racial traumas that he bears are fully healed" (111). Those traumas—racism, violence, alienation—are not his alone, but ours. Noting that readers find

Frank at the novel's outset "still trapped in the maze of a past that prevents him from looking into a future that would not merely repeat the past" such that "he seems unable to move beyond that mental condition in which he simply acts out the disorientation and violence that have taken possession of the best part of his self" (114), Ibarrola recognizes that "Morrison is definitely taking seriously the need to consider all those traces of individual and collective traumatic memories to see how the resulting grieving processes may be resolved—or at least attenuated" (113). It is not only Frank's healing that necessitates his own coming to terms with traumatic memories; it is readers', as well. From Morrison's point of view, one might paraphrase Ibarrola's observation about Frank: The American nation and the world seem unable to move beyond that mental condition in which we simply act out the disorientation and violence that have taken possession of the best part of our selves.

Returning to her analysis of "home" as a concept in the novel, Wall concludes:

> As children, Frank and Cee have witnessed [a black man's] body being dumped; now as adults they restore the murdered man's humanity. In doing so, Frank reclaims his own. Unable to make amends to his victim [the Korean girl], he rights the wrong that others have done to a victim he has not known. His act is private, but not solitary. The last words of the novel belong to Ycidra/Cee: "Come on, brother. Let's go home." By performing the ritual, which conscience demands, they are able to turn the home that has been a source of pain and suffering into a place of redemption and love.... Lotus is finally a place that partakes mainly of the artifice of metaphor. It is transfigured from a rural backwater ... to a site of memory that is stripped of verisimilitude. It centers the encounter of the self with the self that is the ultimate moral drama. Frank ... has waded through deep waters, climbed high mountains, and borne hard burdens, "trying to get home" [63–64].

With Frank and Cee going home, honoring their memories—good and bad—and appreciating the community that formed them in youth and now embraces them in adulthood, readers, too, having co-created the story with Morrison, have been transformed. Morrison has surreptitiously led readers, again, to the unacknowledged ghosts and unmarked graves of American history—in this case in the mid-twentieth century—having been moved, unconsciously, by the music's secret drive.

7

Sula, Tar Baby *and* A Mercy

Although Morrison's narratives typically engender empathy for some characters more than others, the stories interrupt readers' quick judgments as various details of a given character's personality and actions are unvaryingly complex. This collapse of borders and binary oppositions—a type of what Kimberlé Crenshaw has coined "intersectionality,"[1] in which Morrison limns how characters are impacted by multiple forces and then are abandoned to fend for themselves—is central to Morrison's narrative signature. Through *A Mercy*, *Sula*, and *Tar Baby*, we hope to show how Morrison's masterful engagement of and transformation of her readers through this distinctive narrative technique helps condition them for more nuanced understanding of the powerful and the powerless, the perpetrator and the survivor, the hegemonic and the marginalized.

As we have argued throughout this study, communal ways of knowing and acting characterize Morrison's literary works. Morrison leads readers, through irresistible engagement with her texts, to the realization that individual, community, and even national and global healing entails an embrace of traditional ways of knowing integrated with contemporary ones. Whenever an individual such as the title character in *Sula* or a community such as that in *A Mercy* violates this balancing principle, individual sickness and cultural "dis-ease" ensue. As one of this volume's co-authors, Campbell, has written elsewhere, this results in an imbalance "in the relations of the patient to self, the community, and the supernatural world" (213), a prominent African worldview that an African-informed analysis can help explicate. To analyze such intersectionality in literature by writers of color, Campbell advocates the use of what she calls "ethnomedical criticism":

> Ethnomedical systems, healing practices based on the traditions—particularly spiritual practices—of a particular region and herbal medicines created from locally available plants, aim to cure illnesses and diseases through restoring a balance in the relations of the patient to self, the community, and the supernatural world. This mode of analysis,

which I have come to call ethnomedical criticism, focuses on reclaiming wellness through self-worth and the "discredited" knowledge (to quote Toni Morrison) of a culture's healing practices [213].

When such an imbalance has occurred, wellness can be reclaimed only through restoration of self-worth and knowledge of a culture's healing practices. Morrison orchestrates her narratives to show readers that progressively adapting ancestral traditions into contemporary culture and vice versa is the key to wellness and survival for the individual, the community, and the culture. To resort to fully embracing the traditional without evolving with the times or totally abandoning it to embrace contemporary culture will inevitably disconnect individuals from their respective communities and cultures. This communal orientation constitutes one of Morrison's overarching narratives found in in all her works, including *A Mercy*: interdependence with one's community is crucial, but giving complete dominion of oneself to any entity is not only unhealthy, but immoral.

Indeed, *A Mercy* closes with a first-person message from Florens's mother that neither Florens nor those around her are able to comprehend: "...[T]o be given dominion over another is a hard thing; to wrest dominion over another is a wrong thing; to give dominion of yourself to another is a wicked thing" (165). Florens's mother's heartbreaking message to a daughter who will never hear it is that it is an abomination to give dominion of oneself to anyone or anything. This is the *ur* message of all of Morrison's texts as she repeatedly shows what happens to individuals who become enslaved to cultural mores, traditions, and emotions (as well as those who completely abandon such cultural ties). This certainly is true of Florens, who becomes a slave to any type of positive attention because of emotional abandonment issues she has in relationship to her mother, just as it is true of Sula and Nel in *Sula*, who are two sides of the same coin and are not as different from each other as readers might initially suspect. It is true, as well, for Son and Jadine in *Tar Baby*, who are both entrenched in their beliefs of how to best live in the world.

In *Sula*, Morrison continues her message of the perils of giving dominion of oneself over to something or someone else to combat the ways in which the intersection of race and gender are shaping black women's experiences. In this novel she shows readers what happens to individuals who become enslaved by their emotions. By depicting her characters as complex—imperfect but redeemable—Morrison lures readers to identifying with her characters and thereby drawing empathy, understanding, and motivation from them. In *Sula*, Morrison draws readers into the complex dynamics of Nel and Sula by leading them to connect with the narrative's meaning, as she does with all of her fiction.

The narrator establishes connection between readers and the characters of *Sula* immediately at the novel's outset. Just as the African American community members were "mightily preoccupied with … what that little girl Sula who grew into a woman in their town was all about, and what they themselves were all about, tucked up there in the Bottom" (5–6), the text invites readers to wonder about Sula as well as how they, themselves, have constructed their identity. Through this intersectional narrative structure, Morrison moves readers to "recognize [as Sojourner Truth, bell hooks, and Crenshaw have] the importance of considering someone's experience as the encounter of many factors, such as gender, class, and race," as Dayane Evellin de Souza Francisco argues (137). Francisco claims that "[t]o ignore this [intersectional] complexity is to contribute to the spreading of misconceptions and stereotypes, thus reinforcing and reproducing oppressive ideologies" (139). Figuratively enacting Crenshaw's concept of intersectionality, she leads readers to recognize the complex interplay of demographic variables in any given individual and among any given group of people.

Sula did not know that the Nel of their youth would not return. She simply believed that Nel had been polished down into the brown funk Nel's husband described (83), and with Sula's return, Nel would find her shine again and the two of them would become so close that "…they themselves had difficulty distinguishing one's thoughts from the other's" (83). Sula would once again be Nel's respite, but Sula was wrong. Greed had consumed Nel as she no longer measured her worth by what she had but rather by what her neighbors had. At first, readers cannot discern the greed in Nel as most do not recognize that Nel and Sula are two sides of the same coin, or what Alexandra Vasile calls "the pairings" (186), and what Francisco refers to as binary thinking. Furthermore, many readers often interpret Sula as being the tails or "down" side of the coin because they see her as betraying her best friend, Nel, when she has sex with Jude, Nel's husband. This perception marks Sula as a wild woman who has abandoned the prescribed rules of moral conduct in her society to embrace whatever makes her feel good and feeds her feelings of self-worth regardless of whom she hurts. The text leads readers to the impression that Sula has lost touch with her humanity and compassion and with social norms in her selfish pursuits, thus sealing Sula's standing in most readers' and the town's eyes as a woman at the margins living in a town that cannot bear her company because she has set herself adrift from those she knows and has no sense of belonging to the community in which she lives.

Readers later discover that it is not Sula who has changed but Nel, undermining their judgment of Sula and leading them to face the tendency to judge others in general. Sula had always been completely uninhibited: "She was completely free of ambition, with no affection for money, property or things, no greed, no desire to command attention or compliments—no ego" (119). She was surprised when she discovered that she and Nel were no longer one entity sharing two bodies: "They had always shared the affection of other people: compared how a boy kissed, what line he used with one and then the other" (119). For Nel, "[M]arriage, apparently, had changed all that, but having had no intimate knowledge of marriage, having lived in a house with women who thought all men available, and selected from among them with a care only for their tastes, [Sula] ... was ill prepared for the possessiveness of the one person she felt close to" (119). At first, the change in Nel had been indiscernible to Sula. But, as Sula reconsiders the memory of Nel's reaction to finding out Sula had had sex with Jude, the reality that Nel had turned into one of "those spiders whose only thought was the next rung of the web..." seeps into Sula's heart. Nel belonged to the Bottom and all of its ways, something that surprised Sula and deeply saddened her (120). Sula's lesson in regretted judgment becomes a lesson for readers, as well.

On the surface, Nel appears to be the head of the coin, on the right side of societal norms, as she is married, has raised children, has stayed in her hometown, and is community-oriented in helping others. Once married, she sticks to her prescribed cultural role. The text leads readers to judge Nel more benevolently in contrast (e.g., "...Nel seemed stronger and more consistent than Sula..." [53]). However, Morrison is setting readers up to face the drawbacks of quick judgment, having suggested that "...both were unshaped, formless things" that "found relief in each other's personality...." (53). Morrison does not allow readers to comprehend Nel's formlessness until the novel's end, however; the impact is much greater because she enables readers to render judgment first in order to undermine that judgment later. She gives the reader glimpses of it throughout the novel but not the tools to craft wisdom out of information until Nel begins to acknowledge the truth of Miss Eva's accusations as she walks home from the cemetery. When she is with Sula, Nel gives free reign to her aggression (83). Nel initially fails to recognize this because she and Sula were so close. Morrison adds to this obfuscation by playing on cultural mores that are understood by the characters within the novel as well as by the readers. Such mores pronounce Nel as the "good girl" and Sula as a "bad girl." Readers once again forget that there are no good or bad people with Morrison, only people with both good and bad in them—two sides of the same coin. That is why Sula's grandmother, Mrs. Peace, tells Nel that she and Sula are one and the same. Like all human beings, they share at least some common traits. Nel initially rejects that claim but by the novel's end accepts the indictment as she recounts how she and Sula both enjoyed sharing each other's boyfriends and both enjoyed watching Chicken Little's death:

> All these years she had been secretly proud of her calm, controlled behavior when Sula was uncontrollable, her compassion for Sula's frightened and shamed eyes. Now it seemed that what she had thought was maturity, serenity and compassion was only the tranquility that follows a joyful stimulation. Just as the water closed peacefully

over the turbulence of Chicken Little's body, so had contentment washed over her enjoyment [170].

Nel had not wondered in years why she felt so happy to see Chicken Little fall into the water, why she never felt bad about it at all (170). Miss Eva was right: Sula and Nel were the same.

Once Nel embraces this truth she is able to acknowledge another, in a scene of moving pathos:

> "Sula? ... All that time, all that time, I thought I was missing Jude." And the loss pressed down on her chest and came up into her throat. "We was girls together," she said as though explaining something. "O Lord, Sula," she cried, "girl, girl, girlgirlgirl."
> It was a fine cry—loud and long—but it had no bottom and it had no top, just circles and circles of sorrow [174].

When Sula leaves the Bottom, Nel loses her soulmate. She had thought she could replace that loss through a conventional life with Jude and mourns his departure after his affair with Sula. It is not until she begins to examine her reflection using Sula as a mirror that Nel realizes that it is Sula's loss that she truly mourns: "In the safe harbor of each other's company they could afford to abandon the ways of other people and concentrate on their own perceptions of things" (55). Once again, Morrison has led readers to reconsider their harsh judgments of others and to appreciate connections with other people—to empathize.

Morrison has consistently shown readers that when characters become wild, indulging in activities with abandon and diverging from the cultural mores they have known, they inevitably suffer, not because they violate social norms, but because they alienate their communities. Yet Morrison also depicts characters too beholden to social norms and too unforgiving of those who appear to flout them, like the town of Ruby in *Paradise*. By providing enough textual space for readers to fall into the traps of judgment of others and then rebuking them for that judgment through the wisdom gained once the intersectional dynamics have been pieced together, Morrison trains readers to foster empathy—that is, an attitude of compassion and love—instead. This is why we disagree with Vasile's assertion that Morrison purposefully created Sula and Shadrack as a couple "...in order to show the difference in treatment that Shadrack and Sula receive from their community and, at the same time, the oppression that Sula (but not Shadrack) faces that is directly tied to the ... [intersectional] oppression [of Sula] ...," which leaves Sula fighting alone, unable to "connect her oppression with the oppression of the entire community." However, as we note in our chapter on *The Bluest Eye*, Cholly also excludes himself from the community because of the way he violates the norms of black respectability. Indeed, across the range of Morrison's fiction, regardless of gender, characters who become so wild that they pose a danger

7. *Sula, Tar Baby* and *A Mercy*   145

to themselves and to the community effectively exclude themselves from the community rather than become excommunicated by the community.

Morrison depicts intersectionality in *Sula*, and throughout her oeuvre, to help readers dismantle stereotypical concepts. This is most clearly demonstrated, as Francisco asserts, that by reading *Sula* through bell hook's explanation that the characteristics and roles ascribed to women were created for *white* women, not black, and therefore "one could argue that because black women could not perform those roles [assigned to white women] … they could not be considered as women at all, and this is exactly what Sula questions…" (Francisco 146) when she says to Nel, "You say I'm a woman and colored. Ain't that the same as being a man?" (*Sula* 142). We would claim, moreover, that through Morrison's depiction of the intersecting forces that Sula is subjected to, she exposes to readers the flaws in this binary man/woman conception. As Francisco states, "One can say that, consciously, or not[,] Sula engages in deconstruction by exposing how the binary man/woman is flawed since it cannot be used to refer to all women" (146).

Francisco further claims that in order for Sula "…to create her own interpretation of the meanings imposed upon her, … [she] needs first to embrace (white, male) traditional notions of womanhood before she can reject them…," and that Sula is strangled by what Derrida refers to as binary logic such that no matter how hard she tries to break free from its hold she is repeatedly entrapped by the reinscribing of it (148). Nevertheless, Francisco states, Sula does come to a point where she thinks of herself as being as free as a man (Francisco 148).

We disagree with Francisco's declaration that Sula must embrace notions of whiteness before she can reject them, however, for three primary reasons. First, African Diaspora cultures throughout the world have displayed many forms of cultural retention of their African ancestry, that is, Africanisms. Descendants of the African Diaspora practice syncretism—taking what works from the new, discarding what does not, and adding it to their repertoire of what has always been. This has been and still is true in U.S. African diasporic cultures. Moreover, Du Bois's concept of double-consciousness[2] acknowledges ambivalence as an immutable element of living as a black person in America. Consequently, African American culture avoids this privileged need to know with certainty, to have it be either one way or the other, as typically exists in Eurocentric cultures of which Derrida is a product. Africa*n*-Americans[3] have had to negotiate living the enforced twoness of the dark veil and all the ambiguities it represents for centuries, which is why Sula can try on men and discard them as she pleases, just as men have typically done with women. Secondly, we find the mixing of Eurocentric frameworks of analysis, such as Derrida's, with ones more appropriately applied to the African Diaspora, such as

Crenshaw's concept of intersectionality—to make visible that which had been invisible—problematic. Francisco's and Vasile's critical analysis of *Sula* and Schreiner's critical analyses of *Sula, Tar Baby,* and *A Mercy* are emblematic of many other analyses that take a less-consistent theoretical approach in interpreting works created by authors of the African Diaspora.

Eurocentric literary critical analyses of African diasporic texts do not have the foundation of cultural context such that a person outside of the culture can easily make accurate meaning of the behavior. When they attempt to do so, the result is often akin to what Morrison refers to in *Playing in the Dark* as "…the validity or vulnerability of a certain set of assumptions conventionally accepted among literary historians and critics and circulated as 'knowledge'" (4), particularly when critics are not fully aware of their assumptions of universality that actually are particular to cultures deriving from Europe. This is exemplified in what we believe might be Vasile's misunderstanding of Morrison's work when she states, "Morrison's fiction constitutes a critique of race and racism in the United States, by looking at the black experience within the white dominance and resistance to change" (508). If Vasile is suggesting that Morrison critiques American racism from the perspective of white dominance, we would, of course, strongly disagree; Morrison spent her entire career ensuring that the gaze that renders black people invisible was not the dominant one in her work. If, however, she is arguing that Morrison depicts the black experience as it has been brutally altered by white dominance, we largely agree, but would argue that African legacies have persisted through North American slavery to a greater degree than she seems to imply.

Vasile goes on to say, "As Morrison herself has stated in *Playing in the Dark*, most of her work is a 'running commentary on race theory and cultural practice and how each shapes the other'" (508). We would add that Morrison's connotation of her work echoes the five tenets of critical race theory identified for the field of education by Daniel Solórzano: the centrality and intersectionality of race and racism; the challenge to dominant ideology; the commitment to social justice; the centrality of experiential knowledge; and the interdisciplinary perspective ("Images and Words"; see also "Critical Race Theory"). These tenets also undergird critical race theorist Crenshaw's theory of intersectionality.

A second example of "assumptions conventionally accepted … and circulated as 'knowledge'" (*Playing*, 4) and the attempt to integrate Afrocentric theory with Eurocentric theory, which we believe resist such admixture, is Francisco's, Vasile's, and Samantha Schreiner's questionable claims about black people and their identity. "Shadrack is so traumatized," declares Vasile, "that he believes he has 'no past, no language, no tribe, no source, no address book, no comb, no pencil, no clock, no bed, no can opener, no faded postcard, no soap, no key, no tobacco pouch' [(*Sula* 31)], an obvious allusion to slavery and the status of the slaves, *who were required to purge their identities*" (7; emphasis ours). Likewise, Francisco claims that "slavery deconstructed blacks' sense of identity. Black women's sense of identity was even more damaged because they were also discriminated against and oppressed for being women" (144). Schreiner posits: "Enslavement resulted in the severe dismantling of Black individual and communal identity. African slaves were forced into an iniquitous system that severed them from ... their cultural heritage" (38). We believe that a greater understanding of African cultures lead to a different conclusion: Although, as Orlando Patterson documents in his comprehensive history of global slavery,[4] the *attempt* to strip Africans of their culture and language, and to sever their familial and clan ties to Africa, was as horrific as the enslavement of their bodies, contemporary African American culture exhibits abundant African legacies. It would be a mistake to overestimate the success of such attempts to strip Africa from the enslaved Africans and their descendants.

Morrison insists that readers endeavor to identify their own preconceptions and implicit biases. As her work demonstrates, these naturalized ideas arise from lack of knowledge. We literary critics are susceptible, of course. While our ignorance is understandable and inevitable, Morrison teaches us to strive for greater knowledge, deeper understanding, and more compassionate consideration. She asks us as individuals and as a society, as we have noted earlier, to consider who provided any bit of information and why we credulously accepted it. In the present case, we believe some critics underestimate the resilience of pan-African cultures. The absolute dominance necessitated by the enslavement of Africans and their descendants certainly attempted to sever completely the slaves' cultural and familial ties to Africa, and, indeed, much was lost in the Middle Passage, *but the attempt failed*. African Americans have always known who they were and resisted dominant notions and lifeways. It was the oppressors—some intentional and some unwitting—who have often remained unaware of black resistance and of enslaved Africans' and their descendants' ingenious ways of retaining the cultural practices that tie them to their ancestral identity (Dalgish; Barnes; Cole; Creel; Spencer; J. Holloway; and especially Levine). Furthermore, by paying insufficient attention to the lived experiences and histories of those oppressed by institutionalized racism—a core tenet of critical race theory—or pursuing literary studies with insufficient understanding of subcultural groups to which they do not belong, critics will inevitably remain limited by blind spots.[5]

With *Tar Baby*, Morrison extends her prism of intersectionality through emphasizing collective identity and empathy while critiquing racism, sexism, and socioeconomic inequity. As Jean Wyatt states, "*Tar Baby*'s wide-ranging critique targets the ways individual engagement in capitalism deforms self-image, sexual desire, and love; and on a more global level, the novel suggests the ways that capitalism has disadvantaged black people and harmed natural ecosystems through the centuries" ("Economic," 32). Like Wyatt, we see the text's critique of the dangers of a free market society. However, a reader-response approach to the text illuminates how Morrison leads readers to see that one cannot simply blame capitalism in the abstract; personal choice plays a substantial role in the perpetuation of oppressive economies of power. This understanding is crucial to engaging readers in an effort to challenge social inequities. Readers must be prepared—compassionately and lovingly—to examine their own complicity in injustice rather than succumb to the fallacy that they cannot effect change.

Tar Baby critiques individual and collective culpability for capitalist inequities in a variety of ways. For example, according to Andrew Warnes, the black characters' real and symbolic struggle for food against the colonial master is depicted in Son's relationship with the Streets. Son breaks into the Streets' home and steals food because he is literally starving. We contend that there is a triple meaning to this starvation as it also symbolizes Son's financial starvation in relationship to the islanders (Jadine, her Aunt Ondine, and Uncle Sydney—the servants, as well as the Streets), and it symbolizes Jadine's and Ondine's lack of connection to their cultural ancestry. This triple meaning is another example of the way in which Morrison employs critical race theory to reveal how oppressive structures are interconnected and cannot be examined separately if one is to clearly see the marginalizing effects of those structures for black women and black men.

Son, at least on the surface, appears to reject the spoils of the free capitalistic society and venerates living with and in nature. He is often discussed as a model character for his refusal to let go of his connection to his cultural ancestry for the benefits of capitalism. However, the fact that he distances himself from his community suggests that all is not well with Son, as in many ways this cultural/communal disconnection leaves him totally out in the wild—figuratively and literally—unconnected to friends and family in present civilization. Although there is value to Son's positive relationship with his cultural ancestry, with the earth, and, in many ways, with himself, he is also disconnected from present humanity as his relationships with those around him, whether family or friends, do not last. Morrison is once again leading readers to comprehend that an uncritical valuation of one's ancestral roots at the expense of interdependence with one's community leads to alienation. For example, Son derives pleasure from his oppression of the islanders when he eats their precious food and drinks the last of the rum while smoking their cigarettes. Son has some sense of how much he is costing these islanders by enjoying their meager resources, and even derives a sense of satisfaction from the dearness of the items being served to him. By depicting Son giving himself over to this malevolent satisfaction, Morrison shows that Son is neither better than nor worse than Jadine or the Streets. As Cecily E. Hill declares, "Son's character is certainly no more reprehensible than that of Margaret or Valerian. Rather, Morrison's depiction of all their actions reveals the complex means by which foodways may work to oppress" (293). Morrison thus complicates Son's character, who is often held up as an admirable free-market resistor yet one who readily accepts power in ways that are not so different from Valerian's. By complicating readers' view of Son, Morrison leads them to suspend judgment even of the seemingly heroic, and to view all individuals—in texts and in the real world—with a balance between empathy for their flaws and culpability for their actions. In essence, Morrison's readers become more mindful, and less willing to yield self-determination to any person or dogma. She insists that they remain mindful and accountable.

Jadine, a professional model, has given dominion of herself to the capitalist exchange as she worships Eurocentric aesthetics and turns her back on her African ancestral history. As Wyatt states, "Morrison's wording suggests that Jadine's mind and emotions operate according to the protocols of advertising" ("Economic," 34). Through Jadine's relationship with Son, Morrison allows the reader to see that Jadine's rejection of African American traditions is an ambivalent one as Jadine is drawn to her ancestral African roots. Jadine ultimately ends up rejecting them as is foreshadowed by her Paris encounter with the Lady in Yellow spitting in Jadine's face.

The complexity of all these characters opens them to myriad interpretations, but the persistence of Morrison's thematic concerns indicates the importance of a key lesson for readers: They must never yield authority to anything or anybody. Morrison does not resolve how to balance this issue for her readers. "Rather," as Faith Avery declares, "she consistently pushes her reader toward further ethical wrangling, insisting upon the reader's obligation to struggle with moral issues at hand" (4–5). By engaging and training her readers, she better prepares them to take responsibility for actions on behalf of themselves and their communities. Morrison also helps her readers navigate the multiple layers of intersectionality operating within all of her characters who, like readers themselves, are neither wholly good nor wholly bad.

A Mercy features a population of characters who, through the atrocities of the slave trade, have been distanced from their culture. They do not, however, lose all ties to their culture—what Orlando Patterson has famously termed "social death." Neither the individual characters nor the community they form could heal if they lost all ties to their culture. As Gay Wilentz notes, for individuals to be corporally well, they also must be culturally well, and they cannot be culturally well if they are separated from their culture—i.e., their community (5). Alienation from their culture and community often creates such a desperate need for wholeness that individuals might seek it by any means necessary. Often, this quest leads to their figurative, if not literal, enslavement to this desire in some form. The characters in *A Mercy* are in various states of physical and psychic stress as a result of giving the power of their soul to someone or something else and serve as a warning and lesson to readers.

Recovery from such a state comes only from understanding one's own position—knowing what will be protective, knowing when to seek help, and knowing from whom to seek it. However, without a cultural and/or communal foundation helping to orient their perceptions and steps, the characters become lost to the dominion of something or someone else. This is exemplified by Scully's analysis of Sorrow. The novel's narrator states that for Scully, "[t]o dismiss Sorrow as 'the odd one' ignored her quick and knowing sense of her position. Her privacy protected her; her easy coupling a present to herself. When pregnant, she glowed and when her time came she sought help in exactly the right place from the right people" (178). Scully sees Sorrow as "whole." In fact, after the birth of her daughter, Sorrow recognizes her unity and renames herself Complete. It is only after the birth of her daughter that Sorrow, now Complete, is able to reconcile the disparate parts of herself into a coherent whole with a singularity of purpose, motivated to empower herself within rather than in response to some external affliction.

The only characters who are whole at the novel's end are the healer (the Blacksmith) and the patient he healed of a physical and metaphysical ailment (Sorrow/Complete). However, the healer entered the story whole, possessing a sense of cultural and communal rootedness that is the foundation of his self-worth, the very thing he tells Florens she is missing. Initially, "[n]either Sorrow nor Twin had settled on exactly what to think of the blacksmith. He seemed complete, unaware of his effect. Was he the danger Lina saw in him or was her fear mere jealousy? Was he Sir's perfect building partner or a curse on Florens, altering her behavior from open to furtive?" (147–48). "Suffused with the deep insight mothers-to-be claim" after the Blacksmith heals her, Sorrow is sure that the Blacksmith means them no harm and that "Lina was simply wary of anyone who came between herself and Florens" (154–55).

Unlike Sorrow, who finally learns to trust herself after confronting her greatest fears, the other women do not learn to trust themselves after confronting what has the greatest dominion over them and they turn to coldness and cruelty. Scully sees this cruelty in the mistress of the house after her bout with smallpox. She looks to punish things and punish herself and her husband for the happiness that she had. She therefore gives herself over to piety that leads to the sickness of cruelty. Scully sees a coldness in Florens after the Blacksmith puts her out. Whereas Scully once saw Florens as a "combination of defenselessness, eagerness to please and, most of all, a willingness to blame herself for the meanness of others," the Florens he saw marching down the road after being put out by the Blacksmith had become untouchable (179). In Lina, Scully saw a purity that kept her bound to her word (178). Her loyalty to this internal promise blinded her to the fact that the members of her communal family were falling away from each other and that her attempts to hold onto Florens will fail to prevent that (158).

Readers discover that Lina was correct in her assessment that the Blacksmith did not really care about Florens. Florens acknowledges this fact but is unwilling to heed the message because it is given in the wrong spirit and consequently finds herself crushed when the Blacksmith rejects her (167). Morrison characterizes Florens with bird imagery reminiscent of that used to describe Pecola in *The Bluest Eye* after she loses her sanity. Florens holds her feathers from lifting as she cowers before the Blacksmith when he knocks her down upon discovering that, in a fit of jealous rage, she has dislocated the shoulder of the little boy in the Blacksmith's care (165). Florens is cut by the words that follow:

> Why are you killing me I ask you.
> I want you to go.
> Let me explain.
> No. Now.
> Why? Why?
> Because you are a slave.
> What?
> You heard me.
> Sir makes me that.
> I don't mean him.
> Then who?
> You.
> What is your meaning? I am a slave because Sir trades for me.
> No. You have become one.
> How?
> Your head is empty and your body is wild.
> I am adoring you.
> And a slave to that too.
> You alone own me.
> Own yourself, woman,[6] and leave us be. You could have killed this child.
> No. Wait. You put me in misery.
> You are nothing but wilderness. No constraint. No mind.
> You shout the word—mind, mind, mind—over and over and then you laugh, saying as I live and breathe, a slave by choice [165–66].

This exchange enables readers to realize that Lina's instincts about the Blacksmith are correct (71). Despite his healing powers, he also brings a sickness that "would spread like mold among them all" which would prove to be "much longer lasting and far more lethal" than the smallpox, especially for Florens (150).

Will and Sorrow also question the Blacksmith's moral character even though they both also see him as complete. Will is bewildered by the sharp change in Florens's behavior after the Blacksmith's arrival (178), and Sorrow is ambivalent about his character but ultimately decides he is essentially good after he heals her from smallpox. Sorrow and Will are right to question the Blacksmith's moral character because, like all of Morrison's characters, he is flawed but not evil. These characters thus help readers recognize the moral ambiguity within the Blacksmith, particularly in relationship to Florens. Whereas the Blacksmith takes the time and effort to heal Sorrow, he makes no attempt to effect any remedy for the malady he sees in Florens. Instead, he allows her to become feral, chastises her, and then casts her out. Readers expect the Blacksmith, as a healer, to help Florens free her mind from her emotional enslavement to abandonment fears as it would seem he had the wisdom and psychological power to do so. He clearly understands that she is enslaved to worshipping him as well as by the darkness of an unenlightened mind that chooses to be a slave to societal ideology of her time (82). Yet, he chooses to cast Florens out instead of leading her to a place of wholeness, leaving readers to wonder why he declines to take her in and care for her as he does the little boy he finds. Instead, the Blacksmith takes advantage of Florens's sickness—her empty mind—and uses her willing body to satisfy his sexual needs.

Although some might read Florens's empty mind to be connected to racism, we see it as a connection to religious dogma and the inability to define the invisible aspects of herself. Consequently, we agree with Barbara Christian when she writes, "In every society where there is the denigrated *Other*[,] whether that is designated by sex, race, class, or ethnic background [—to which we would add 'religion'—], the *Other* struggles to declare the truth and therefore create the truth in forms that exist for her or him. The creation of that truth also changes the perception of all those who believe they are the norm" (*Black Feminist*, 160). We distinguish identity loss from the struggle to declare one's identity and its value in one's society. The struggle is not in self-identification because of loss of identity, as Schreiner argues (40). Rather, the struggle is to declare the value of a lived identity that differs from the hegemonic norm.

Moreover, we postulate that it is also crucial to understand the historicity of the settings in literary works. For example, *A Mercy* was set in the late seventeenth century, long before current, Western meanings were ascribed to what we now call "race," and before the institution of slavery came to apply primarily to Africans. In his seminal work, *Man's Most Dangerous Myth: The Fallacy of Race*, Ashley Montagu notes that "the rise of racism as an endemic disorder is associated with slavery and the growing opposition to it, so that it is not until the second half of the eighteenth century that one begins to encounter its development" (55–56). White Europeans certainly discriminated against darker-complected peoples long before then, but the convenient argument that Africans (and indigenous peoples of the Americas, et al.) deserve to be enslaved—that is, an unquestioned association of race and slavery—emerged much later than the setting of *A Mercy*.

In fact, it is European, Christian theology, more than racism, that undergirded seventeenth-century societal value and norms. Therefore, Schreiner misinterprets Florens's encounter with a radical group of Christians when she interprets it as a moment of racist—rather than religious— oppression when the group orders Florens to strip so that they can examine her body for demonic signs (45). The group finds no telltale signs aside from the darkness Florens is born with (*A Mercy*, 109). However, it is not the darkness of Florens's skin that is the referent here but the darkness of her mind. Florens struggles is in trying to figure out where her self-worth lies in light of the Christians' *religious*, not racist, prejudice. Through Florens's struggle, Morrison leads the reader to see that nothing is more dangerous than a destructive ideology sustained and validated by a theology as it later serves in the foundation of the United States.

Barbara Christian's discussion of the struggle black women have had in defining themselves also provides an interesting perspective on the question of the Blacksmith's moral character. Christian declares that "the struggle of black women, then, to define themselves rather than being defined (which is the major thread in contemporary Afro-American women's literature) is critical to the struggle of white women, of all American women. As poor, woman, and black, the Afro-American woman had to generate her own definition in order to survive.... It is primarily in the expressions of herself that she could be her totality" (*Black Feminist*, 161). Insofar as intersectionality aims to make visible previously unacknowledged interrelationships among demographic factors, Schreiner correctly asserts that Christian's concept of intersectionality (although she was writing before Crenshaw coined the term) helps black women define themselves rather than be defined (*Black Feminist*, 40).

Thus, it makes sense when the ultimate indictment of the Blacksmith's moral ambiguity comes from Florens herself. She writes to the Blacksmith on the walls of the grand house Sir had built and died in without having a chance to live there:

> I am remembering what you tell me from long ago when Sir is not dead. You say you see slaves freer than free men. One is a lion in the skin of an ass. The other is an ass in the skin of a lion. That is the withering inside that enslaves and opens the door for what is wild. I know my withering is born in the Widow's closet. I know the claws of the feathered thing did break out on you because I cannot stop them wanting to tear you open the way you tear me. Still, there is another thing. A lion who thinks his mane is all. A she-lion who does not. I learn this from Daughter Jane. Her bloody legs do not stop her. She risks. Risks all to save the slave you throw out [187–88].

This passage echoes Morrison's Nobel lecture in that the Blacksmith's words to Florens are like a dead language, unyielding and "content to admire its own paralysis[,] ... [r]uthless in its policing duties...," with no desire or purpose "...other than to maintain the free range of its own narcotic narcissism, its own exclusivity and dominance" (13–14). The knowledge of the Blacksmith makes him the caretaker who, holding the feathered, bird-like thing Florens in his hands, is free to decide if he will give her life or kill her. Florens perceives the Blacksmith's words as choosing to kill her, as do readers, and there is some truth to this interpretation. However, to stop at that perspective would not present the whole truth. The Blacksmith's words do kill the foolish hedonism Florens falls into because of her obsession with the Blacksmith. Yet, the murderous words also give birth to a Florens who becomes wiser because of the symbolic death she has experienced.

The ways in which the Blacksmith (59) and minha mãe attempt to bring Florens into womanhood are mixed with a cruelty and kindness she does not understand. Although the Blacksmith provides Florens with the message about not giving up dominion over oneself that minha mãe could not, readers question whether she receives it. When Florens says, "I am become wilderness but I am also Florens. In full. Unforgiven. Unforgiving. No ruth, my love. None. Hear Me? Slave. Free. I last" (189), it would seem that she does receive the message as she has hardened herself to life. Yet, in the very next paragraph, Florens confesses that "I will keep one sadness. That all this time I cannot know what my mother is telling me. Nor can she know what I am wanting to tell her. Mãe, you can have pleasure now because the soles of my feet are hard as cypress" (189). Maria Rice Bellamy believes that Morrison offers no evidence that the words of Florens's mother will ever reach her because they are truly intended for readers (15). Although we concur with Bellamy's assessment that minha mãe's words are meant for readers, we disagree with her conclusion that Morrison offers no evidence that minha mãe's words will ever reach Florens. Florens has already begun to toughen up as is evidenced by her own words above as well as by Scully's observation of the change in Florens after the Blacksmith kicks her out. Although she has not yet made the connection between the Blacksmith's words and the plea in her mother's eyes, she has come to understand that she must own herself and not give ownership of herself to another, which is the essential message of minha mãe and the Blacksmith, and she is able to read the hatred in the Blacksmith's eyes (162). Heretofore, she had been unable to read the look that was in her mother's eyes, and had longed to understand what her mother was trying to say. Unfortunately, the hatred in the Blacksmith's eye combined with his command that she be a woman who owns herself acts as an obstacle to her youthful ignorance of self-dominion. ("You your best thing," as Paul D tells Sethe in *Beloved* [273].) In time, however, surrounded and supported by a healing community, she can come to learn this truth as Sethe does in *Beloved*.

On the other hand, we endorse Bellamy's supposition that minha mãe's words are ultimately intended for the audience as Morrison is leading readers to connect with the communal and familial losses of American slavery (15). Minha mãe's words to her daughter are meant for those who, three centuries later, need to comprehend their own agency in order to confront the legacy of the global slave trade but also their ability to make a difference here and now. Morrison has spent her career combatting both the tendency to erase or ignore the enormity of the institution of slavery and the equally troubling tendency to wallow, paralyzed, in guilt. In *Paradise* she shows readers how a town gives dominion of itself to tradition and the wickedness that ensues includes killing four women. In *The Bluest Eye*, she shows readers how Pecola gives dominion of herself over to Aryan beauty ideals and the wickedness of that folly ends with her losing her sanity. And, in *A Mercy*, she shows us how Florens gives dominion of herself to the Blacksmith because of her insatiable need to be loved, to be wanted, and to feel belonging, which leads her to treat a young boy cruelly. Bellamy therefore is right in the sense that Morrison leaves these words to haunt her readers. She presses readers of African descent to resist giving dominion of oneself to anyone or anything, and admonishes other readers to hold themselves accountable for the legacy of racism and responsible for movement toward social justice. Morrison also makes it clear that the Blacksmith believes himself to be superior to all of the other characters, as indicated by Florens when she says of him, "A lion who thinks his mane is all" (188). This supremacist thinking prevents the Blacksmith from leading Florens towards healing and instead to exploit her, thus affirming Crenshaw's view that "the experiences of women of color are frequently the product of intersecting patterns of ... [oppression]" ("Mapping," 1243).

As Morrison leads readers to identify with the Blacksmith, they also may have initially applauded Jacob (also referred to as Sir) for his unwillingness to enjoy dominion over his slaves. However, Morrison makes it clear that Jacob, like the Blacksmith, is not without his flaws when she has him die before he is able to enjoy the fruits of his labor. As admirable as it may be that Jacob was "...determined to prove that his own industry could amass the fortune, the station D'Ortega claimed without trading his conscience for coin," in doing so, he trades one form of dominion for another. He had become obsessed with the idea of building a house the size of D'Ortega's on his own property, thereby giving dominion of himself over to materiality—a lesson for readers against self-congratulatory moral stances that ignore greed and pride. Sir simply cannot get over the wealth of the D'Ortega slave estate: "... [I]n spite of himself, [he] envied the house, the gate, the fence" (31). His epiphany that it is only things, not bloodlines, that separate him from the rich gentry leads to his downfall, as it is during his crazed quest to acquire his outward material desires that he contracts smallpox.

Materialistic greed and pride constitute a common theme for Morrison. Wilentz notes that narratives by women of color typically value cultural wealth, not material wealth: "The overarching vision of all the works ... is that to be well at all one needs to be well culturally" (5), and to be well culturally, one must be part of a community. Protagonists who return "to the healing traditions of his/her own culture" are able to "cure their dis-ease" (5), whereas those who eschew their cultural roots are eventually destroyed by their unrootedness. Such is the case with Jacob and Rebekka, who believed that they could live in isolation. The narrative voice in the novel reveals that they "leaned on each other root and crown. Needing no one outside their sufficiency. Or so they believed" (102). However, Morrison makes it clear to readers through narration that the pair did indeed pay a price for such apparent self-sufficiency:

> Their drift away from others produced a selfish privacy and they had lost the refuge and the consolation of a clan. Baptists, Presbyterians, tribe, army, family, some encircling outside thing was needed.... Pride alone made them think they needed only themselves, could shape life that way, like Adam and Eve, like gods from nowhere beholden to nothing except their own creations [68–69].

"Their own creations" refers to Lina, Florens, and Sorrow, the women who would form a makeshift family and pseudo-community for Jacob and Rebekka after they lose child after child to various natural forces. As long as Jacob was alive this truth was easily veiled. His death, however, makes it plain to the characters within the novel and the readers outside of it that they were not a family at all but a group of orphans forging a life of coexistence. Like Cholly (*The Bluest Eye*), Sula (*Sula*), and Son (*Tar Baby*), they had chosen to put themselves out of their community. They are not, as Schreiner says of Sula, Denver [*Beloved*], and Florens, "a people searching for someone to master them..." (45); they are a people who foolishly lose themselves in a hedonist sensuality they believe can conquer all.

Conclusion

In this concluding piece, we first discuss how "Recitatif," *The Bluest Eye, Song of Solomon, Beloved, Paradise,* and *Home* fit together and exemplify Toni Morrison's oeuvre. Second, we recapitulate our argument in earlier chapters that Morrison clears an ideological space for new ideas about race in America while also clearing a space in American literature for her own art. This clearing gesture is necessary in order to establish a *tabula rasa*; contemporary ideas about race are so misguided, intractable, and insidious that no new vision can emerge through its miasma. We discuss the significance of Morrison's self-styled position as a *griot*, or storyteller, particularly how and to what effect this tactic involves her readers, and we recapitulate our principal argument that her work deconstructs race and recruits readers to combat contemporary racism. Her artful combination of African and European cultural elements in her work helps her accomplish this task and is appropriate to her position as a premier African American artist, we argue. We also explain how this study fits into and extends existing scholarship on Morrison's work. Finally, we consider the limits of this study and suggest areas for further research.

Although they sometimes vary in their specific tactics, the texts we explicate share features that mark them as distinctly Morrison's. One commonality is that each challenges the generally unquestioned and seemingly natural social assumptions about race. Each work helps undermine and deconstruct race as a concept and as a meaningful way of categorizing human beings while it testifies to the terrible, oppressive power of the concept. Her position is similar to that of Tshembe, a character in Lorraine Hansberry's play, *Les Blancs*, who explains thus the device of race:

> I am simply saying that a device is a device, but that it also has consequences: once invented it takes on a life, a reality of its own. So, in one century, men invoke the device of religion to cloak their conquests. In another, race. Now, in both cases you and I may recognize the fraudulence of the device, but the fact remains that a man who has a sword run through him because he refuses to become a Moslem or a Christian—or who is shot in Zatembe or Mississippi because he is black—is suffering the utter *reality*

of the device. And it is pointless to pretend that it doesn't *exist*—merely because it is a *lie*! [122, emphases in original]

One of Morrison's purposes in these three works is to expose the "fraudulence" of the device of race without denying its "utter reality."

Dwight A. McBride comments that Morrison's use of discourse is apparently "essentialist"—that is, operates rhetorically as if black people and white people were essentially different. Michael Omi and Howard Winant define "essentialism" as *"belief in real, true human, essences, existing outside or impervious to social and historical context"* (181n6, italics in original). Such a rhetorical turn is curious for someone like Morrison who, in her fiction and non-fiction, undercuts essentialist notions. Yet, McBride argues (757), Morrison speaks in the first-person plural when discussing African Americans in her well-known essay, "Unspeakable Things Unspoken: The Afro-American Presence in American Literature." He concludes that Morrison's use of racial essentialism in her rhetoric is necessitated by a black person's "attempt to represent one's experience in a language that is not intended to do that work" (774). In other words, as Morrison herself points out in *Playing in the Dark*, our language "can powerfully evoke and enforce hidden signs of racial superiority, cultural hegemony, and dismissive 'othering' of people and language" (x), so, if they are "othered" anyway by dominant discourse, African Americans can at least co-opt and subvert the essentializing language. McBride states the political usefulness of this tactic:

> It allows us to speak categorically in a discourse that seems to demand and respect labels. It enables us to speak to and about a people whose individual lives may be markedly different, but who nonetheless suffer from a common form of racial hegemony. It permits us to hold up the possibility of a unity, albeit fictitious, that makes our burdens more manageable because the load is shared. It empowers us to be able to speak (through the discourse available to us) about the oppressive material and political manifestations of a racialized hegemony in our lives [774].

McBride analyzes this counter-hegemonic use of racial essentialism only in "Unspeakable Things Unspoken." As we have shown in previous chapters, Morrison undermines hegemonic racial essentialism in each of her fictional works in a variety of ways.

The Bluest Eye's principal tactic for challenging the concept of race while insisting on its power is to impart to readers an overwhelming sense of tragedy stemming from some African Americans' internalized, white standards of value and beauty. The novel demonstrates how the rigid social hierarchy, based on race, unremittingly humiliates Cholly Breedlove until he breaks free from any constraints on human behavior. Told by his father (when Cholly finally tracks him down), by the white hunters who find him having sex in a field, and by his mother's absence that he is less than human, he behaves inhumanly, turning against his wife and his daughter. The daughter, Pecola, is so obsessed with white standards of beauty that, betrayed by her father who rapes her and rejected by the mother who also desires not to be black, she falls prey to a misanthrope who persuades her that she now has the blue eyes she so fervently craves. She ultimately descends into madness. The narrator implicates not only herself, but readers, too, for perpetuating white cultural hegemony.

"Recitatif" also calls readers to task for their role in black oppression. Its principal tactic, however, is to lead readers to expose their own racial prejudices. By suppressing the racial identity of the two characters and providing a mixed set of clues, the story essentially traps readers into conjecturing the characters' racial identities. As the "real readers" discussed in Chapter 1 demonstrate, readers do not hesitate to hazard guesses based on what actually is inconclusive evidence. Only by attaching extra-textual meaning—brought to the text by the readers themselves—to the clues in the text can readers render judgment concerning race. The text thus leads readers to expose to themselves their own preconceptions about race. After disquieting readers this way, "Recitatif" releases them into their world altered and introspective.

Song of Solomon extends the bildungsroman form to carry readers through a sensitizing lesson and personal growth analogous to that which its protagonist, Milkman Dead, undergoes. By enticing readers to figuratively assist Milkman in his quest for truth and identity, the novel prepares readers for the truth as the quest prepares Milkman. The journey is fraught for both, but, by the end of the extraordinary story—to paraphrase the novel's stunning conclusion—readers now know what Milkman knows: If you surrendered to the air, you could *ride* it.

Compelling readers to face the shameful history of slavery and, indirectly, its contemporary legacy is the primary tactic of *Beloved*. By initiating readers' sympathy with Paul D and especially Sethe, the novel exposes the absolute power of the slaveholder and utter powerlessness of the slave, even to the extent that families are rent within and throughout generations. Although the loss of one's family—past, present, and future—is certainly painful to anyone, the text makes it clear that such loss is especially devastating to those whose origins lie in the traditional societies of Africa. To them, ancestors and descendants constitute life's meaning. As John S. Mbiti notes, family is one of the things that composes and sustains human life in African religion and philosophy (43). The text pushes readers to comprehend that the horrors of slavery are so severe, the logic of the institution so warped, that, albeit greatly disturbing, Sethe's killing of her own baby makes sense. As the black community ultimately dispatches the haunting presence of Beloved so the characters can heal and move on as a family, readers are led by the text to confront the awful history of slavery so they can heal and, eventually, actively counter the continuing legacy of slavery: racial prejudice and discrimination. Thus, as candid and thoughtful discussions of race in the United States become increasingly lost in a fog of rhetoric and disingenuousness, Morrison's voice is a beacon. In her fiction and nonfiction, she passionately and insistently calls the nation's attention to the force of race in history and in contemporary society. Like Baby Suggs preaching in the Clearing, Morrison clears an ideological space, stripping old, unquestioned, and unproductive thinking about race and races. Also like Baby Suggs, she counts on her auditors to build with her, upon the newly cleared space, a new vision of a society in which all members, regardless of age, gender, race, and class, are liberated.

Continuing her use of and revision of African themes, motifs, and forms, Morrison signifies upon African ritual inheritances as a core, innovative feature of *Paradise*. Rife with characters who misunderstand spoken and written texts, *Paradise* bears less legibility to readers unfamiliar with the trope of the African healing ritual, although, in typical care and generosity, Morrison provides guidance to readers, just as *dabtaras*—itinerant individuals, primarily in Ethiopia and Eritrea, who sing hymns and perform dances for church congregations to help heal them—require effort on the part of readers (auditors). Without resolving all—perhaps even most—textual enigmas in *Paradise*, Morrison lays out a courageous pathway toward love and compassion as demonstrated by the Reverend Misner, who concludes that "because there was no better battle to fight, no better place to be than among these outrageously beautiful, flawed and proud people" (306).

In her tenth novel, *Home*, Morrison inspires readers to consider what makes a home, fleshing out in fiction what she explores in her influential essay of the same title. Uprooted from a solid identity, the protagonist, Frank Money, must overcome terrible trauma from his experiences in the Korean War before he can literally and figuratively go home to his origin, Lotus, Georgia. Significantly, what readers discover—while Frank himself discovers—is that sometimes the most devastating, debilitating trauma comes not from awful experiences visited upon us, but by unconscionable actions we ourselves have perpetrated. As painful as it is to face such truths, we cannot begin to heal until we do so. This holds true not just for individuals, but for societies. Without facing the agony of slavery and the legacy of racism—as descendants of slaves and as descendants of slaveholders—the United States and the world will not find moral footing. Again the loving *griot*, Morrison fortunately provides a model, as Frank witnesses and experiences the healing power of community. Notably, the community who provide succor to Frank and his sister, Cee, comprises women, just as a community of women exorcises Sethe's tormenting spirit, Beloved, in *Beloved*. Because *Home* carefully prepares readers to comprehend the truth along with Frank, they become instruments in Morrison's lifelong mission to deconstruct the violence of racism.

Not only do critics often neglect to explicate Morrison's rhetorical strategy of recruiting readers in her political and social project; few apply appropriate critical techniques for analyzing her artistic forms. Henry Louis Gates, Jr., argues that African American literature cannot be understood or appreciated in the terms of dominant modes of Western literary criticism. "The Western critical tradition has a canon, as the Western literary tradition does" ("Writing 'Race'" 13), Gates writes. The Western literary canon tends to recapitulate the assumptions about race found in Western literature: Blackness is a sign of absence in Western figurative language, and black people are invisible or are caricatures, which, as Morrison asserts in *Playing in the Dark* (e.g., "American means white" [47]), are used as an unacknowledged background against which whiteness, an ostensibly superior "race," is constructed and measured.

Several contemporary black writers and critics recognize and respond to the irony of trying to assert black presence in this context. Gates, for example, rhetorically asks: "[H]ow can the black subject posit a full and sufficient self in a language in which blackness is a sign of absence?" ("Writing 'Race'" 12). Morrison and others accomplish this seemingly paradoxical task by overturning the assumptions of language, exposing and then clearing it of its hidden assumptions before enveloping readers in their interactive sermons in the Clearing. What Gates prescribes for critics applies also to black artists: he states that "our task is to utilize language more precisely, to rid ourselves of the dangers of careless usages of problematic terms which are drawn upon to delimit and predetermine the lives and choices of human beings who are not 'white'" ("Talkin'" 403).

Gates advocates drawing upon the "black vernacular" to "step out of the discourse of the white masters" ("Talkin'" 408). Morrison accomplishes this task in her critical work, especially in *Playing in the Dark*, in which she exposes the masked construction of whiteness found in the American literary tradition. She also relies upon the black vernacular in her fiction to the same end. One strategy for achieving her desired liberation from the "discourse of the white masters" is to draw greatly upon the African aspects of African American culture. She states that African literature has influenced her technique more than have European and Euro-American works (*Toni Morrison Interview*), so it is fitting that she also relies upon African symbolism, mythology, themes, and literary forms.

The texts we have discussed combine African and American elements, expanding the recognized scope of American literary themes and forms. Morrison's self-cast role of *griot* is most significant. As a storyteller representing in written form the African (and subsequently African

American) oral tradition, she casts her readers in the role of listeners. In the African storytelling tradition, listeners are expected to participate in making meaning with the teller. The experience is cooperative and communal, an experiential precursor to the call-and-response pattern of African American religious services. As Lawrence W. Levine notes, the antiphonal call-and-response patterns in the music carried by slaves from Africa was incorporated into their cultural practices in America (24). Hence, Morrison states often that her work demands readers' active participation, and she writes her fiction accordingly—leaving puzzles, mysteries, and gaps with which readers must contend. Morrison's use of textual and meta-textual enigmas is her most distinguishing trademark and her most important formal contribution to American and world literature, as her unflinching exposure of racism—overt and covert—and its effects is her most significant thematic contribution. Form and theme complement each other.

Proponents of Black Aesthetics advocate exactly what Morrison accomplishes. Her use of distinctively African American cultural forms, such as jazz music (see, for example, *The Bluest Eye* 125 and *Jazz* esp. 65) contributes to her treatment of themes that come from, validate, and promote the experiences of African Americans. In fact, Morrison has stated categorically that she writes principally for black people (*Toni Morrison Interview*); her artful fusion of African and Western elements is apropos.

In the preceding analyses of her works, we argue that Morrison's fiction is intentionally structured to guide readers to introspection (about their own prejudices), retrospection (about the national legacy of slavery), and action (toward dismantling prejudice and discrimination based on race). This strategy is absolutely crucial to understanding her works' significance. That is why, as we state in our introduction, we chose to title this book *The Music's Secret Drive*, a phrase taken from Morrison's novel, *Jazz*. In that book, the music of 1920s Harlem leads its listeners to dance, guiding their movements, all the while making them believe that they themselves are determining their bodies' motion. Like "the music's secret drive" that she evokes in the novel, her fiction has a "secret drive" that guides readers' responses, typically without their awareness.

Although many critics comment upon Morrison's involvement of readers in her fiction, few delineate how she accomplishes this task. We have tried to show more specifically how her texts disrupt readers' expectations about her themes (race, racism, history, whiteness, blackness, Western cognitive categories) and her forms (non-linear plots; incredible, undependable, and ignorant narrators; complex textual authority) in order to clear a space in the minds of readers. Having undermined readers' expectations and thus leaving them open to new ideas, the texts then guide readers to fresh understandings of race, races, history, and society.

Conclusion 163

Morrison's texts do not direct readers to respond, but rather inspire and enlist readers to co-create, with the texts, both meaning and meaningful responses. "Recitatif" builds upon that project by leading readers to expose their own prejudices. By tricking readers into making conjectures about the characters' racial identities, the story reveals readers' predilection for stereotyping. *The Bluest Eye* guides readers to question their previous assumptions about race, poverty, dignity, and violence, and, most significantly, their own complicity in the creation and perpetuation of African American oppression. Conducting readers toward the disgraceful history of slavery—previously a topic conveniently disregarded by Americans, according to Morrison (Broad 193)—*Beloved* initiates readers' psychic healing just as the novel's characters heal only after facing, and coming to terms with, Beloved. Morrison finds it imperative that both black and white readers learn about slavery. Harris notes that this defining institution is a common theme among black writers: "Clearly the history of slavery in this country, and the permanent psychological stamp it has made upon all of us, is one explanation for the persistence of black writers in keeping history alive in their works" (Preface ix). *Beloved* goes beyond calling attention to this history; it also inspires readers to combat contemporary racism as they realize its source in slavery's legacy.

Numerous critics discuss the difficulty that Morrison's texts present to readers (e.g., James Phelan admits that, despite his training as a literary critic, *Beloved* "eludes me" [710]). Several write, for example, about the fragmented narratives, the unconventional use of time, the ambiguous diction, and the complex symbolic systems present in her fiction. Unfortunately, most critics attempt to resolve these textual challenges, an inclination prevalent in Western criticism. We have argued that the gaps and puzzles in her texts should be analyzed (in terms of their effects on readers) but not resolved—that their ambiguity is their *raison d'etre*. William R. Handley and co-authors Wendy Harding and Jacky Martin are exceptions. Handley notes the irony of most Morrison criticism, "for whereas Morrison wants her readers to experience otherness, interpretation, like allegory, wants to see sameness in place of difference. Whereas Morrison wants us to read gaps as gaps, interpretation seeks to fill the gap in allegory" (680 n4). Harding and Martin concur: "As long as we construe the critic's role as the solution to problems raised in the text, we seek to unify our impressions and thereby reduce its complexity" (87). Like Harding and Martin and like Handley, we have tried to avoid reducing the complexity of Morrison's work, focusing on how the texts' complex features holistically influence readers.

Even critics sensitive to the enormous complexity of Morrison's work pay scant attention to the way she undermines the authority of her works by calling readers' attention to the texts as texts. Postmodern texts often playfully and directly refer to themselves or to their readers as a way of challenging the modernist reification of texts. Richard Beach notes that Henry Green's novels feature the former tactic, speaking directly to readers, and *Mulligan Stew* by Gilbert Sorrentino includes the author's comments about the novel as well as rejection letters from publishers (42). Such postmodern texts—also called *metafiction*—"invite readers to reflexively examine their own processes of reading" (42). Readers thus "become self-consciously aware of how they apply realist text conventions and the attitudes associated with a realist, modernist worldview" (42), Beach states.

Although she, too, attempts to disrupt readers' application of conventions, Morrison's revision of the postmodern text takes a subtler approach. Her texts do not refer directly to themselves or to readers, but present readers with puzzles about the texts that prod readers to consider the texts' artifice. These puzzles, which we have called *meta-textual enigmas*, challenge the texts' authority, a tactic consistent with Morrison's desire for readers to question *all* authority and instead to think independent of received knowledge. The most outstanding example of her use of this tactic comes at the conclusion of *Jazz*, which is not examined in depth in this study. The mysterious, unidentified, first-person narrator, personifying the implied author, states in the novel's closing lines, "If I were able I'd say it. Say make me, remake me. You are free to do it and I am free to let you because look, look. Look where your hands are. Now" (229). As readers look, they see that their hands are holding a book—her book. The narrator figuratively becomes the text itself, telling readers that it is mute without them, and alive only when they make it so. The text, with readers' cooperation, almost literally becomes a talking book, a trope that, according to Gates, dates back to eighteenth- and nineteenth-century slave narratives (*Signifying Monkey* 130). In employing this trope, Morrison honors and revises an African American literary tradition more than two hundred years old.

Morrison's texts' solicitation of readers' cooperation is crucial. The preceding chapters have tried to explicate the myriad ways in which Morrison's literary works instigate readers' collaboration. We have argued that Morrison deliberately and masterfully engages readers in this manner. The texts themselves, obviously, can make no difference in contemporary American society. Only readers, carefully trained by the texts to uncover prejudice within themselves and in their neighborhoods and nation, can carry out her grand project: to deconstruct the concept of race while appreciating its pervasive power to oppress, and to dismantle the social institutions that perpetuate racial oppression.

Morrison often acknowledges her awareness of the importance of her readers. As we note in our introduction, in her lecture upon receiving the Nobel Prize for Literature in 1993, Morrison offers a parable in which some youngsters, holding a bird, ask an old woman to demonstrate her wisdom by determining whether the animal is alive or dead. She replies, "I don't know whether the bird you are holding is dead or alive, but what I do know is that it is in your hands" (*Lecture* 11). Although she cannot know whether the texts her readers hold are "alive" or not, Morrison recognizes that they, and their fate, rest in her readers' hands.

Morrison's work is so rich and complex that no study of it can be comprehensive. Indeed, studies that focus on any one of her works necessarily miss the important patterns that emerge intertextually in her work. Conversely, broader critical pieces cannot treat sufficiently the fine detail that her work merits. This work, too, has limitations; we suggest areas into which we hope Morrison scholarship will expand.

We have privileged race in our study of Morrison's work. Many scholars, particularly from a perspective of feminist theory, study her treatment of gender, a topic as important to Morrison as is race. Some critics, studying certain novels, find gender even more central than race. Critics ideally will work toward integrating the dual concerns of race and gender in Morrison's work. Her treatment of class deserves greater attention, too. We encourage Morrison scholarship grounded in intersectionality; the complex interplay of identity categories provides a rich framework for Morrison studies.

We identified our theoretical assumptions about the reading process in this book's introduction. We also discussed how our concept of Morrison's textual and meta-textual enigmas extend Wolfgang Iser's theory of textual "gaps." Having distinguished "real readers" from Iser's conception of the "implied reader" in the introduction, we examined in Chapter 1 the responses of sixty-seven "real readers" of Morrison's "Recitatif." This analysis led to our explication of the story's reader-directed rhetorical devices, including an unreliable narrator—similar in significant ways to the narrator of Hawthorne's "Rappaccini's Daughter," discussed by Steven Mailloux in his book, *Interpretive Conventions* (73–92)—and other textual and meta-textual enigmas. Other chapters extended our discussion of these tactics to five key Morrison novels: *The Bluest Eye*, *Song of Solomon*, *Beloved*, *Paradise*, and *Home* respectively—roughly half of her oeuvre.

We have limited our attempt to place our study of how Morrison's texts guide readers' responses into a context of contemporary reader-response theory. We cite two reasons: First, we have sought to explicate Morrison's particular rhetorical strategies as she sees them—as illuminated by her own critical writing and by her statements in essays and interviews about how and why she involves readers. How critics theorize hypothetical readers' responses to generic texts, especially if they claim that their imagined readers and their texts are somehow universal, interests us somewhat less.

Second, as Robert B. Stepto forcefully argues, contemporary

reader-response theories tend to ignore the ways in which race affects both literary production and literary reception (205). African American writers like Morrison often take into account the races of their potential readers and write accordingly, but reader-response theories that generalize about readers of various "interpretive communities" (Fish, *Is There a Text* 171–73) all but ignore race as a factor in interpretation. Moreover, Stepto asserts, the predominantly white critics who posit theories of reading fail to recognize that texts in the black tradition must be analyzed as performances as well as texts (200).

Morrison's fiction certainly fits Stepto's paradigm of the black written/spoken tale. We have tried, in Chapter 1, to demonstrate in detail how Stepto's own model of reading/listening, based on the performative elements of the African American tradition, helps illuminate "Recitatif." We also have endeavored to show, in Chapter 4, how Gates's theory of African American literary criticism based on the African figure of the Signifying Monkey reveals aspects of *Beloved* that some "white" criticism fails to clarify. Beyond these two theories of reading and writing African American literature—both based on the African American vernacular—one finds little explanatory power in contemporary reader-response theories. Stepto and Gates concur that such theories, although they typically claim universality, cannot do justice to black texts.

Finally, we have made little attempt to place Morrison in either a specific, African American literary history or a general American one. We have trained our focus upon the internal workings of the fiction and how particular features of the texts guide readers' responses, and to what ends. Morrison clearly is well-versed in the American literary canon, as her analyses of several canonical texts—particularly in *Playing in the Dark*—demonstrate. Gates claims that she also owes a debt to some of the American writers, especially African American writers, who precede her. Gates notes:

> Grounded in Faulkner, and informed by James Baldwin's densely lyrical experiments with a fictional prose rooted in the religious vernacular ... as well as jazz, blues, and the whole range of black secular vernacular speech rituals and discourses, Morrison has evolved a register of representation that we might think of as a magical naturalism [Preface ix].

Although Morrison rejects the "magical naturalism" label for her fiction (*Toni Morrison Interview*), she recognizes that her work builds upon and revises her predecessors'. Interestingly, however, she states that Baldwin and Ralph Ellison "were good for information, for data, but nothing else" (qtd. in Madden 591), and that for style she is much more influenced by African writers (*Toni Morrison Interview*). In any case, her work undoubtedly has influenced American fiction that follows it. Wilfred D. Samuels and Clenora Hudson-Weems rank her among "such eminent writers as Henry David Thoreau, Sherwood Anderson, Sinclair Lewis, and William Faulkner" and, internationally, in company with Dostoevsky and Gabriel García Márquez (142). Danille Taylor-Guthrie states that with the publication of her first novel, *The Bluest Eye*, Morrison "became an integral part of a nascent group of black women writers who would alter the course of African American, American, and world literature" (vii).

Such intertextual relationships deserve greater study. Gates's analysis in *The Signifying Monkey* (239–58) of how Alice Walker revises ("Signifies upon," to use Gates's phrase) Zora Neale Hurston can serve as an excellent model. In fact, Gates includes Morrison among the black writers who revise other African American texts and who "afford subsequent writers tropes and topoi to be revised" (256). Extended analyses of her place in American and international letters are beyond the scope of this book.

In *Beloved*, Sethe is censured by the black community for declining to share her pain and horror upon her baby's death by her own hand. The townsfolk implicitly accuse her of the sin of pride. Similarly, they lose respect for Baby Suggs for her immodest display of generosity at an impromptu banquet. Andrew Levy notes that

> Morrison's closing words, that *Beloved* "is not a story to pass on," is also a recognition of her kinship with Baby Suggs, an awareness of the risk that her novel might overstep, give too much, or offend by excess as well. The fact that Morrison distances herself, however slightly, from even her own telling of *Beloved*, also suggests the depths of her understanding of the limits of narrative [121].

Our hope is that we have contributed to a collective understanding of, and appreciation of, Morrison's work without overstepping or offending, and that we have correctly gauged and acknowledged the limits of our own narrative.

Chapter Notes

Preface

1. Morrison also published a story, "Sweetness," in the *New Yorker* on 9 Feb. 2015, which later became the first chapter of *God Help the Child*.
2. As of this writing, hundreds of high school and college courses and many thousands of academic articles have focused on Morrison's work. Contrast this post-Nobel attention with Barbara Christian's complaint in 1987 that "in no way is the literature Morrison, [Paule] Marshall, or [Alice] Walker create supported by the academic world.... For there is no reason, given who controls these institutions, for them to be anything other than threatened by these writers" (61–62).

Introduction

1. Many—perhaps most—authors claim that they intend to engage readers, of course. Fellow winner of a Pulitzer Prize and a National Book Critics Circle Award, John Cheever famously said in an interview, "I can't write without a reader. It's precisely like a kiss—you can't do it alone" (Unger 17). Author John Fowles notes in his foreword to Harald William Fawkner's book on him, "A word ... is never the destination, merely a signpost in its general direction; and whatever ... body that destination finally acquires owes quite as much to the reader as to the writer." In our estimation, no Anglophone writer surpasses Morrison in eliciting readers' responses.
2. Although Morrison invokes jazz-like themes and techniques in all of her novels, they are most apparent in her 1992 novel, *Jazz*. Surprisingly, despite being set in the Jazz Age in Harlem, the novel mentions no well-known African American jazz musicians (Goulimari, 191). Instead, Morrison adapts the originality and the experimental and improvisational nature of jazz as a narrative structure for the novel in order to convey themes of love, betrayal, and redemption, rather than to produce an homage to jazz itself. Morrison's continuous campaign to thwart, in disconcerting and thrilling ways, readers' expectations of narrative conventions as well as ethical themes finds perfectly appropriate form in *Jazz*. As Chad Jewett observes, "The narrative strategies and constructive principles on display in *Jazz* reflect the attempted freedom from the page that served as one of the tenets in modal theory. Modal jazz frees the performance, which remains the focus, from any strict sense of composition or written notation besides a beginning prompt, a few bars of melody to set a path for the performance" (445). Like modal jazz, in which a theme or mood remains consistent throughout a piece but the structure remains stubbornly unpredictable, *Jazz* squarely fits into Morrison's characteristic approach that resists readers' confidence in their own assumptions and worldviews. In other words, here, again, Morrison's narrative techniques intentionally discomfort readers, engaging them to co-create complex meaning with the text.
3. For a thorough analysis—from a woman-centered, psychological perspective—of the ways in which Morrison depicts community, see Gillespie and Kubitschek.
4. Responding to writer Junot Díaz's appreciation of *Song of Solomon*, Morrison has said, "I like the notion of being suddenly thrown into a text, with no information or

predilection. It's like being thrown into the sea and then learning to swim" (Glass).

5. For a thorough analysis of Morrison's use of African history, culture, and mythology, see Jennings.

6. Following Franz Fanon's groundbreaking work and reaching a broader audience in George Yancy's philosophical writings, we take the "white gaze" to mean the hegemonic perspective that "white" is universal and non-white is specific; that black and brown bodies have "race" but white bodies do not; that people of color have significance only in contrast to white people—defined as what they are *not* rather than who they *are*. The concept of the white gaze has some analogy to that of the male gaze—the idea that the male perspective is universal and female bodies and lives have meaning only for men's viewing pleasure. See, for example, bell hooks's influential essay, "The Oppositional Gaze: Black Female Spectator."

7. Kwame Anthony Appiah ("Race") provides a particularly useful explanation of the concept of race in the context of literature.

8. For alternative and expanded perspectives on reader-response criticism, see Stanley Fish's work, particularly "Interpreting the *Variorum* and *Is There a Text in This Class?*"

Chapter 1

1. The story has since been reprinted in a few anthologies, including *Calling the Wind: Twentieth-Century African-American Short Stories*, ed. Clarence Major (New York: HarperPerrenial, 1993); *The Oxford Book of Women's Writing in the United States*, ed. Linda Wagner-Martin and Cathy N. Davidson (New York: Oxford UP, 1995); and the children's literature volume, *Leaving Home: Stories*, sel. Hazel Rochman and Darlene Z. McCampbell (New York: HarperCollins, 1997).

2. See Rebecca Aanerud's discussion of how literary texts by white authors tend to be seen as racially neutral, and characters who are not specifically labeled as persons of color are presumed to be white.

3. We view the empirical results as valuable only insofar as they suggest ways in which Morrison's text acts upon readers; that is, they appear to corroborate our assertions regarding Morrison's ability to elicit varying responses from readers who bring disparate backgrounds to her texts. Because reader-response criticism typically focuses on theoretical or imagined readers—as Iser calls them, "implied readers" (*Implied Reader*)—what actual readers do with texts is, in fact, of marginal relevance. We appreciate a comment from Marilyn S. Mobley, professor of English and African American Studies at Case Western Reserve University, who notes that "for many Morrison scholars, including myself, the quantitative study is unnecessary ... [but] it has relevance for what it reveals about readers and their cultural presuppositions. Put another way, Morrison might say that the study itself is evidence of the narrative 'trap' she has set for her readers, not the least of which includes literary/cultural critics" ("Manuscript Reader Report"). We acknowledge that we have fallen voluntarily into that trap and contend that our captivity is worth exploring.

4. The character of "high yellow" Maureen Peal in the novel, *The Bluest Eye*, is described as an atypical black girl in that she "even bought and liked white milk," the narrator states (53).

5. Morrison herself mentions Flack in an interview (Morrison, "Talk" 237); she might have had the singer in mind when naming her character Roberta.

6. Sander L. Gilman presents a disturbing account of a nineteenth-century Hottentot woman exhibited in life and after death as the Hottentot Venus. What European audiences found "riveting" was "the steatopygia, or protruding buttocks, ... which captured the eye of early European travelers" (232). He notes that the woman's "genitalia and buttocks summarized her essence for the nineteenth-century observer, or, indeed, for the twentieth-century one, as they are still on display at the Musée de l'homme in Paris" (235). The connotative meaning attached to this single physical trait is thus disproportionately great.

7. In the story's language usage, too, the less-emphasized factor of gender contributes to the text's task of concentrating readers' attention on race. In "Cognitive Research on Gender and Comprehension," Mary Crawford and Roger Chaffin report that readers' gender (which they view as socially defined and constructed and which is usually but not necessarily congruent with chromosomal sex [13]) affects the interpretation of

language that is masculine but meant to be generic, such as the nouns "man" and "mankind" standing in for "person" and "humankind" and the pronoun "he" used to mean "he or she" (15). They cite a study by Wendy Martyna which found that men tended to interpret "he" as referring only to men, while for women the male pronoun called up neither male nor female images (15).

Crawford and Chaffin also discuss their own research that indicates differences in how men and women remember the content of texts that use supposedly generic—but actually masculine—language. Half of their subjects read an essay titled, "The Psychologist and His Work," which always referred to "the psychologist" as "he." The other half of their subjects read an otherwise identical essay but which was titled, "Psychologists and Their Work," and referred to a singular psychologist as "he or she" or used the plural "they" to refer to the plural "psychologists." Crawford and Chaffin found that men who had read the essay using masculine pronouns in an ostensibly generic manner recalled more than those who had read the gender-inclusive one. Women, however, "recalled better the essay form that specifically included them" (16).

8. Morris does err, though, when she claims in a footnote that "Goldstein-Shirley ... notes that Roberta is black in 'Race/[Gender]: Toni Morrison's 'Recitatif'"" (178). In point of fact, Goldstein-Shirley's claim is *conditional*: "*If* [Robert] Stepto's model fits 'Recitatif' as well as we have argued it does, one must conclude that Roberta, as the master storyteller, is black and therefore Twyla is white" (103; emphasis added).

9. Sandra Kumamoto Stanley offers a persuasive, alternative, disability- and Africanist-based reading of Maggie. See esp. pages 82–83.

10. The tactic of an unreliable narrator in "Recitatif" functions much like that in Hawthorne's short story, "Rappaccini's Daughter." Steven Mailloux's analysis of that story indicates that, as readers realize that the narrator is unreliable, they learn to "go beyond appearances" to pass the story's trial of their powers of discernment (*Interpretive Conventions* 81). "To judge for oneself—this self-reliance is the ultimate goal in the test of the reader's discernment" (83), Mailloux notes. Ultimately, Hawthorne's story tries readers' moral judgment (81), as they must decide for themselves who is responsible for the death of the title character (88). In "Recitatif," the unreliable narrator tries readers' powers of discernment as they must decide what to believe, and tries their moral judgment as they must decide who is responsible for Maggie's torment.

11. Ivan Delazari disagrees that "Recitatif" is a framed narrative as outlined by Stepto.

12. Stelamaris Coser, citing a Morrison interview with Claudia Tate conducted in the same year in which "Recitatif" was published, states: "Storytelling was 'a shared activity between the men and women' in her family, and she attempts to write within that oral tradition. Morrison deliberately pursues an 'oral quality' in order to 'capture the vast imagination of black people'" (Coser 88). Stepto himself includes Morrison in his list of African American writers known for telling—rather than writing—stories (207). It therefore seems appropriate to apply Stepto's model to "Recitatif."

13. See, for example, Dana Nelson Salvino's "The Word in Black and White: Ideologies of Race and Literacy in Antebellum America."

14. The line near the end of *Beloved*, "This is not a story to pass on" (275), is similarly ironic, as we discuss in Chapter 4.

15. No less an authority than opera singer Leontyne Pryce says of Morrison's fiction that "reading or hearing those words is like listening to music" (Strouse 52).

16. As is a common problem in social science research, these respondents might have ascribed racial identities to the characters simply because they were asked to do so (Cook and Campbell 66–67). Nevertheless, not one respondent, even given the opportunity to express concern about any aspect of the study in a questionnaire item, noted any discomfort with the requested task.

Chapter 2

1. For a detailed analysis of the power of the gaze, see Guerrero.

2. Trudier Harris ("Preface") usefully connects lynching in history and literature.

3. Morrison has told interviewers, "I'm writing to, about, and for other black people. And if it's good enough, it will be read by and appreciated by people who are not

African-Americans. That's the simple way to put it" (Kaiser and Manyinka). To put it mildly, we certainly believe Morrison's work is "good enough" to engage readers of any so-called "race."

Chapter 3

1. For an enlightening conversation about Morrison's choice of names in *Song of Solomon*, see Anatol.

2. We continue in this chapter to focus upon readers—especially black and white, when the text suggests differing lessons for different readers—implied by the text. "Real" readers might respond differently than the ways we suggest; we are interested in how the text guides the responses of the readers it theoretically constructs.

3. See TuSmith, esp. 16–20.

4. Although we refer principally to non-black readers, the kind of reader implied by the text might include African American readers alienated from their inherited culture, perhaps because they have been isolated from it or because, like Milkman, they have turned consciously away from it.

5. "Concern with verbal art is a dominant theme in Black culture," notes Claudia Mitchell-Kernan (9).

6. Notwithstanding some of the essentializing reviews published upon its publication. Hortense J. Spillers pulls no punches, stating that "what was said of the novel ... could be applied to a repertoire of black events.... To identify the novel in no more differentiated terms than that is to accommodate oneself to the least tense assumpions which suggest that 'Black Experience,' a monolith down to death, has been exhausted" (694).

7. Phiri notes: "Morrison's intimation of, and mourning for, a 'safe' blackness conservatively presupposes an authentic, homogenous culture, a 'pure, unalloyed tradition from which to draw' (Rushdie 1991, p. 67) that potentially elides the complex plurality and mutability of black subjectivity. In this regard, and in the observation that, 'modern black political culture has always been more interested in the relationship of identity to roots and rootedness than in seeing identity as a process of movement and mediation that is more appropriately approached via the homonym of routes,' Gilroy argues that blackness be regarded as 'a matter of politics rather than a common cultural condition' (1993, p. 27)" (124). Although we ourselves run the risk of overgeneralizing ethnic groups and other demographic variables, we see Morrison's oeuvre as richly complicating, rather than simple generalizations, making a reader-response approach to her work that much more challenging (and rewarding).

8. See Middleton 35.

9. Again, the text shows how alienated from his ethnic heritage Milkman has been: he knows not a single ode, folksong, or spiritual.

10. In this regard, Spillers connects *Song of Solomon* to Morrison's earlier novel, *Sula*, in which "the narrator explains that the population of Medallion, Ohio—the scene of Sula's misdeeds and subsequent victimization—never learned what to do 'with the wings, a way of holding the legs and most of all a full surrender to the downward flight....'" (697).

11. That Milkman's primary teacher is a woman is, of course, no accident. The novel exemplifies Morrison's mastery of intersectionality—depicting the complex, interacting, dialectical dynamics of race, ethnicity, gender, and sexuality long before Kimberlé Crenshaw coined the term in 1989. As Phiri points out, "*Song of Solomon* ... offers a critique of, and reads as a disruption to, a potentially androcentric reading, for while the novel sings of or about Solomon, it is the women who, left behind and abandoned, bear witness to, and the weight of, this 'botherin'' (p. 318) cultural legacy by transmitting to their children the complex, gender-inflected story of blackness" (130).

12. Wendy W. Walters writes extensively of the African legends about flying humans. Morrison is clearly drawing, again, upon African folklore. Phiri notes: "... Milkman's journey parallels somewhat his ancestor Solomon's flight but segues into a necessary route backwards in a southward trajectory into his cultural past and African heritage in order to achieve in the present subjective roots and rootedness" (127–28).

13. Phiri insightfully ties the flying motif to the quest trope, arguing that "Milkman's flight ... reads like a rite of passage to a particular mode of African-American subjectivity. *Song of Solomon* here puts forward an originary, 'linear progress narrative of Middle Passage Blackness' in which the individual is embedded in a relationship

of causality that delineates itself through 'a direct connection to the etiology that first defines and necessarily frames that collective" (Wright 2015, p. 12, 73) (127).
14. Morrison's own maternal grandparents made the trek (Century 59).
15. Phiri further states that "Morrison, in a novel infused with supernatural figures, pointedly advocates black mythology and folklore as necessary 'cultural information' and education (Washington 1994, p. 238) that has a collective unifying and validating effect" (Bascom 1965, Dorson 1972)" (126).
16. Linda Wagner-Martin, for example, advocates teaching the novel as such (153–54).
17. Marilyn Sanders Mobley makes this point ("Call" 43). Kimberly W. Bentson notes that Pilate expresses and performs a communal, as opposed to an individual, orientation (99).
18. Phiri is referring here to the song itself, not to the novel.
19. See Phiri for an illuminating analysis of how Chimamanda Ngozi Adichie's 2013 novel, *Americanah*, expands some of the key themes of *Song of Solomon*.

Chapter 4

1. Carol E. Schmudde develops this idea; see esp. 412.
2. See Broad 190.
3. "All the empirical evidence, in other words, points to a good, old-fashioned, unified spectral identity," Broad notes (190).
4. Broad points out that "the challenge of decoding and interpreting this spirit is severe, since the section in which Beloved encodes her supernatural autobiography (210–13) is another of those 'excessively demanding' and 'incomprehensible' passages to which Morrison refers in 'Unspeakable Words [sic] Unspoken'" (190).
5. As Carl D. Malmgren points out, the novel's dedication, "Sixty Million and more," lends credence to this explanation (98).
6. Malmgren notes, "Beloved is in this reading the ultimate victim of slavery, a living reminder of the brutality of the institution" (99).
7. As Page notes, "Since neither the telling nor the listening character can tolerate the whole truth at once, the reader must wait" (36).

8. Linda Krumholz notes that "Morrison's fragmented revelation of Sethe's terrible act works to postpone the reader's judgment" (406).
9. See A. Appiah, esp. 23–24.
10. See Carabi 89.
11. For an illuminating analysis of Morrison's "reconstruction" of the South to counter hegemonic understandings of its history, see Deborah H. Barnes, "Myth, Metaphor, and Memory in Toni Morrison's Reconstructed South."
12. Krumholz notes that "Morrison indirectly critiques historical and pedagogical methods prevalent in the United States" (405).
13. As Malmgren notes, "It is the institution of slavery that supplies the logic underwriting the novel, the thematic glue that unifies this multifaceted text" (96), but the white characters in the novel fail to grasp the distorted logic of slavery.
14. "Discovering through Denver who it is visiting at 124, Ella convinces the others 'that rescue was in order' because 'the past [was] something to leave behind' 256). But one never leaves the past behind; the past is always present. One must face the past and learn from it," argues Angelyn Mitchell (105).
15. Berger states that Bodwin "remains blind to the interests and culture of African Americans," including those in his own home (417).
16. For a more detailed development of this idea, see Rafael Pérez-Torres 695.
17. Pamela E. Barnett notes that this incident represents an inversion of rape in that a man rather than a woman is victimized (425).
18. "Morrison constructs history through the acts and consciousness of African-American slaves rather than through the perspective of the dominant white social classes" [395], notes Krumholz. Our comments here are based on Harding's and Martin's extended analysis of the novel's symbolism, esp. 93.
19. In her play, *Desdemona*, a musical and dramatic collaboration with Rokia Traoré, Morrison figuratively speaks for Barbary, the title character's mother's African maid, whose voice is conspicuously absent in Shakespeare's *Othello*.
20. Scarpa notes, "The reader is progressively made the narrator's accomplice and

knows more than some of the characters ... but there are always surprises even for the well-informed reader" (95).

21. The destructive power of townspeople's adoption of white norms about "uppity" blacks that this episode evidences (Harris, "Escaping Slavery" 335) reiterates the lesson about black self-hatred found in *The Bluest Eye*.

22. Heller notes that "the family cannot survive in isolation but requires the strength and protection of a much wider network of 'kinfolk'" (115).

23. The "ritualistic sacrifice of Beloved" is "a ceremony that frees the community from this pervasive haunting" (189), as David Lawrence notes. Bell finds the lesson at the novel's conclusion to be that "the struggle to survive with justifiable self-respect rather than inordinate self-esteem or self-debasement prevails for those who affirm ties to their ethnic community" (14).

24. Also see Bell, *The Contemporary African American Novel*.

25. Scarpa notes that "the characters become the narrators of their story and fill in one another's gaps" (97).

26. This reading is consistent with our analysis of Morrison's strategy of enlisting readers to carry forth into their world the issues and concerns depicted in her fictional worlds.

27. As Harding and Martin put it, "Rather than subsuming complexity in unity, Morrison's symbolism reveals ambivalence in multiplicity" (89).

28. Handley points out that Beloved "inhabits both West African and American cultural spaces; she is at once found and then lost, visible and then invisible, tangibly alive and then part of language, emblematic of both African survival and American loss" (679).

29. See Krumholz, esp. 401.

30. Malmgren notes that "some of its generic forms seem to rub against one another, to co-exist uneasily, in a state of tension, if not antagonism" (96).

31. James Phelan observes that the text's "stubbornness" serves an important purpose: it "helps reveal the limitations of interpretation's desire for mastery" (724).

32. "Denver is Morrison's precursor, the historian with her roots in African-American history and culture" (405), according to Krumholz.

Chapter 5

1. Morrison's 2003 novel, *Love*, opens with this mystifying line: "*The women's legs are spread wide open, so I hum* (3; emphasis in original). Who is speaking? Who are the women? How many are there? Why would someone hum because of women's spread legs? Of course, Morrison declines to resolve these questions quickly, but instead undermines readers' faith in this enigmatic narrator, as she does in her earlier novels, forcing readers to weigh for themselves what is true and what is not. As Jean Wyatt notes, "From the start, L disqualifies herself as reliable narrator," her narrative's credibility "marred by the eccentricity of their content and delivery" ("*Love's Time*," 205–06).

2. For example, what Ralph Reckley, after Robert Rogers, calls the "opposing self" such as "the bad self and guardian angel, the normal self and the diabolical self" (449).

3. African ritual inheritance novels heavily incorporate African-based cultural and historic rituals, especially metaphysical practices, into their narrative.

4. Ethiopian healing scrolls are created by dabtaras, unordained clerics practicing traditional medicine in its most varied aspects. The scrolls incorporate written prayers, talismans, and other images that work synergistically to cure the patient. For more details about the healing process see Jacques Mercier's *Art That Heals*.

5. We use the terms "rhetorical imagery" and "visual rhetoric" interchangeably. Visual rhetoric is a theoretical framework used to analyze how visual images—including written words—communicate. The term is approached differently depending upon the academic field of study. Our use of it includes the analysis of images as well as the images created by the narrative of the written word.

6. "Text of the body" is a term this book's second author created to describe the stories that can be written and shared only as the person in need of healing untangles the mental chains that perpetuate pain and starts a journey leading to wholeness.

7. The setting of an all-black community intertextually recalls the Bottom in *Sula*, Harlem in *Jazz*, and Son's hometown of Eloe, Florida, in *Tar Baby*, which itself pastiches another noble but flawed Floridian town:

Eatonville in Zora Neale Hurston's *Their Eyes Were Watching God*.

8. Anthracite (8-rock) coal also is, significantly, the hardest grade of coal. Like the 8-rock citizens of Ruby, it lasts a long time in its hot crucible.

9. See McBride for an extended analysis of essentialist rhetoric in Morrison.

10. The modernist multivocality of this passage in *Paradise* recalls, for example, *Light in August* and *The Sound and the Fury*. For a detailed comparison of the Faulkner and Morrison, see Weinstein as well as Kolmerten, Ross, and Wittenberg.

11. Although it is not central to our present study, we recommend reading Linda Krumholz's essay on *Paradise* and Sean Grattan's critique of Krumholz and his expansive analysis of the novel's title in light of utopian literary criticism. Most notably, he argues that the title is not as ironic as it might seem: "In writing *Paradise* Morrison draws a map for a kind of subjectivity searching for a more inclusive world, a search that is continually frustrated but also productive of a politics outside typical sociopolitical organizational sites" (372). We see in Grattan's observation a confirmation of our reading: The neighborly love that emerges at the novel's conclusion serves as a model for readers, particularly in a racially fraught American nation.

Chapter 6

1. As we take a reader-response approach to Morrison's work, we theoretically eschew author's stated intentions because we privilege what readers actually *do* with the texts they read, irrespective of authors' designs. As we state in our Introduction, we believe readers co-create meaning with the texts they read; texts are mute until activated by readers' minds as they are influenced by the texts. However, we also know that Morrison is extraordinarily reflective about how her texts move readers, and we therefore feel it is illuminating to consider her authorial intentions not as the final word but as clues to how her novels might operate. We would argue that, more than any other Anglophone author, she has succeeded in her effort to "enunciate race while depriving it of its lethal cling" ("Home," 3), which has entailed her "efforts ... to carve away at the accretions of deceit, blindness, ignorance, paralysis, and sheer malevolence embedded in raced language so that other kinds of perception were not only available but were inevitable" ("Home," 7). Resisting the white gaze embedded in American English, Morrison develops a fresh lexicon to describe a more just national home, calling to mind Audre Lorde's famous 1979 essay, "The Master's Tools Will Never Dismantle the Master's House." The link between language and home is powerful.

2. Because the epigraphical poem prefigures Frank's story, readers naturally will assume that the narrator of the poem is male, not to mention the sexually suggestive analogy of the narrator's phallic "key" fitting the house's "lock."

3. Both horses are male, based on the pronouns Frank uses for them. As the victor begins "nudging the mares before him" (4), one can presume he is not gelded.

4. The psychic cost of repressed memory, the healing of which comes only after compassionate assistance resurfaces the trauma in order to come to terms with it, reminds us of *Goodbye, Farewell and Amen*, the television movie that served as the final episode (1983) of the television drama *M*A*S*H*, in which Hawkeye, like Frank Money in *Home*, must face his own complicity in Korean War tragedies. See Diffrient and Chung.

5. For example, Americans typically think of lynching as a phenomenon of Reconstruction through the 1920s, but at least six African Americans were lynched in the United States in the 1950s ("Lynching Statistics").

6. Martin also notes, interestingly, that the first time he "really took note of the clash between the beauty of nature and the trauma of lynching was in Toni Morrison's *Beloved*" (94).

7. See Katha Pollitt's moving poem, "Lilacs in September," in which a storm-split tree (a lilac) has bloomed out of season, with its flowers. It is hard to imagine a poem more fitting for Frank and Cee.

8. Stave contrasts Frank, as a dynamic, evolving character, with Son in *Tar Baby*, whom she identifies as the only static male character in Morrison's oeuvre to date. She sees Frank, in fact, as something of a revision of Son, whose misogyny never abates.

Chapter 7

1. See esp. her landmark essay, "Demarginalizing."
2. We refer here to Du Bois's famous essay, "Of Our Spiritual Strivings," in his classic text, *The Souls of Black Folk*, esp. 5.
3. Hyphenated here for emphasis.
4. See our discussion of Patterson's work in our chapter on *Beloved*.
5. This is not to say, in reductionist fashion, that critics may not study literary works of writers outside their own demographics—in fact, they should learn from such work—but they need to do so with abundant care and humility. In fact, in writing this book, Goldstein, who identifies as white, had much to learn, especially about African traditions, from Campbell, who identifies as African American.
6. This line echoes Paul D's declaration to Sethe in *Beloved*, as we point out below: "You your best thing, Sethe. You are" (273).

Works Cited

Aanerud, Rebecca. "Fictions of Whiteness: Speaking the Names of Whiteness in U.S. Literature." *Displacing Whiteness: Essays in Social and Cultural Criticism*. Ed. Ruth Frankenberg. Duke UP, 1997. 35–59.

Abel, Elizabeth. "Black Writing, White Reading: Race and the Politics of Feminist Interpretation." *Critical Inquiry* 19 (Spring 1993): 470–98.

Ahmad, Soophia. "Women Who Make a Man: Female Protagonists in Toni Morrison's *Song of Solomon*." *Atenea* 27.2 (Dec. 2008): 59–73.

Alexandru, Maria-Sabina Draga. "Love as Reclamation in Toni Morrison's African American Rhetoric." *European Journal of American Culture* 27.3 (2008): 191–205.

Anatol, Giselle Liza. *Song of Solomon*. Language Matters II: Reading and Teaching Toni Morrison. Online. http://www2.ku.edu/~langmtrs/lmII/discussions/song.html. Retrieved 1 Jan. 2020.

Androne, Helane Adams. "Revised Memories and Colliding Identities: Absence and Presence in Morrison's 'Recitatif' and Viramontes's 'Tears on My Pillow.'" *MELUS* 32.2 (Summer 2007): 133–50.

Appiah, Kwame Anthony. "Race." *Critical Terms for Literary Study*. Ed. Frank Lentricchia and Thomas McLaughlin. U of Chicago P, 1990. 274–87.

Appiah, [Kwame] Anthony. "The Uncompleted Argument: Du Bois and the Illusion of Race." *"Race," Writing, and Difference*. Ed. Henry Louis Gates, Jr. U of Chicago P, 1986. 21–37.

Avery, Faith M. "'Let Loose the Dogs': Messiness and Ethical Wrangling in Toni Morrison's *Tar Baby*." *Iowa Journal of Cultural Studies* 16.1 (2014): 4–21.

Awkward, Michael. *Inspiriting Influences: Tradition, Revision, and Afro-American Women's Novels*. Columbia UP, 1989.

Azizmohammadi, Fatemeh, and Hamedreza Kohzadi. "A Study of Racism in Toni Morrison's the [sic] *Song of Solomon*." *Australian Journal of Basic and Applied Sciences* 5.12 (2011): 2260–64.

Bambara, Toni Cade. *The Salt Eaters*. Random House, 1980.

Bao, Jinping. "On Magic Narrative Technique in Toni Morrison's *Beloved*." *Cross-Cultural Communication* 8.3 (2012): 1–7.

Baraka, [Imamu] Amiri (LeRoi Jones), and Amina Baraka, eds. *Confirmation: An Anthology of AfricanAmerican Women*. Morrow, 1983.

Barnes, Deborah H. "Myth, Metaphor, and Memory in Toni Morrison's Reconstructed South." *Atlanta: Studies in the Literary Imagination* 31.2 (Fall 1998): 17–35.

Barnes, Paula. *Tradition and Innovation: Toni Morrison and the Flight Motif in Afro-American Literature*. Greenwood, 2000.

Barnett, Pamela E. "Figurations of Rape and the Supernatural in *Beloved*." *PMLA* 112 (May 1997): 418–27.

Beach, Richard. *A Teacher's Introduction to Reader-Response Theories*. NCTE, 1993.

Bell, Bernard W. "*Beloved*: A Womanist Neo-Slave Narrative; or Multivocal Remembrances of Things Past." *African American Review* 26 (1991): 7–15.

———. *The Contemporary African American Novel: Its Roots and Modern Literary Branches*. U of Massachusetts P, 2004.

Bellamy, Maria Rice. "'These Careful Words ... Will Talk to Themselves': Textual Remains and Reader Responsibility in

Toni Morrison's *A Mercy*." In *Contested Boundaries: New Critical Essays on the Fiction of Toni Morrison*. Ed. Maxine Montgomery. Cambridge Scholars, 2013. 14–32.

Belsey, Catherine. *Critical Practice*. Methuen, 1980.

Benjamin, Shanna Greene. "The Space That Race Creates: An Interstitial Analysis of Toni Morrison's 'Recitatif.'" *Studies in American Fiction* 40.1 (Spring 2013): 87–106.

Bennett, Juda. "Toni Morrison and the Burden of the Passing Narrative." *African American Review* 35.2 (Summer 2001): 205–17.

Bentson, Kimberly W. "Re-Weaving the 'Ulysses Scene': Enchantment, Post-Oedipal Identity, and the Buried Text of Blackness in Toni Morrison's *Song of Solomon*." *Comparative American Identities: Race, Sex, and Nationality in the Modern Text*. Ed. Hortense J. Spillers. Routledge, 1991.

Berger, James. "Ghosts of Liberalism: Morrison's *Beloved* and the Moynihan Report." *PMLA* 111 (May 1996): 408–20.

Bérubé, Michael. *Marginal Forces/Cultural Centers: Tolson, Pynchon, and the Politics of the Canon*. Cornell UP, 1982.

Boswell, Barbara. "Re-Memory and an African Ecofeminist Poetic of Healing in Malika Ndlovu's Poetry." *Scrutiny2: Issues in English Studies in Southern Africa* 16.2 (2011), 32–41.

Bouson, J. Brooks. "Uncovering 'the Beloved' in the Warring and Lawless Women in Toni Morrison's *Love*." *Midwest Quarterly* 49.4 (2008): 358–73.

Broad, Robert L. "Giving Blood to the Scraps: Haints, History, and Hosea in *Beloved*." *African American Review* 26 (1991): 189–96.

Brownmiller, Susan. *Against Our Will: Men, Women and Rape*. Bantam, 1976.

Bump, Jerome. "Racism and Appearance in *The Bluest Eye*: A Template for an Ethical Emotive Criticism." *College Literature* 37.2 (Spring 2010): 147–70.

Busia, Abena P.A. "What Is Your Nation?: Reconnecting Africa and Her Diaspora Through Paule Marshall's *Praisesong for the Widow*." *Changing Our Own Words: Essays on Criticism, Theory, and Writing by Black Women*. Ed. Cheryl A. Wall. Rutgers UP, 1989. 196–211.

Butler-Evans, Elliott. *Race, Gender, and Desire: Narrative Strategies in the Fiction of Toni Cade Bambara, Toni Morrison, and Alice Walker*. Temple UP, 1989.

Campbell, Shawnrece D. "Using Ethiopian Healing Scrolls as Ethnomedicine to Read Healing in African American and Contemporary American Literature by Women." In *Multiethnic American Literatures: Essays for Teaching Context and Culture*. Ed. Helane Adams Androne. McFarland, 2015. 205–22.

Carabi, Angels. "Toni Morrison." *Belles Lettres: A Review of Books by Women* 9.3 (Winter 1994): 38–39, 86–90.

Carden, Mary Paniccia. "'Trying to Find a Place When the Streets Don't Go There': Fatherhood, Family, and American Racial Politics in Toni Morrison's *Love*." *African American Review* 44.1–2 (Spring/Summer 2011): 131–47.

Casey, Robert Pierce, Trans. *The Excerpta Ex Theodoto of Clement of Alexandria*. Studies and Documents 1. Christophers, 1934. 40–91. Retrieved 6 Feb. 2019 from Http://www.gnosis.org/library/excr.htm.

Castro, Quassan. "Made of Shade: Dr. Bell Hooks on Zimmerman Effect." Jet.com (24 Jul. 2013). Online. <http://www.jetmag.com/made-of-shade/bell-hooks/>. Retrieved 17 Feb. 2014.

Century, Douglas. *Toni Morrison*. Chelsea, 1994.

Christian, Barbara. *Black Feminist Criticism: Perspectives on Black Women Writers*. Pergamon, 1985.

———. "The Race for Theory." *Cultural Critique* 6 (Spr. 1987): 51–63.

Cole, Johnnetta B. "Africanism in the Americas: A Brief History of the Concept." *Anthropology and Humanism Quarterly* 10.4 (1985): 120–26.

Cook, Thomas D., and Donald T. Campbell. *Quasi-Experimentation: Design and Analysis Issues for Field Settings*. Houghton, 1979.

Coser, Stelamaris. *Bridging the Americas: The Literature of Toni Morrison, Paule Marshall, and Gayl Jones*. Temple UP, 1995.

Crawford, Mary, and Roger Chaffin. "The Reader's Construction of Meaning: Cognitive Research on Gender and Comprehension." *Gender and Reading: Essays on Readers, Texts, and Contexts*. Ed. Elizabeth A. Flynn and Patrocinio P. Schweickart. Johns Hopkins UP, 1986. 3–30.

Creel, Margaret Washington. "Gullah Attitudes Toward Life and Death." *Africanisms in American Culture*. Ed. Joseph E. Holloway. Indiana UP, 1990, 69–97.

———. *A Peculiar People: Slave Religion and Community Culture Among the Gullahs*. New York UP, 1988.

Crenshaw, Kimberlé. "Demarginalizing the Intersection of Race and Sex: A Black Feminist Critique of Antidiscrimination Doctrine, Feminist Theory and Antiracist Politics." *Chicago Legal Forum* 1989.1: 139–67.

———. "Mapping the Margins: Intersectionality, Identity Politics, and Violence Against Women of Color." *Stanford Law Review* 43.6 (Jul. 1991): 1241–99.

Cristea, Ileana. "Changing Places (and Not Only) in *Home* by Toni Morrison." *East-West Cultural Passage* 2 (2014): 117–129.

Dalgish, Gerard M. *A Dictionary of Africanisms: Contributions of Sub-Saharan Africa to the English Language*. Greenwood P, 1982.

Delazari, Ivan. "Voicing the Split Narrator: Readers' Chores in Toni Morrison's 'Recitatif.'" *Audionarratology: Interfaces of Sound and Narrative*. DeGruyter, 2016. 199–215.

Derrida, Jacques. "Racism's Last Word." Trans. Peggy Kamuf. *"Race," Writing, and Difference*. Ed. Henry Louis Gates, Jr. U of Chicago P, 1986. 329–38.

Diffrient, David Scott and Hye Seung Chung. "TV Hybridity: Genre Mixing and Narrative Complexity in *M*A*S*H*." *Quarterly Review of Film and Video* 29.4 (2012): 285–302.

Drieling, Claudia. "Constructs of 'Home' in Gloria Naylor's Quartet." Königshausen and Neumann, 2011.

Du Bois, W.E.B. *The Souls of Black Folk*. 1903. Penguin, 1989.

Ethnic Notions. Dir. and screenplay by Marlon Riggs. California Newsreel, 1986.

Fanon, Franz. *Black Skin, White Masks*. 1967. Trans. Charles Lam Markmann. Grove, 1991.

Feagin, Joe R., and Clairece Booher Feagin. *Discrimination American Style: Institutional Racism and Sexism*. 2nd ed. Kreiger, 1986.

Fish, Stanley E. "Interpreting the *Variorum*." *Reader-Response Criticism: From Formalism to Post-Structuralism*. Ed. Jane P. Tompkins. Johns Hopkins UP, 1980. 164–84.

———. *Is There a Text in This Class?* Harvard UP, 1980.

Foster, Frances Smith. *Witnessing Slavery: The Development of Ante-bellum Slave Narratives*. Greenwood, 1979.

Foucault, Michel. *Madness and Civilization: A History of Insanity in the Age of Reason*. Trans. Richard Howard. Pantheon, 1965.

Francisco, Dayane Evelline de Souza. "'Ain't That the Same?' Intersectionality and the Supplements in Toni Morrison's *Sula*." *Estudos Anglo Americanos* 47.1 (2018): 137–52.

Freund, Elizabeth. *The Return of the Reader: Reader-Response Criticism*. New Accents. Methuen, 1987.

Fuller, Hoyt W. "Towards a Black Aesthetic." *Afro-American Writing: An Anthology of Prose and Poetry*. Ed. Richard A. Long and Eugenia W. Collier. 2nd ed. Pennsylvania State UP, 1985. 582–88.

Furman, Jan. *Toni Morrison's Fiction*. U of South Carolina P, 1996.

Gates, Henry Louis, Jr. *Figures in Black: Words, Signs, and the "Racial" Self*. Oxford UP, 1987).

———. Preface. *Toni Morrison: Critical Perspectives Past and Present*. Ed. Henry Louis Gates, Jr., and K[wame] A[nthony] Appiah. Amistad. ix–xiii.

———. *The Signifying Monkey: A Theory of African-American Literary Criticism*. Oxford UP, 1988.

———. "Talkin' That Talk." *"Race," Writing, and Difference*. U of Chicago P, 1986. 402–09.

———, ed. "Writing 'Race' and the Difference It Makes." Editor's Introduction. *"Race," Writing, and Difference*. U of Chicago P, 1986. 1–20.

Genovese, Eugene D. *Roll, Jordan, Roll: The World the Slaves Made*. Vintage, 1976.

Gibson, Donald B. "Text and Countertext in *The Bluest Eye*. *Toni Morrison: Critical Perspectives Past and Present*." Ed. Henry Louis Gates, Jr., and K[wame] A[nthony] Appiah. Amistad, 1993. 159–74.

Gillespie, Diane, and Missy Dehn Kubitschek. "Who Cares? Women-Centered Psychology in *Sula*." *Black American Literature Forum* 24.1 (Spring1990): 21–48.

Gilman, Sander L. "Black Bodies, White

Bodies: Toward an Iconography of Female Sexuality in Late Nineteenth-Century Art, Medicine, and Literature." *"Race," Writing, and Difference.* Ed. Henry Louis Gates, Jr. U of Chicago P, 1986. 223–61.

Glass, Joshua. "Literary Giants Junot Díaz and Toni Morrison on Their Unwillingness to Surrender." *Document* 10. Web. Retrieved 16 Jun. 2017 from http://www.documentjournal.com/article/junot-diaz-and-toni-morrison.

Goldstein-Shirley, David. "Preacher in the Clearing: Toni Morrison at the Turn of the Millennium." *Fake-City Syndrome: American Cultural Essays.* Ed. Kate Gale and Charles Rammelkamp. Red Hen, 2002. 184–99.

Goulimari, Pelagia. "'Something Else to Be': Singularities and Scapegoating Logics in Toni Morrison's Early Novels." *Angelaki: Journal of the Theoretical Humanities* 2.2 (Aug. 2006): 191–204.

Grattan, Sean. "Monstrous Utopia in Toni Morrison's *Paradise*." *Genre* 46.3 (Fall 2013): 367–92.

Greenfield-Sanders, Timothy. *Toni Morrison: The Pieces I Am.* Film. Magnolia Pictures, 2019.

Guernin, Wilford L., et al. *A Handbook of Critical Approaches to Literature.* 3rd ed. Oxford UP, 1992.

Guerrero, Edward. "Tracking 'The Look' in the Novels of Toni Morrison." *Black American Literature Forum* 24 (Winter 1990): 761–73.

Hall, James, and Kenneth Clark. *Dictionary of Subjects and Symbols in Art.* Harper & Row, 1979.

Handley, William R. "The House a Ghost Built: *Nommo*, Allegory, and the Ethics of Reading in Toni Morrison's *Beloved*." *Contemporary Literature* 36 (1995): 676–701.

Hansberry, Lorraine. *Les Blancs: The Collected Last Plays of Lorraine Hansberry.* Ed. Robert Nemiroff. Random, 1973.

Harack, Katrina. "'Not Even in the Language They Had Invented for Secrets': Trauma, Memory, and Re-witnessing in Toni Morrison's *Love*." *Mississippi Quarterly* 66.2 (2013): 255–78.

Harding, Wendy, and Jacky Martin. "Reading at the Cultural Interface: The Corn Symbolism of *Beloved*." *MELUS* 19 (Summer 1994): 85–97.

Harris, Trudier. "Escaping Slavery but Not Its Images." *Toni Morrison: Critical Perspectives Past and Present.* Ed. Henry Louis Gates, Jr., and K[wame] A[nthony] Appiah. Amistad, 1993. 330–41.

———. *Fiction and Folklore: The Novels of Toni Morrison.* U of Tennessee P, 1991.

———. Preface. *Exorcising Blackness: Historical and Literary Lynching and Burning Rituals.* Indiana UP, 1984. ix–xiii.

Heinze, Denise. *The Dilemma of "Double-Consciousness": Toni Morrison's Novels.* U of Georgia P, 1993.

Heller, Dana. "Reconstructing Kin: Family, History, and Narrative in Toni Morrison's *Beloved*." *College Literature* 21 (June 1994): 105–17.

Hill, Cecily E. "Three Meals: Eating Culture in Toni Morrison's *Tar Baby*." *Midwest Quarterly* 53.3 (2012): 283–98.

Holloway, Joseph E., ed. *Africanisms in American Culture.* Indiana UP, 2005.

Holloway, Karla F.C. "*Beloved*: A Spiritual." *Callaloo* 13 (1990): 516–25.

Holloway, Karla F.C., and Stephanie A. Demetrakopoulos. *New Dimensions of Spirituality: A Biracial and Bicultural Reading of the Novels of Toni Morrison.* Greenwood, 1987.

Holton, Robert. "Bearing Witness: Toni Morrison's *Song of Solomon* and *Beloved*." *English Studies in Canada* 2.1 (March 1994): 79–90.

hooks, bell. "The Oppositional Gaze." *The Feminism and Visual Cultural Reader.* Routledge, 2003: Amelia Jones. 94–105.

———. "Representing Whiteness in the Black Imagination." *Displacing Whiteness: Essays in Social and Cultural Criticism.* Ed. Ruth Frankenberg. Duke UP, 1997. 165–79.

Humann, Heather Duerre. "Family and Violence in *Love*." *Women's Studies* 43 (2014): 246–62.

Ibarrola, Aitor. "The Challenges of Recovering from Individual and Cultural Trauma in Toni Morrison's *Home*." *International Journal of English Studies* 14.1 (2014): 109–24.

Illes, Judika. Foreword. *A Healing Grove: African Tree Remedies and Rituals for the Body and Spirit.* Stephanie Rose Bird. Lawrence Hill, 2009.

Iser, Wolfgang. *The Act of Reading: A Theory of Aesthetic Response.* 1976. Johns Hopkins UP, 1978.

———. *The Implied Reader: Patterns of Com-*

munication in Prose Fiction from Bunyan to Beckett. 1972. Johns Hopkins UP, 1974.

Jackman, Mary R. *The Velvet Glove: Paternalism and Conflict in Gender, Class, and Race Relations*. U of California P, 1994.

Jauss, Hans Robert. *Toward an Aesthetic of Reception*. Trans. Timothy Bahti. Theory and History of Lit. 2. U of Minnesota P, 1982.

Jennings, La Vinia Delois. *Toni Morrison and the Idea of Africa*. 2008. Cambridge UP, 2010.

Jewett, Chad. "The Modality of Toni Morrison's *Jazz*." *African American Review* 48.4 (Win. 2015): 445–56.

Joly, Claire Helene. *"A Bridge of Words": The American Critical Reception of Richard Wright, 1938–1945*. Diss. U of California, Irvine, 1994. Ann Arbor: UMI, 1994. 9506824.

Jones, LeRoi [Imamu Amiri Baraka]. "State/Meant." *Home: Social Essays*. Morrow, 1966. 251–52.

Kaiser, Mario, and Sarah Lapido Manyinka. "Toni Morrison in Conversation." *Granta*. Web. 29 Jun. 2017. Retrieved 4 Jul. 2017 from https://granta.com/toni-morrison-conversation/.

Kolmerten, Carol A., Stephen M. Ross, and Judith Bryant Wittenberg. *Unflinching Gaze: Morrison and Faulkner Re-Envisioned*. UP of Mississippi, 1997.

Krumholtz, Linda. "The Ghosts of Slavery: Historical Recovery in Toni Morrison's *Beloved*." *African American Review* 26 (1992): 395–408.

———. "Reading and Insight in Toni Morrison's *Paradise*." *African American Review* 36.21 (2002): 21–34.

Kubitschek, Missy Dehn. *Toni Morrison: A Critical Companion*. Greenwood, 1998.

Lawrence, David. "Fleshly Ghosts and Ghostly Flesh: The Word and the Body in *Beloved*." *Studies in American Fiction* 19 (Autumn 1991): 189–201.

Lawrence, Elizabeth Atwood. *Rodeo: An Anthropologist Looks at the Wild and the Tame*. 1982. U of Chicago P, 1984.

Leitch, Vincent B. *American Literary Criticism from the Thirties to the Eighties*. Columbia UP, 1988.

Levend Water. "The Spiritual Significance of Numbers." Online. http://levendwater.org/companion/append10.html. Retrieved 12 Dec. 2013.

Levine, Lawrence W. *Black Culture and Black Consciousness: Afro-American Folk Thought from Slavery to Freedom*. Oxford UP, 1977.

Levy, Andrew. "Telling *Beloved*." *Texas Studies in Literature and Language* 33 (Spring 1991): 114–23.

Li, Stephanie. "'Paradise Lost': Reconciling the Semiotic and Symbolic in Toni Morrison's *Love*." *Studies in the Literary Imagination* 47.1 (Spr. 2014): 27–47.

Lilienfeld, Jane. "'To Have the Reader Work with the Author': The Circulation of Knowledge in Virginia Woolf's *To the Lighthouse* and Toni Morrison's *Jazz*." *Modern Fiction Studies* 52.1 (Spring 2006): 42–65.

Łobodziec, Agnieszka. "Toni Morrison's Discredited Magic: Magical Realism in *Beloved* Revisited." *Brno Studies in English* 38.1 (2012): 103–21.

López Ramírez, Manuela. "The Shell-Shocked Veteran in Toni Morrison's *Sula* and *Home*." *Journal of the Spanish Assn. of Anglo-American Studies* 38.1 (Jun. 2016): 129–47.

Lorde, Audre. "The Master's Tools Will Never Dismantle the Master's House." 1979. Rpt. In *Sister Outsider: Essays and Speeches*. Crossing P, 2007. 110–14.

Lubiano, Wahneema. "The Postmodernist Rag: Political Identity and the Vernacular in *Song of Solomon*." *New Essays On Song of Solomon*. Ed. Valerie Smith. Cambridge UP, 1995. 93–116.

"Lynchings: By Year and Race." U of Missouri-Kansas City. Retrieved 22 Dec. 2018 from http://law2.umkc.edu/Faculty/projects/ftrials/shipp/lynchingyear.html.

Madden, Mary. "Necessary Narratives: Toni Morrison and Literary Identities." *Women's Studies International Forum* 18 (1995): 585–94.

Mailloux, Steven. *Interpretive Conventions: The Reader in the Study of American Fiction*. Cornell UP, 1982.

———. "Misreading as a Historical Act: Cultural Rhetoric, Bible Politics, and Fuller's 1845 Review of Douglass's *Narrative*." *Readers in History: Nineteenth-Century American Literature and the Contexts of Response*. Ed. James L. Machor. Johns Hopkins UP, 1993. 3–31.

———. *Rhetorical Power*. Cornell UP, 1989.

Major, Clarence, ed. *Calling the Wind: Twentieth-Century African-American Short Stories*. HarperPerennial, 1993.

Malmgren, Carl D. "Mixed Genres and the Logic of Slavery in Toni Morrison's *Beloved.*" *Critique* 36 (Winter 1995): 97–106.

"Manuscript Reader Report." Anonymous. Received via e-mail on 23 Sept. 2019.

Martin, Daniel J. "Lynching Sites: Where Trauma and Pastoral Collide." In *Coming into Contact: Explorations in Ecocritical Theory and Practice.* U of Georgia P, 2007. Project MUSE. Web. 14 Dec. 2013. http://muse.jhu.edu/.

Mbiti, John S. *African Religions and Philosophy.* Anchor, 1970.

McBride, Dwight A. "Speaking the Unspeakable: On Toni Morrison, African American Intellectuals and the Uses of Essentialist Rhetoric." *Modern Fiction Studies* 39 (Fall/Winter 1993): 755–76.

McIntosh, Peggy. "White Privilege: Unpacking the Invisible Knapsack." *Experiencing Race, Class, and Gender in the United States,* 2nd ed. Ed. Virginia Cyrus. Mayfield, 1996. 194–97.

Medoro, Dana. "Justice and Citizenship in Toni Morrison's *Song of Solomon.*" *Canadian Review of American Studies* 32.1 (2002): 1–15.

Mellard, James M. "Unimaginable Acts Imagined: Fathers, Family Myth, and the Postmodern Crisis of Paternal Authority in Toni Morrison's *Love.*" *Mississippi Quarterly* 63.1–2 (2010): 233–67.

Meyer, Lakeisha. "Testimony and Transformation: An Exploration of the Intersection of the Arts of Toni Morrison and the Potential Therapeutic Uses of Narrative." *Toni Morrison: Forty Years in the Clearing.* Ed. Carmen R. Gillespie. Bucknell UP, 2012. 238–44.

Middleton, Joyce Irene. "From Orality to Literacy: Oral Memory in Toni Morrison's *Song of Solomon.* New Essays on *Song of Solomon.* Ed. Valerie Smith. Cambridge UP, 1995. 19–39.

Miner, Madonne M. "Lady No Longer Sings the Blues: Rape, Madness, and Silence in *The Bluest Eye.*" *Conjuring: Black Women, Fiction, and Literary Tradition.* Ed. Marjorie Pryse and Hortense J. Spillers. Indiana UP, 1985. 176–91.

Mitchell, Angelyn. *The Freedom to Remember: Narrative, Slavery, and Gender in Contemporary Black Women's Fiction.* Rutgers UP, 2002.

_____. *Love.* Language Matters II: Reading and Teaching Toni Morrison. Online. http://www2.ku.edu/~langmtrs/lmII/discussions/love.html. Retrieved 24 Dec. 2019.

Mitchell-Kernan, Claudia. *Language Behavior in a Black Urban Community.* Working Paper 23. Language-Behavior Research Laboratory. U of California, Berkeley, 1969.

Mobley, Marilyn Sanders. "Call and Response: Voice, Community, and Dialogic Structures in Toni Morrison's *Song of Solomon.*" New Essays on *Song of Solomon.* Ed. Valerie Smith. Cambridge UP, 1995. 41–68.

_____. "A Different Remembering: Memory, History, and Meaning in *Beloved.*" *Toni Morrison: Critical Perspectives Past and Present.* Ed. Henry Louis Gates, Jr., and K[wame] A[nthony] Appiah. Amistad, 1993. 356–65.

_____. *Folk Roots and Mythic Wings in Sarah Orne Jewett and Toni Morrison: The Cultural Function of Narrative.* Louisiana State UP, 1991.

Montagu, Ashley. *Man's Most Dangerous Myth: The Fallacy of Race.* 6th ed. AltaMira, 1997.

Mori, Aoi. "Rewriting the History in Toni Morrison's Trilogy of *Beloved, Jazz* and *Paradise.*" *Bulletin of Hiroshima Jogakuin University* 51 (Dec. 2001): 35–45.

Morris, Susana M. "A Past Not Pure but Stifled: Vexed Legacies of Leadership in Toni Morrison's *Love.*" *South Atlantic Quarterly* 112:2 (Spr. 2013): 319–38.

_____. "'Sisters Separated for Much Too Long': Women's Friendship and Power in Toni Morrison's 'Recitatif.'" *Tulsa Studies in Women's Literature* 32.1 (Spring 2013): 159–80.

Morrison, Toni. *Beloved.* Penguin, 1987.

_____. *The Bluest Eye.* Washington Square-Pocket, 1970.

_____. *The Dancing Mind: Speech Upon the Acceptance of the National Book Foundation Medal for Distinguished Contribution to American Letters on the Sixth of November, Nineteen Hundred and Ninety-Six.* Knopf, 1997.

_____. *Desdemona.* Oberon, 2012.

_____. "Friday on the Potomac." Introduction. *Race-ing Justice, En-Gendering Power: Essays on Anita Hill, Clarence Thomas, and the Construction of Social Reality.* Ed. Toni Morrison. Pantheon, 1992.

——. *God Help the Child*. Knopf, 2015. Kindle Edition.

——. "Home." In *The House That Race Built: Original Essays by Angela Y. Davis, Cornel West, and Others on Black Americans and Politics in America Today*. Ed. Wahneema Lubiano. Vintage, 1998. 5-12.

——. *Home*. Knopf, 2012.

——. *Jazz*. Penguin, 1992.

——. *Lecture and Speech of Acceptance, Upon the Award of the Nobel Prize for Literature, Delivered in Stockholm on the Seventh of December, Nineteen Hundred and Ninety-Three*. Knopf, 1997.

——. *Love*. Vintage, 2003.

——. *A Mercy*. Knopf, 2008.

——. "The Official Story: Dead Man Golfing." Introduction. *Birth of a Nation'Hood*. Ed. Toni Morrison and Claudia Brodsky Lacour. Pantheon, 1997.

——. *Paradise*. Knopf, 1998.

——. *Playing in the Dark: Whiteness and the Literary Imagination*. Vintage, 1993.

——. "Recitatif." *Confirmation: An Anthology of AfricanAmerican Women*. Ed. [Imamu] Amiri Baraka (LeRoi Jones) and Amina Baraka. Morrow, 1983. 243-61.

——. "Rootedness: The Ancestor as Foundation." *Black Women Writers (1950-1980): A Critical Evaluation*. Ed. Mari Evans. Anchor, 1984. 339-45.

——. *Song of Solomon*. Penguin, 1977.

——. *Sula*. Plume-NAL, 1973.

——. "Talk with Toni Morrison." Interview by Elsie B. Washington. *Conversations with Toni Morrison*. Ed. Danille Taylor-Guthrie. UP of Mississippi, 1994. 234-38.

——. *Tar Baby*. Knopf, 1981.

——. *Toni Morrison Interview with Kay Bonetti*. Audiotape. American Audio Prose Library, 3112, 1983.

——. "Unspeakable Things Unspoken: The Afro-American Presence in American Literature." *Michigan Quarterly Review* 28 (1989): 1-34.

——, and Charlie Rose. Interview. *Charlie Rose*. Television. 7 May 1993. Online. https://youtu.be/F4vIGvKpT1c. Accessed 24 Dec. 2019.

Murphy, Anne N. *A Narrative of Her Own: Appropriating Aesthetics for Postcolonial Feminism*. MA Thesis, Georgetown U, 2011.

Naylor, Gloria, and Toni Morrison. "A Conversation." *Southern Review* 21 (1985): 589-90.

Neal, Larry. "And Shine Swam On." Afterword. *Black Fire: An Anthology of Afro-American Writing*. Ed. LeRoi Jones [Imamu Amiri Baraka] and Larry Neal. Morrow, 1968. 638-56.

——. "The Black Arts Movement." *The Drama Review* 12 (Summer 1968): 29-39.

"Nobel Prize for Literature 1993—Press Release." *Nobelprize.org*. Nobel Media AB 2014. Web. 21 Sep 2017. http://www.nobelprize.org/nobel_prizes/literature/laureates/1993/press.html.

Omi, Michael, and Howard Winant. *Racial Formation in the United States: From the 1960s to the 1990s*. 2nd ed. Routledge, 1994.

Page, Philip. "Circularity in Toni Morrison's *Beloved*." *African American Review* 26 (1992): 31-39.

Palmer, Robert. *Deep Blues*. Penguin, 1982.

Patterson, Orlando. *Slavery and Social Death: A Comparative Study*. Harvard UP, 1982.

Pérez-Torres, Rafael. "Knitting and Knotting the Narrative Thread—*Beloved* as Postmodern Novel." *Modern Fiction Studies* 39 (Fall/Winter 1993): 689-707.

Phelan, James. "Toward a Rhetorical Reader-Response Criticism: The Difficult, the Stubborn, and the Ending of *Beloved*." *Modern Fiction Studies* 39 (Fall/Winter 1993): 709-28.

Philyaw, Deesha. Review of *God Help the Child* by Toni Morrison. *Bitch* 15.67 (Summer 2015): 59.

Phiri, Aretha. "Expanding Black Subjectivities in Toni Morrison's *Song of Solomon* and Chimamanda Ngozi Adichie's *Americanah*." *Cultural Studies* 31.1 (2017): 121-42.

Pollitt, Katha. "Lilacs in September." *The New Yorker* (22 Sept. 2003): 189.

Powell, Timothy B. "Toni Morrison: The Struggle to Depict the Black Figure on the White Page." *Black American Literature Forum* 24 (Winter 1990): 747-60.

Previn, André, and Toni Morrison. *Honey and Rue: Six Songs for Soprano and Orchestra*. Chester Music, 1993. Musical score.

Prose, Francine. "Growing Up Too Black." Review of *God Help the Child* by Toni Morrison. *New York Review of Books* 62.8 (7 May 2015): 11-13.

Rabinowitz, Peter J. "Reader-Response Theory and Criticism." *The Johns Hopkins Guide to Literary Theory and Criticism*. Ed. Michael Groden and Martin Kreiswirth. Johns Hopkins UP, 1994.

Rashomon. Dir. Akira Kurosawa. Daiei, 1950.

Reckley, Ralph. "The Use of the Doppelganger or Double in Chester Himes' [sic] *Lonely Crusade*." *CLA Journal* 20 (June 1977): 448–58.

Rochman, Hazel, and Darlene Z. McCampbell, Selectors. *Leaving Home: Stories*. HarperCollins, 1997.

Rogers, Robert. *A Psychoanalytic Study of the Double in Literature*. Wayne State UP, 1970.

Romero, Channette. *Activism and the American Novel: Religion and Resistance in Fiction by Women*. U of Virginia P, 2012.

Roye, Susmita. "Toni Morrison's Disrupted Girls and Their Disturbed Girlhoods: *The Bluest Eye* and *A Mercy*. *Callaloo* 35.1 (Winter 2012): 212–27.

Ryan, Judylyn S. "Language and Narrative Techniques in Toni Morrison's Novels." In Tally, Justine, ed. *Cambridge Companion to Toni Morrison*. Cambridge UP. 151–61.

Salvino, Dana Nelson. "The Word in Black and White: Ideologies of Race and Literacy in Antebellum America." *Reading in America: Literature and Social History*. Ed. Cathy N. Davidson. Johns Hopkins UP, 1989. 140–56.

Samuels, Wilfred D., and Clenora Hudson-Weems. *Toni Morrison*. Twayne, 1990.

Saunders, James Robert. "Why Losing a Tooth Matters: Shirley Jackson's 'The Tooth' and Toni Morrison's *The Bluest Eye*." *The Midwest Quarterly* 53.2 (2012): 193–204.

Scarpa, Giulia. "Narrative Possibilities at Play in Toni Morrison's *Beloved*." *MELUS* 17 (Winter 1991–92): 91–103.

Schmudde, Carol E. "The Haunting of 124." *African American Review* 26 (1992): 409–15.

Schreiber, Evelyn Jaffe. *Race, Trauma, and Home in the Novels of Toni Morrison*. Louisiana State UP, 2010.

Schreiner, Samantha. "Naming, Identity and Intersectionality in Toni Morrison's *Sula*, *Beloved* and *A Mercy*." *English Academy Review* 36.2 (3 Jul. 2019): 38–48.

Schwab, Gabriele. "Reader-Response and the Aesthetic Experience of Otherness." *Stanford Literature Review* 3 (1986): 107–36.

Shange, Ntozake. "Interview with Toni Morrison." *American Rag*. Nov. 1978: 48–52.

Shepperd, Rene. E-mail to the author. 12 Mar. 1997.

Sherard, Tracey. "Women's Classic Blues in Toni Morrison's *Jazz*: Cultural Artifact as Narrator." *Genders* 31 (2000). Online. https://www.atria.nl/ezines/IAV_606661/IAV_606661_2010_51/g31_sherard.html. Retrieved 25 Sept. 2015.

Skerrett, Joseph T., Jr. "Recitation to the *Griot*: Storytelling and Learning in Toni Morrison's *Song of Solomon*." *Conjuring: Black Women, Fiction, and Literary Tradition*. Ed. Marjorie Pryse and Hortense J. Spillers. Indiana UP, 1985. 192–202.

Sklar, Howard. "'What the Hell Happened to Maggie?' Stereotype, Sympathy, and Disability in Toni Morrison's 'Recitatif.'" *Journal of Literary and Cultural Disability Studies* 5.2 (2011): 137–54.

Smith, Valerie. "'Circling the Subject': History and Narrative in *Beloved*." Ed. Henry Louis Gates, Jr., and K[wame] A[nthony] Appiah. Amistad, 1993. 342–55.

_____. *Toni Morrison: Writing the Moral Imagination*. Blackwell, 2012.

Solórzano, Daniel. "Critical Race Theory, Racial and Gender Microaggressions, and the Experiences of Chicana and Chicano Scholars." *International Journal of Qualitative Studies in Education* 11.1 (1998): 121–36.

_____. "Images and Words That Wound: Critical Race Theory, Racial Stereotyping and Teacher Education." *Teacher Education Quarterly* 24.3 (Summer 1997): 5–19.

Spencer, Jon M. *The Rhythms of Black Folk: Race, Religion, and Pan-Africanism*. Africa World P, 1995.

Spillers, Hortense J. "Formalism Comes to Harlem." *African American Review* 50.4 (Winter 2017): 692–97.

Spivak, Gayatri Chakravorty. *In Other Worlds: Essays in Cultural Politics*. Routledge, 1988.

Stanfield, John H. II. "Racism in America and in Other Race-Centered Nation-States: Synchronic Considerations." *Journal of Comparative Sociology* 32 (1991): 243–60.

Stanley, Sandra Kumamoto. "Maggie in Toni Morrison's 'Recitatif': The Africanist

Presence and Disability Studies." *MELUS* 36.2 (Summer 2001): 71-88.

Stave, Shirley A. "Growing Up to Be a Man: Son Revisited." *Mosaic* 50.4 (Dec. 2017): 17-32.

Stepto, Robert B. *From Behind the Veil: A Study of Afro-American Narrative.* 2nd ed. U of Illinois P, 1991.

Strouse, Jean. "Toni Morrison's Black Magic." *Newsweek* (30 Mar. 1981): 52-57.

Stuckey, Sterling. *Slave Culture: Nationalist Theory and the Foundations of Black America.* Oxford UP, 1987.

Sweeney, Megan. "'Something Rogue': Commensurability, Commodification, Crime, and Justice in Toni Morrison's Later Fiction." *Modern Fiction Studies* 52.2 (Summer 2006): 440-69.

Tate, Claudia. "Conversation with Toni Morrison." *Black Women Writers at Work.* Continuum, 1983. 117-31.

Taylor-Guthrie, Danille. Introduction. *Conversations with Toni Morrison.* Ed. Danille Taylor-Guthrie. UP of Mississippi, 1994. xii-xiv.

Thorsson, Courtney. "James Baldwin and Black Women's Fiction." *African American Review* 46.4 (Win. 2013): 615-31.

Tolnay, Stewart E., and E.M. Beck. *A Festival of Violence: An Analysis of Southern Lynchings, 1882-1930.* U of Chicago P, 1995.

Travis, Molly Abel. "Beyond Empathy: Narrative Distancing and Ethics in Toni Morrison's *Beloved* and J.M. Coetzee's *Disgrace*." *J of Narrative Theory* 40.2 (Sum. 2010): 231-50.

Troyna, Barry. "Busing." *Dictionary of Race and Ethnic Relations.* 3rd ed. Routledge, 1994.

TuSmith, Bonnie. *All My Relatives: Community in Contemporary Ethnic American Literatures.* U of Michigan P, 1993.

Vasile, Alexandra. "Intersectional Approach to Toni Morrison's Intercultural Word." *Cogito: Multidisciplinary Research Journal* 4 (2011): 186-94.

Visvis, Vikki. "Alternatives to the 'Talking Cure': Black Music as Traumatic Testimony in Toni Morrison's *Song of Solomon*." *African American Review* 42.2 (Summer 2008): 255-26.

Wagner-Martin, Linda. "'Closer to the Edge': Toni Morrison's *Song of Solomon*." *Teaching American Ethnic Literatures: Nineteen Essays.* Ed. John R. Maitano and David R. Peck. U of New Mexico P, 1996. 147-57.

Wagner-Martin, Linda, and Cathy N. Davidson, eds. *The Oxford Book of Women's Writing in the United States.* Oxford UP, 1995.

Wall, Cheryl A. "Taking Positions and Changing Words." Introduction. *Changing Our Own Words: Essays on Criticism, Theory, and Writing by Black Women.* Rutgers UP, 1989. 1-15.

———. "Trying to Get Home: Place and Memory in Toni Morrison's Fiction." In *Toni Morrison.* Ed. Adrienne Lanier Seward and Justine Tally. UP of Mississippi, 2014.

Wallace, Cynthia R. "L as Language: Love and Ethics." *African American Review* 47.2-3 (Summer-Fall 2014): 375-90.

Walters, Wendy W. "'One of Dese Mornings, Bright and Fair,/Take My Wings and Cleave De Air': The Legend of the Flying Africans and Diasporic Consciousness." *MELUS* 22 (Fall 1997): 3-30.

Ward, Jervette R. "In Search of Diversity: Dick and Jane and Their Black Playmates." *Making Connections: Interdisciplinary Approaches to Cultural Diversity* 13.2 (Spring 2012).

Wardi, Anissa Janine. "A Laying on of Hands: Toni Morrison and the Materiality of Love." *MELUS* 30.3 (Fall 2005): 201-18.

Warnes, Andrew. *Hunger Overcome? Food and Resistance in Twentieth-Century African-American Literature.* U of Georgia P, 2004.

Weinstein, Philip M. *What Else but Love? The Ordeal of Race in Faulkner and Morrison.* Columbia UP, 1996.

White, Evelyn C. Review of *God Help the Child* by Toni Morrison. *Herizons* 29.1 (Summer 2015): 35.

Wilentz, Gay. *Healing Narratives: Women Writers Curing Cultural Dis-ease.* Rutgers UP, 2000.

Willis, Susan. "Eruptions of Funk: Historicizing Toni Morrison." *Toni Morrison: Critical Perspectives Past and Present.* Ed. Henry Louis Gates, Jr., and K[wame] A[nthony] Appiah. Amistad, 1993. 308-29.

Wong, Shelley. "Transgression as Poesis in *The Bluest Eye*." *Callaloo* 13 (Summer 1990): 471-81.

Wright, Richard. "How 'Bigger' Was Born."

Introduction. *Native Son*. 1940. Harper, 1987. vii–xxxiv.

Wyatt, Jean. "The Economic Grotesque and the Critique of Capitalism in Toni Morrison's *Tar Baby*." *MELUS* 39.1 (2014): 30–55.

———. "Love in the Novels of Toni Morrison." *Angelaki* 22.1 (Mar. 2017): 261–70.

———. "*Love*'s Time and the Reader: Ethical Effects of *Nachträglichkeit* in Toni Morrison's *Love*." *Narrative* 16.2 (May 2008): 193–221.

Yancy, George. "Walking While Black in the 'White Gaze.'" *New York Times* 1 Sept. 2013. Online. Retrieved 24 Dec. 2019 at https://opinionator.blogs.nytimes.com/2013/09/01/walking-while-black-in-the-white-gaze/.

Zebialowicz, Anna, and Marek Palasinski. "Probing Racial Dilemmas in *the* [sic] *Bluest Eye* with the Spyglass of Psychology." *Journal of African American Studies* 14 (2010): 220–33.

Index

Aanerud, Rebecca 170
Abel, Elizabeth 24
abolitionism 12, 41, 95–96
African American literary tradition: expressive tradition 13, 16, 39, 73, 104; memory 4, 7, 14, 21, 33, 51–53, 87, 89, 103, 109, 130–131, 135, 173, 175; myth and folklore 14, 78, 80–84, 161, 170, 172–173; revision 15, 69, 160, 164; storytelling 13–16, 35–39, 49–50, 84, 103–104, 161–162, 171; textual and meta-textual enigmas or gaps 9, 20–21, 23, 30, 32, 34, 38, 44, 48, 60, 75, 83, 88, 90, 104, 108–109, 114–116, 127, 133–134, 159–160, 162–165; vernacular black dialect 13–15, 72–73, 161, 166
African ritual inheritances 119–120, 160, 174
Ahmad, Soophia 78, 81
Alexandru, Maria-Sabina Draga 84
Anatol, Giselle Liza 172
Androne, Helene Adams 1–6, 33
Appiah, Kwame Anthony 43, 170, 173
authors' relationship to Morrison's work: Campbell 2–4, 7–8; Goldstein 2–4, 7
Avery, Faith M. 149
Awkward, Michael 15, 47, 49–50, 69
Azizmohammadi, Fatameh 78

Bambara, Toni Cade 2, 8, 178
Bao, Jinping 89, 109
Baraka, [Imamu] Amiri (LeRoi Jones) 5, 13, 23
Barnes, Deborah H. 173
Barnes, Paula 147
Barnett, Pamela E. 173
Beach, Richard 19, 164
Beck, E. M. 55
Bell, Bernard W. 97
Bellamy, Maria Rice 154–155
Beloved (1987): Amy Denver 94–99, 107, 113, 174; Baby Suggs 110–111, 119, 167; Beloved (character) 88–90, 98, 101, 103–104, 106, 109, 159; Bodwin family 93–95, 173; community as concept 103–104; epigraph 87; family as concept 101–102, 159; Garner family 91–92, 108; as genre 112–113; irony 105; love as concept 92, 111; "... not a story to pass on..." passages 104–106, 128; omniscient narrative voice and unreliable narration 107; 124 Bluestone Road 87–89, 101, 109; Paul D 89–91, 94–95, 102, 106–108; readers' responsibilities 103, 106–107, 113; schoolteacher 88, 91, 93, 110; Sethe 91–94, 98–103, 107–108, 167; Sixo 110; Stamp Paid 98–100, 106–107; Sweet Home 88, 90–92, 107; symbolism 108–109, 174
Belsey, Catherine 39–40, 51
Benjamin, Shanna Greene 33
Bennett, Juda 44, 119, 122
Bentson, Kimberly W. 173
Berger, James 94, 96–97, 173
Bérubé, Michael 23
binary codes and dichotomies 18, 33–34, 78, 88–89, 96–98, 118–119, 132, 140, 142, 145
Black Aesthetics movement 13, 16, 162
The Bluest Eye (1970): Breedlove family 47, 53, 101; character-as-narrator 46–53, 67–68; Cholly Breedlove 61–65; Dick-and-Jane reading primer 46–48, 69, 101; generational cycle of racial self-hatred 56–60; irony 53–56, 63, 67; Maureen Peal 53–55; Morrisonian lyricism 50–51; Mrs. Breedlove 57–60, 65–68; narration 48–51; omniscient narrative voice and unreliable narration 46, 49–53, 68; Pecola Breedlove 55–60, 65–67; readers' responsibilities 48, 65, 68–70
Boswell, Barbara 131
Bouson, J. Brooks 48, 83–84
Broad, Robert L. 87, 89–90, 163, 173
Brownmiller, Susan 62
Bump, Jerome 70
Busia, Abena P.A. 104
Butler-Evans, Elliott 50

Campbell, Donald T. 171
Campbell, Shawnrece D. 2–4, 7–8, 140, 170–171, 176
Carabi, Angels 173
Carden, Mary Paniccia 127
Castro, Quassan 34
Century, Douglas 173
Chaffin, Roger 170–171
Christian, Barbara 152, 169
Chung, Hye Seung 175

Index

Clarke, Kenneth 136
Cole, Johnetta B. 147
Cook, Thomas D. 171
Coser, Stelamaris 14, 16, 63, 171
Crawford, Mary 170–171
Creel, Margaret Washington 119, 147
Crenshaw, Kimberlé 16, 140, 142, 145–146, 155, 172
critical race theory 146, 148

Dalgish, Gerard M. 147
Davidson, Cathy N. 170
deconstruction theory 18
Delazari, Ivan 171
Demetrakopoulos, Stephanie A. 24
Derrida, Jacques 18, 145
diaspora 85, 145–146
Diffrient, David Scott 175
"discrimination" (definition) 17
double-consciousness 145
"dozens" 74–75
Drieling, Claudia 131
Du Bois, W. E. B. 15

"essentialism" 99, 158
Ethiopian healing scrolls (*dabtaras* or *debtaras*) 120–122, 160, 174
"ethnomedical criticism" 140–141

Feagin, Clairece Booher 99
Feagin, Joe R. 99
feminist perspective on rape 62
Fish, Stanley E. 166
Foster, Frances Smith 112
Foucault, Michel 18
Francisco, Dayane Evelline de Souza 142, 145, 147
Freund, Elizabeth 20
Fuller, Hoyt W. 13
funkiness as blackness 55–56
Furman, Jan 30, 37, 57, 105, 112

Gates, Henry Louis, Jr. 14–15, 17, 39, 44, 49, 64, 108, 161, 164, 166–167
Genovese, Eugene D. 94, 111
Gibson, Donald B. 47–49, 61, 69
Gillespie, Diane 169
Gilman, Sander L. 170
Glass, Joshua 170
Goldstein-Shirley, David 2–4, 7, 22, 24, 111, 171, 176
Goulimari, Pelagia 169
Grattan, Sean 175
Greenfield-Sanders, Timothy 17
griot tradition 14, 16, 79–80, 85, 104, 106, 157, 160–162
Guerrero, Edward 171

Hall, James 85, 136
Handley, William R. 103, 109, 163, 174
Hansberry, Lorraine 157

Harack, Katrina 84
Harding, Wendy 88, 108, 163, 174
Harris, Trudier 37, 42, 49, 54, 57, 59, 64, 70, 104, 163, 171, 174
Heinze, Denise 68, 103, 105
Heller, Dana 91–92, 95, 101, 174
Hill, Cecily E. 148
Holloway, Joseph 147
Holloway, Karla F.C. 24, 100
Holton, Robert 82, 102
Home (2012): Cee 130–132, 135, 137–138; Frank Money 128–139, 160, 175; home as a place and concept 126, 128, 131–133, 139, 160; irony 129, 137; Lotus, Georgia 128, 130–132, 137–139; love as concept 126–127, 129, 131, 136; narrative structure 129–130, 135; omniscient narrative voice and unreliable narrator 129–130, 134, 136; readers' responsibilities 127, 129; symbolism 136–138
hooks, bell 2–5, 34, 142
horizon of expectation 20, 44; *see also* reader-response criticism/theory
Hudson-Weems, Clenora 112, 166
Humann, Heather Duerre 83, 102, 136
Hurston, Zora Neale 13, 49, 167

Ibarrola, Aitor 129, 138–139
Illes, Judika 119
"implied reader" 19–20, 44–45, 165, 170, 172; *see also* reader-response criticism/theory
"interrogative text" 39–40
intersectionality 2, 16, 124–125, 140–147, 149, 153, 155, 165, 172
Iser, Wolfgang 19, 44, 165; *see also* reader-response criticism/theory

Jackman, Mary R. 58–59
Jauss, Hans Robert 20, 43–44
Jazz (1992) 11, 21–22, 162, 164, 169
Jennings, La Vinia Delois 81, 92, 170
Jewett, Chad 169
Joly, Claire Helene 64
justice as concept 126–127

Kaiser, Mario 11, 13, 172
Kohzadi, Hamedreza 78
Kolmerten, Carol A. 174
Krumholz, Linda 97, 103, 112, 173–175
Kubitschek, Missy Dehn 73, 85, 169

Lawrence, David 174
Lawrence, Elizabeth Atwood 56
Leitch, Vincent B. 13, 18
Levend Water 130
Levine, Lawrence W. 73, 75, 147, 162
Levy, Andrew 104–105, 111, 167
Li, Stephanie 102
Lilienfeld, Jane 21
limits in studying Morrison's work 165–167
Łobodziec, Agnieszka 99
López Ramírez, Manuela 138

Index

Lorde, Audre 175
Love (2003) 83, 102, 126–127, 135–136, 174
Lubiano, Wahneema 72–73, 82

Madden, Mary 62, 166
Mailloux, Steven 21, 40–41, 43, 68, 165, 171; *see also* reader-response criticism/theory
Malmgren, Carl D. 100, 103, 173–174
Manyinka, Sarah Lapido 11, 13, 172
Martin, Daniel J. 137, 175
Martin, Jacky 88, 108, 163, 174
"master narrative" 93–94, 106, 128
Mbiti, John S. 100, 159
McBride, Dwight A. 158, 175
McCampbell, Darlene Z. 170
Medoro, Dana 77
Mellard, James M. 84
A Mercy (2008): Blacksmith 150–155; community 111, 140, 149–150, 156, 174; dominion 141, 150, 154–155; readers' responsibilities 155; Scully 150–151; Sorrow 150–152, 156
Meyer, Lakeisha 129
Middleton, Joyce Irene 79–80, 172
Miner, Madonne M. 62
Mitchell, Angelyn 89, 113, 126, 173
Mitchell-Kernan, Claudia 172
Mobley, Marilyn Sanders 71, 85, 170, 173
Montagu, Ashley 17, 152
Mori, Aoi 123
Morris, Susana M. 30, 84, 171

Naylor, Gloria 2, 15
Neal, Larry 13, 100
neo-conservative discourse 97
Nobel Prize speech 12, 164–165
nommo 109

Omi, Michael 158

Page, Philip 90, 104–105, 107, 173
Palasinski, Marek 57
Palmer, Robert 39
Paradise (1997): Consolata 118–119, 121–122, 124–125; Convent 115, 120–122, 124–125; doppelganger or double 117–118; irony 115–116, 124, 175; omniscient narrative voice and unreliable narration 114–116; Oven inscription 116–117; readers' responsibilities 117, 122, 125; the Reverend Misner 115–118, 124–125; the Reverend Pulliam 115–118; Ruby, Oklahoma 123–124
Patterson, Orlando 92–93, 110, 147, 149
Pérez-Torres, Rafael 100, 104, 108, 112, 173
Phelan, James 163, 174
Phiri, Aretha 82–83, 85, 172–173
Playing in the Dark (1992) 37, 40, 96–97, 100, 146, 158, 161, 166
Pollitt, Katha 175
Powell, Timothy B. 47
"prejudice" (definition) 17
Previn, Andreï 127–128

Rabinowitz, Peter J. 44
"race" (definition) 17
"racialism" 44
"racism" (definition) 17–18
Rashomon (1950) 33
reader-response criticism/theory 1, 8–9, 12, 19, 35, 43, 148, 165–166, 170, 172, 175
readers' responsibilities in "Conclusion" 159, 162–164
"real readers" 19–20, 22, 25–28, 30–31, 34, 44, 159, 165, 172; *see also* reader-response criticism/theory
"Recitatif": cultural enigmas 25–28, 33, 43; framework of Goldstein's empirical study 24–25, 170; Maggie 31–33, 36, 42, 171; physical enigmas 24–28, 32–33, 43, 171; Roberta 24–38, 42–44, 57; school desegregation and mandatory busing 23, 26, 28, 31–32, 34, 41–42; Twyla 24–40, 42–44, 52, 171
Reckley, Ralph 174
Rochman, Hazel 170
Rogers, Robert 174
Romero, Channette 120
Ross, Stephen M. 174
Roye, Susmita 69
Ryan, Judylyn S. 127

Salvino, Dana Nelson 171
Samuels, Wilfred D. 112, 166
Saunders, James Robert 53
Scarpa, Giulia 88, 102, 109, 112, 173–174
Schmudde, Carol E. 109, 112, 173
Schreiber, Evelyn Jaffe 129
Schreiner, Samantha 146–147, 152–153, 156
Schwab, Gabriele 20
scientific racism 93–94, 100
Seven Days (organization) 75–77
Shange, Ntozake 96
Sherard, Tracey 21
Skerrett, Joseph T., Jr. 80, 103
skin-color hierarchy 54–57, 59, 69, 123–124
Sklar, Howard 32
Smith, Valerie 48, 105, 132
Song of Solomon (1977): as bildungsroman 84–85; Guitar 77, 81, 85; love as concept 72, 76–81, 83; Milkman Dead 74–75, 78, 80–82, 172; models of justice 77–78; Pilate 77–80, 85; readers' responsibilities 71–72, 77, 83, 86
Spencer, Jon M. 147
Spillers, Hortense J. 80, 172
Spivak, Gayatri Chakravorty 99
"staged" debate 41–42
standards of beauty and value 46, 53, 63, 65, 69–70, 111, 158–159
Stanfield, John H. II 44
Stanley, Sandra Kumamoto 171
Stave, Shirley A. 175
Stepto, Robert B. 35–37, 64, 106, 165–166, 171
Strouse, Jean 29, 171
Stuckey, Sterling 104

Sula (1973): community as concept 144–145; narrative structure 142; relationship between Nel and Sula 141–144
Sweeney, Megan 83, 127

Tar Baby (1981) 148–149
Tate, Claudia 12, 171
Taylor-Guthrie, Danille 167
Their Eyes Were Watching God (1937) 15, 49, 175
Thorsson, Courtney 83
Tolnay, Stewart E. 55
transcendent sisterhood 124–125
Travis, Molly Abel 103
Troyna, Barry 42
TuSmith, Bonnie 63, 172

Vasile, Alexandra 142, 144, 146
Visvis, Vikki 73, 84

Wagner-Martin, Linda 170, 173

Wall, Cheryl 61, 132, 135, 138–139
Wallace, Cynthia R. 135
Walters, Wendy W. 172
Ward, Jervette R. 47
Wardi, Anissa Janine 127
Warnes, Andrew 148
Weinstein, Philip M. 175
western literary tradition 14, 161
white gaze 17, 146, 170, 175
white liberalism 95–97
Wilentz, Gay 149, 156
Willis, Susan 59
Winant, Howard 158
Wittenberg, Judith Bryant 174
Wong, Shelley 48, 63
Wright, Richard 64–65, 173
Wyatt, Jean 102, 127, 136, 147–149, 174

Yancy, George 170

Zebialowicz, Anna 57

www.ingramcontent.com/pod-product-compliance
Lightning Source LLC
Chambersburg PA
CBHW020837020526
44114CB00040B/1241